MW00427555

LEADERSHIP FROM BELOW

Leadership From Below

Paradoxes of Submarine Leadership

JEFF FLESHER

Dave Oliver

Wisdom Mates Press

Contents

Acknowledgments

I am extremely thankful to the twenty-two submariners who graciously allowed me to tell their stories and share their insights into leadership: Doug Ackley, Bud Atkins, Harry Baker, John Buffery, Rob Davis, Jack Gallimore, Mike Gray, Ron Gordon, Chris Groves, Bob Hogue, Dave Hulin, Greg Kane, Niall Kilgour, Al Konetzni, Stan Mathis, Bill McGonegal, Dave Oliver, Tim Oliver, Frank Stewart, Steve Thorpe, Pat Urello, and Joe Tofalo. I have also found inspiration and support from the United States Submarine Veterans Inc., the Naval Submarine League, and the Royal Navy Submarine Association.

I would also like to thank my editor Dr. Scott Johnson who provided critical feedback for enhanced readability and clarity of important points. Dr. Johnson introduced me to the study of problem solving and the development of expertise and has been a primary research and teaching mentor and role model.

My deep appreciation also to Dave Oliver who contributed his story and wrote the forward to the book. His writing on leadership and performance includes *Lead On, A Practical Approach to Leadership, Against the Tide, Rickover's Leadership principles and the Rise of the Nuclear Navy,* and *A Navy Admirals Bronze Rules, Managing Risk and Leadership.*

I would also like to thank my wife Bonnie who has heard all my submarine stories. Thank you for always listening.

Jeff Flesher, PhD
Fire Control Technician Ballistic Missiles Second Class, USN

Forward

Rear Admiral David R. Oliver Jr. USN (Ret.)

As you read this book, for a few hours you will enter the uncommon world Jeff Flesher was part of when he and his friends fought and won the Cold War. You may find its citizens fascinating, you may find them distracting, but Jeff has a much grander game in mind. He is introducing you to a new neighborhood to exhibit old problems from the new perspective of the immense pressures that exist down deep below the sea. Jeff's lifetime of leadership experience reinforces that, in that process, you will gain fresh perspectives for your practice.

In my own work, I have spent thirty-six years in the Navy, ten in industry and four as a political appointee in Washington, D.C. The same leadership and management principles were applicable to each environment and were grasped the same way, through experience or self-reflection. But no matter how seasoned, none of us can ever have the full range of experiences we need. We all owe Jeff a great debt for pulling these valuable leadership perspectives together.

Every one of us owes it to become a great manager,
to do the very best, and if circumstances arise that some of us
great managers will become a great leader because we'll have the
background. We don't need to sort of worry about if that hap-
pened because you'll reach down and grab that part of yourself
that you need. Dave Oliver

Chapter 1

Charting a Course

This book leads to enhanced leadership performance; if that is your intention. I can lead you to the ocean but you have to pick up an oar and push off into a new place to explore. That paradox underlies all efforts at describing leadership no matter how simple or complex. Ideas and experiences are personal and situational and wisdom is earned, just like the Dolphin badges submariners receive following qualification. There is significant effort required. I am convinced that those of us who choose leadership as our calling also accept it as our life's work and it is work worth doing.

Submarines are a paradoxical extreme environment. The strategic advantage of submarines is the mastery of the paradox of being able to hide at sea in ships designed to sink. Submarines are inherently dangerous and yet operated safely by many navies. Modern boats have no deck guns or other outward appearances of a warship while a ballistic missile boat with its nuclear missiles is the most lethal weapon ever created with more destructive power than all of human conflict combined.

The submarine's role in nuclear deterrence is the ultimate performance paradox. Success comes from not doing the job but being constantly alert and ready to accomplish the un-thinkable. Submarines are the most survivable component of the nuclear triad (land-based, airborne and submarine launched nuclear weapons). Strategic deterrence is based on the theory of mutual self-destruction. In effect any launch will be met by a massive counterstrike creating a balance of power and ultimate deterrent to a first-strike attack.

Submarines are also great environments to practice and study leadership. There is no question that effective leader-ship and continuous high performance are baseline require-ments in the submarine services. They are also closed environments and that lack of familiarity creates a space where we can look into their world with an open mind; a pre-requisite to learning.

In the next fifteen chapters you will meet twenty-two sub-mariners. They are veterans from the United States Navy and the British Royal Navy. In order to better understand a person's unique contribution and perspective it is important to share some context. Who are they? What was their experience? Some important memories shared by them about their own life and the people that they respect and value. Each chapter in-cludes these personal leadership contexts along with some of their impressions, lessons learned, and valued principles based on their similar and yet diverse experience.

These leaders represent every level of management from the first line leader to the Captains and Admirals responsible for the entire submarine forces of their countries. The com-bined naval service of this group is more than 400 years and spans the timeframe from 1954 to 2021; more than half of the history of the Submarine Service in both navies. Their terms of service ranged from one enlistment of four years to more than 40 years in the military. One was in fact the longest serving submarine qualified officer still at sea before his retirement.

Many served on World War II era boats with veterans from that war including one who was a crewmember on the last boat still in active service in the Royal Navy that had fired a torpedo in anger during that war. They were also there at the dawn of the age of nuclear power, the Cuban missile crisis, the Cold War, and the first US war patrol after World War II firing the first Tomahawk missile in action during operation Desert Storm.

They come from council houses and the inner city. They also come from boarding schools and military academies. They grew up in the Navy as sons of war heroes and heroines, sat on their father's knee onboard a sub as a small boy, and dreamed of joining the Navy at the tender age of six. One told his father while fishing on the Thames River in Groton Connecticut that "Someday that will be me," as they watched a diesel boat go by on its way to the Submarine Base. Some joined with best friends to see the world and have adventures while others planned to join the Navy to provide for a later college education or to learn a trade. Most volunteered and some were volun-told.

They started in the Navy in Boy's Service as a 15 year old and participated in rituals that sometimes were on the edge (or a bit over) of hazing. They have experienced fire, flooding, collisions, grounding and survived hurricanes, gales and poor leaders. They were on active duty when the pride of the US fleet, the USS Thresher, went down on sea trials and they assisted in locating and rescue operations for the ill-fated Russian submarine *Kursk* and the Argentinian submarine *San Juan*.

They are humble heroes. More than one said "I'm not comfortable talking about myself." Even while hesitant to seek praise, they are quick to recall, share and honor the great leaders they learned from and to offer help and support where they can. They have run toward fires because that was their job. They have stayed until the job was done because people depended on them. They and their families have shouldered the burden of long periods at sea often with little communication in isolation from the most basic of things like sunlight and fresh air.

During their service they were Torpedomen, Interior Communications Technicians, Nuclear Machinist Mates, Missile Technicians, Sonar Technicians, Electricians, Yeomen, and Radiomen. They operated the nuclear reactor, manned the weapons systems, navigated and drove the boat and helped prepare the meals. They loaded torpedoes and cans of food and cleaned and painted and practiced every emergency condition and warfighting need until their response was immediate and unwavering.

Following their submarine service they worked to make electricity at hydroelectric dams and nuclear power plants, rebuilt war-torn Iraq, produced baseball bats, fixed critical medical equipment, taught at-risk youth, and kept the steam engines running at the zoo. They were volunteer fire fighters, bartenders, middle school teachers, and an Inspector General. Their legacy of leadership and service has extended to government, corporate and non-profit organizations. They serve on Boards, judge technical competitions for students, and bring encouragement to critically ill children.

Most still have deep connections to the Submarine Service and actively share the experience and importance of submarines in national defense. Some still work in the defense industry in shipyards or software systems development supporting the next generation of submarine and naval warfighting capability. Some have written books and served as technical advisors to submarine related productions. Others have leadership roles in submarine professional organizations and veterans groups. Many are involved in community efforts related to veterans and within these groups they promote a

close link to current submariners and honor the
before creating a continuity of service, tradition

I encourage you as you read to listen to the..
you were sharing a drink at the submarine veteran's clubhouse
in Groton, CT. These are leaders who chose to learn, practice
and perform. Several almost left the service because of poor
leaders but instead used that experience to guide their pursuit
of excellence. Maintaining the paradox theme, I know there is
great value for you in reading these leadership cases and I can't
tell you exactly what it is. This may seem absurd and yet each
reader brings unique needs and experiences and while it is impossible to know exactly, I can predict with some certainty
that you will find personal value and insight in these stories
and leadership perspectives. Listen, agree or not, consider their
wisdom and find what you can leverage to accelerate your own
leadership practice.

In the final chapters of this book I share ten examples of
leadership paradoxes from the submarine service that transfer
to any context. While they may be new to you, I'm sure they
will be a familiar frame to transfer the collected knowledge for
your benefit. It is my honor to give you a peek inside this environment without windows. I hope that you enjoy and are inspired by these stories as much as I am. They have encouraged
me in my work and remind me of some of the qualities I aspire
to in my practice of leadership. We are brothers and sisters of
the Phin; confidants that know the secrets of life in the deep
of the oceans and the depths of ourselves. These members of
the Silent Service have a million stories and more than a few
they still can't tell you.

1

At the Deck Plates

Chapter 2

Entrepreneur

Robert F. (Bob) Hogue
Sonar Technician First Class, USN

Mr. Robert F. Hogue is the Chief Executive Officer and President of In-Depth Engineering Corporation. With over forty years of experience in business management, systems and software engineering design and development, Mr. Hogue is a recognized national expert in the development of combat, radar, sonar, ESM, and air traffic control systems. Prior to forming In-Depth Engineering in 2007, Mr. Hogue served as the Chief Executive Officer for The Consulting Network Incorporated (TCNI). Prior to that, he held senior engineering and management positions at Raytheon Company's Submarine Signal Division, IBM Corporation's Federal Sector Division, and at DRS Technologies, Inc.

Robert F. Hogue, President and CEO
http://www.in-deptheng.com/about.html

How did I get in the Navy? My best friend. I was a pretty good student in school and I had a scholarship to a Christian college, a university in Ohio. I had partial scholarships to a couple of other places. I grew up in the inner city with my father, he was black, my mother was white. She had left years and years before, right after I was born. It's a long story, that's sort of irrelevant, but it was my father and stepmother that raised me. It was a very loving family. It was great. We had no particular issues but we were poor. Neither of my parents had gone to college and could offer little by way of direction for college. There was no doubt about that and I honestly didn't understand loans and programs of that sort very well in those days. I didn't want to tax my father with the financial burden of my college. I thought it was the right choice.

My best friend decided that he was going to join the Navy or wanted to join the service. We went to the Recruiting Station and took the armed services test. We applied to Air Force and Navy. The Navy's programs seemed better for us so that's where we went. We joined under the buddy program. When we got to boot camp he couldn't swim, I could, so we were split up on day two and we didn't see each other again for two years. By the way, the Vietnam War was going on, that was `72. My perspective was if you failed out of college you could be drafted, so that was another consideration. I did not want to go into the Army. The Navy was our choice, and I knew that I would get the GI bill if I went into the service. That was my objective, 100%, to find a course to go to college.

I was in the Navy from '72 to '78 and I served on board USS Skate and USS Sea Devil with some absolutely fantastic people, the skippers in particular. It was just an amazing experience. It sort of set the course for my life. Afterwards, I went to work for Raytheon, building or working on combat systems. I concurrently went to school to get my degree. It was the combination of those things in order (Navy, Raytheon and College) that helped propel me forward. It plotted a course for me, so it was very, very good.

I started as a Sonar Technician Submarines without really realizing that I had actually volunteered for the submarine service. The next thing I knew I was in a dive tank doing a pressure test with one other guy who coincidentally failed the pressure test. I just remember he had a filling pop out of a tooth during the test. I was the only one in my boot camp company that went to submarines and that was sort of interesting. I knew it was special, I just didn't understand why. As a Sonar Technician it was the standard Navy pipeline program. We went to basic electronics and then to "A" school in those days. Then we went to our first assignment. We stayed on board for about eighteen months then we went back to "C" school, then onboard your final ship for about three years. That was basically the rotation and my path.

It's hard to talk about those days without thinking about the people and the things that you've learned. I was impressed always with the Captains on board and most everyone for that matter. The crew was knowledgeable about the operation of the boat. That whole notion of learning and being able to do your job or stand in, in order to help in lots of different ways, whether it's damage control or operating certain systems. I qualified in every system forward. Not machinist's systems, but all the electronic systems. I stood the ESM [electronic sensing] watch, the radar watch, and the sonar watch. I was a sonar supervisor at some juncture. I just loved it all; there was so much to learn. I think that was the thing that helped me the most, my thought was, I'm on this ship and the Navy has given me this billion-dollar platform (I have no idea how much it cost in those days, but I was just saying), a billion-dollar platform and given me the charter to learn everything I could.

I didn't understand pneumatic systems or any others but through the course of qualifying you understood pneumatics, hydraulics, electrical systems, control valves, indicators, actuators, every imaginable part of all of these systems and you started to understand their interrelations. There was the notion while you were on board you were learning, and you were always learning. That was the number one thing that I got out of being in the Submarine Service; I started to understand, loosely, roughly, how systems fit together, how things interrelated in terms of making very complex systems out of a whole bunch of very simple parts. That became clear to me while I was qualifying and then in the work we did in the submarine. I thought that was just a fantastic learning experience.

I think the Captains were amazing, and I only cite them because they were very prominent in the decisions and the things that they did were obvious. I always thought that they were pretty spectacular. I served under three skippers, but two principally. One was Commander Ron Eytchison on the USS Skate. The thing about him, well I remember lots about him, but he was such a simple, elegant person, with a great sense of humor. He was such a good storyteller. Never lost his temper, never shouted. I never heard him even say a bad word, even during times when things were pretty dicey.

One time we submerged with the hatch open, the hatch going up to the bridge. I don't know if you're familiar with Skate, but Skate was an old SSN. She was the first production SSN, the third nuclear boat in the Navy. She had bow planes that were up front, obviously. But in order to rig them into the superstructure, they went to a 25 degree down angle and then they would rig in-board. One time we were surfacing, don't remember where, I think it was the North Atlantic, but we were surfacing without air because it just took so long to recharge the air banks, so we surfaced without air often. They cracked the lower hatch, opened the lower hatch and cracked the upper hatch, opened the other upper hatch and then rigged-in the bow planes in relatively short order. All of these evolutions are going on and it turns out a swell caught the boat and forced it back underwater with both hatches open, bow planes at 25 down being rigged in. It was pretty amazing.

I was standing in the sonar door which is exactly across from the hatch about to go man the radar. I was young, that was my first assignment really. I had no real idea what to do. All of a sudden water started pouring in. At first, I thought it was just a wave breaking over the sail but it just kept coming and coming. It was just a column of water. In that moment, everyone did exactly what they were supposed to do. I mean, you had this column of water dropping down into the control room, it's this big rush of water going by. You heard the flooding alarm "flooding in the control room" was announced. The next thing you know, it was the XO. His name was Porter, John Porter. He comes dashing out of the wardroom and then straight up the hatch. While inside that column of water, he grabbed the lanyard for the lower hatch and pulled the hatch closed.

Now, it wasn't two seconds later the Skipper was right behind him. We had gear that was shorted out, we lost some stuff in the IC space, but the bottom line was in the moment everything was calm even though the boat had taken on a lot of water. We were pretty heavy and the Skipper said, "I have the conn," and he just took control. We did an EMBT [emergency main ballast tank] blow and increased speed. We got light enough to surface and did. Throughout the evolution there was no shouting, there was no panic. He knew exactly what to do and he just calmly took control of everything and then it all worked out. When flooding was announced the crew in the operation's compartment immediately put blankets and pillows and mattresses over the battery well hatch to ensure no saltwater got into the battery well. Everyone knew what to do; it was just such an impressive reaction. We could have lost the ship because there was so much water. It was just a few seconds, but everyone reacted immediately. That experience stuck with me, I was firsthand right there.

Afterwards there was no retribution, no witch hunt. We found out who did what and what was wrong. There was no blame. The skipper wasn't mad. There were just discussions. We had talks about the course of actions that happened to cause this to occur and what things should we do to not have this re-occur. We had repairs, repairs in the fan-room and there were some switches on the IC switchboards that needed to be repaired and so forth but it just went on.

I thought it was just sort of fantastic and it set a tone to understand that these guys were effective because they were decisive, they were passionate, but they did so without emotions. They moved forward without getting encumbered by or asserting blame or some other thing. So, I thought that was memorable. I think that was directly from the submarine service. It's a lesson that I learned in watching those kinds of events occur. I can tell you a different story with Commander Chabot, where there was a live torpedo in the water. It wasn't one of ours, but he knew what to do. I just found that over and over again, when things happened, the more severe it was, the cooler the skipper got.

The friend that I told you I joined the Navy with, he wound up on board the USS Forestall [an aircraft carrier]. Two years later, I met up with him on board his ship. It was in the dry dock at Norfolk Naval Shipyard in Portsmouth, VA. He took me on board for a tour and while I was on board there was a fire alarm. I don't know exactly what they're saying, but, you know, "Fire! Fire! Fire! Away, the damage control team!" I said, "Don't, you have to do something?" But he's like, "Nah, the damage control team will take care of it." That was a foreign notion to me at that point. Their jobs were so compartmentalized. The ship was on fire and nobody else had a worry or concern. His reaction was so strange to me. It was never like that on the submarine. Everyone would participate in any casualty. I can remember even if we had a problem with the sonar, nukes were asking, "Hey, did we get that fixed?" Or, "Do we need some help?" They would do stuff if you needed. I'm just saying as far reaching as the ends of the ship everyone was concerned about the ship and its mission and things going forward. So, I think that was another big thing I learned from being in the Navy, in the Submarine Service. I don't think the surface guys, and I don't think other branches use an idea like qualifying on-board a submarine and understanding how these systems fit together. If you take that to heart how valuable that is in terms of learning.

I've also observed in the Navy, at least in the submarine service, that the people were very authentic and I thought that was important. What I mean by that is they weren't worried so much about impressing you. They weren't worried about show-ing how much they knew. They were worried about you learn-ing and they would help you. Anyone you approached would sit down and talk you through the systems, draw them out with you, quiz you on it, help you learn. What I'm saying is I just felt this focus on learning was unique in the submarine service.

We had this sort of camaraderie where people were helping you learn. We would test each other in lots of different ways. Sometimes it would be humorous and sometimes they were just doing it to goof off, but we would always challenge each other with what we knew. It was just amazing. I felt like I was around a lot of very smart dedicated people. There were times where people messed up, obviously. But I felt like everyone was carrying their weight. I mean, everyone on board the boat was doing their best. Everyone was contributing in a meaningful way so you felt like you should do your part. The crew was try-ing to help you and they were setting you on a course to make sure you can do your job by giving you all of these tools in or-der to help learn.

I learned a lot to qualify on Skate. Then I went off to school again and then went on board Sea Devil. I had made first class at four years. It turns out that I was the second senior person in the gang, our Chief was a surface convert who readily admitted he had a lot to learn. The skipper would come to me and talk about what was happening through the Division Officer, but sometimes just casually ask, "What's going on?" For the search plan we had to answer the questions "What should we do in particular?" "How should we employ sensors?" "How should we set up?" "What is the best depth for detection?" We reviewed it and he reviewed it. It wasn't that he just reviewed it with the division officer, he had his lead sonar guys there to help.

It was great because you felt empowered or something, right? I couldn't say that he actually decided to do those things that we were suggesting in most cases, I think it happened, it worked out that way but the point is he included you and made you feel like you were part of the decision process, which I thought was fantastic. I'm still awestruck by it and you get the sense of saying you've had a chance to participate in those decisions.

My division officer, who later became the weapons boss onboard Sea Devil was Siegfriend Shalles. They called him Siggy, affectionally. I don't know what happened, but he and I hit it off. I loved doing the performance predictions and I also did the sound silencing. I became the sound silencing guy on board the ship. I just loved to do stuff like that. We got into this formula where I understood what he needed and it just worked. I spent hours doing these things. I would work in off hours and so forth to develop the sonar predictions. Performance predictions were a big deal because the skipper sort of lived and died by them. We were on a hunter killer kind of mission if you will.

We were always out searching for something and we were pretty successful. So, my marks, my performance reviews were spectacular, it was fun, and they made it fun. It's sort of the lesson that I keep talking about where the leadership invited your participation. Because of that it made you want to do it better. It made you want to work harder to make it more effective, more encompassing, just more. It wasn't just getting it done. I'm saying that in particular because it was such a rewarding experience. I think I walked away with the idea of inviting participation during my civilian life.

I think that those experiences set a tone for me going forward when I left the Navy, which was a hard decision because I loved what we did in the Navy. Of course, I wanted to go back to college and move forward in that way. So I did. When I got out of the Navy and I got a job at Raytheon Company, in Portsmouth, Rhode Island. I didn't have my degree obviously but I was going to school part time. I was working full time and that worked out very well for me.

Importantly, when I took physics courses, math courses, the things that we had to do for engineering, I was interested in engineering principles. They were pretty easy at that juncture. I understood how things physically fit together because I had studied systems and lots of ocean physics in the sonar context. Those experiences just helped. So, what I want to try to point out is that the Navy was such a springboard for me. Learning how systems fit together and having those experiences with such great men that taught me how to control situations and what to do.

I worked for Raytheon for thirteen years. I met a young woman whose name was Sandy who worked at Raytheon also and had gone back to school in Virginia for her master's degree. She decided that she wanted to stay in the Washington Metropolitan Area. She was my girlfriend at the time so I decided to leave Raytheon and go to the Washington Metropolitan area. She's now my wife of 32 years. It was a good decision.

After Raytheon I worked at IBM for three years and then I went to work at DRS, Diagnostic Retrieval Systems, and then started my own company called TCNI with another guy named Tim. We worked on that for 10 years. It was a virtual corporation, which was amazing and was certainly a good idea. It kept our overhead and our costs very low. But it was hard to oversee what everyone was doing. This is why Tim and I split. I was managing engineers and he was managing the bookkeeping and the enterprise; the business of running the business. I was managing the new business and the engineering. It was just too hard to communicate with everyone virtually in those days. So, we wound up making the decision to split. He kept the company TCNI and I formed In-Depth Engineering.

During the course of our work we worked with a lot of leadership in the Navy to start the APB process. The APB process was a notion, about the time when we were just starting to transition into commercial off-the-shelf equipment, of periodically updating, then building capability for the ships and systems about to deploy. We were involved at the onset of the APB process and that's sort of how the business took off. I realized you didn't have to be a big company anymore to build systems or build software that could go on board submarines or surface ships. Once we started using commercial equipment, I felt anyone could build software if you knew how the systems worked and how they fit together; exactly what I had focused on in the Navy. You can buy a box, a computer system, like you buy PCs now. That was the impetus to start this company to start building our own software and applying it to these systems. Ultimately, we wound up being the principal software developers for the BYG combat system that was deployed and is currently deployed on a lot of submarines.

That was about twelve years ago. In-Depth Engineering has grown quite a bit in those years. We're supplying services to various organizations other than the Navy. We do a lot of sub-contract work with Lockheed, with General Dynamics, with other large organizations. We sort of diversified outside of doing systems for the Submarine Service in which we were involved in; the Sonar system, the EW system, the Imaging system and the Combat system. Those are the principal electronic systems onboard. We started doing the same kind of services for IUSS, which is the Integrated Undersea Surveillance Systems. Then for the Aegis Program. So, we're going like gang busters with these new initiatives with lots of development roles and lots of service roles including working in shipyards. That puts us up to about 200 people now.

I think command at sea must be amazing, I can't imagine. Growing up I had teachers, of course. There were no direct notions of leadership, maybe the pastor at my church and leaders in the community. It was my Navy commanders who I think set the first example that I ever personally or directly witnessed. The fact that they included me as I got a little more senior in decisions, particularly Commander Chabot. He would talk to you. He would make you feel like you were included. You would see those attributes in particular, in the Submarine Service over and over again. I think the skippers set the model of what it would take to lead people. Be technically competent and capable, be kind, and to include those that work for you in the decision process. I think beyond that, in my own experience I reflected on this idea of learning. What I've come to find, and I'm sure you do too, the more I learned, the more I've learned what I don't know. The more I studied, the more expert in the particular field I became, the more I realized that there's so much more that I need to learn in order to excel.

I don't know how I wound up in the Submarine Service but I thank God I did. Since then, I've met guys like Tim Oliver. He was on board Skate. He was a junior engineering officer, and I tend to think of him as a "Mr. Roberts" because he was so easy to talk to. Everyone was. He was always cheerful, always friendly. There were two XOs, McGonegal and Porter, and they were both exceptional. I can't think of anyone that I could say I would not want to serve with or that was unfair in any way.

I also realized, in the course of managing the companies that I have, and the skippers demonstrated this, that it's about the people, it's not about me per se. Our company's doing well, we're relatively small and things are working well for us. We're growing but it's the people that make you succeed. At first it was a few people and I taught them explicitly and then they reached out and they started doing things that I didn't imagine. Once I really started to understand, and reflecting back on Peter Chabot in particular, where he would invite people to participate, it was those people that kept him straight. It was those people that kept the ship out of trouble. It was those people that helped us succeed in whatever our mission requirements were.

I came to realize that as soon as you pass managing about ten or twelve people you can't understand what's going on completely. They have to contribute. I find that if you participate or rather you include them in the decisions, they contribute freely. They're in it for their community, for the company, and you're trying to reward them, you try to give them recognition. It's just a self-perpetuating thing. So, we help each other succeed more than focusing on our individual success. I certainly believe it. I think that everyone is important and I know that we couldn't do the jobs that we do without the team that completes our capability. It has very little to do with me at this point. I think that is what you get out of working together in an environment like the submarine service, the importance of working together and the successes you achieve. It was just an amazing experience.

Chapter 3

Go-To Guy

David A. (Dave) Hulin
Missile Technician Second Class, USN

"My dad always told us, 'Do the job that no one else will do and you're always going to have a job. And do the job so they don't have to ask who did it.' That's how I always tried to work."

Unemployment was tough, back in the early-mid 70s. I went to all the recruiters. I was looking more for education because I needed to go to school and I couldn't afford it. The Navy had the best package for training and also for advancement because I was married and we were thinking of having kids. I chose submarines because I thought I might get seasick. I figured, well, the best place to be is underwater rather than being on top of it.

The day I went down to swear in I got there a little bit early. This Marine guy comes out and he's like, "what are you here for?" I said, "I'm here to enlist in the Navy." "Oh, you haven't enlisted yet?" He puts his arm around me, we start walking. "Let me tell you the programs the Marines have to offer." The Navy recruiter comes out, and he said, "Hey, what are you doing?" The Marine said "I'm going to steal one of your boys." The Navy recruiter said, "Hey, did he tell you what he wants to do?" And the guy goes, "No," and he says, "He volunteered for submarines." This guy couldn't get his arm off my shoulders quick enough. He looks at me and says, "What are you, nuts?"

When I got to boot camp, I was so lucky. I had two guys leading my company. One was a boiler tech. That guy was Navy all the way. You could have cut paper on the sleeves on his shirt. The guy who was in charge was a senior chief submariner. In boot camp there were 79 of us and three had volunteered for subs. So he kind of put his arm around us every chance he got and told us what we were going to get into, what we could expect, things like that. Automatically, it was like hey I made the right decision. I know where I'm going. From there on in it was go to school because they would give it to you for nothing. That's how I looked at it and that's why I went to as many schools as I did.

I was an LPO [Leading Petty Officer] at boot camp for seventeen guys. Seventy guys were divided into sections. On our fourth or fifth day the kid who was in charge of us marched us in the side of these buses that were leaving for Orlando. Our CC [Company Commander] went bonkers. He came out, "You're in charge now." And I was like, "I'm a section leader, I already have a job." I remember him freaking out. "Attention! You are in the goddamn Navy. You don't tell me you've got a job. I'm telling you what you're going to do." I'm like, oh, man. They looked through my service record; they gave me that job in part because I was the oldest guy and I was in the marching band in school so they figured I knew how to march.

I remember this very well. We had a Master at Arms. We'd come in at nighttime and he would not let the guys smoke but he would smoke in front of them. I remember when I was a section leader and I'm thinking that's not right. You shouldn't do that. First night I was RCPO [Recruit Chief Petty Officer] he pulled that. "Uh-uh, no, that's not flying. You smoke, they smoke." That guy went down and woke some chief up and this guy kicks the door open. I thought he'd cracked the ceramic behind it. He wanted to see the RCPO and this guy in his office. Turns out I was right, I asked him to stop for just a second, I opened the door, I said, "Yo, the smoking lamp's lit." You know what, there's nothing I could do afterwards that was wrong. Those guys were like, hey, you stuck up for us. That's all they needed to hear. That's the way it was. It's kind of the way it should be. If you've got someone who's in charge you've got to let him lead. If he's doing it wrong listen to the guys who are helping. They'll steer you straight and together you get it all figured out.

The guy I took over from was kind of goofy and every night would just get up and walk up and down on the tables and just espouse his view on whatever was going on. I remember thinking I don't want to listen to this clown. When they put me in charge that changed. You know what? Anybody got something to say you get up on a table and you talk. And when you're done anybody else got something to say? It brought so many people together. Because up until then we weren't working together too well. In the end those guys carried that guy across the finish line when we had to do that run. I was so proud of those guys for doing that because they could have left him. He was such a dick to them and they didn't do that and that was pretty cool.

Being a missile tech, sometimes you walked around with a tweaker [small screwdriver] and sometimes you walked around with a pipe wrench that might hit the floor from your waist. It was a varied career; hydraulics, pneumatics, and electronics; all I was looking for. I'm a hands-on type of person. I have to get my hands in there or I'm just not right with things. I'm not the quickest or sharpest knife in the drawer but I will still butter bread and cut beef. I picked all that stuff up while I was in the service. Lot of cool people. Lots of guys to learn from; how to work, take the good put it in your box, take the bad make sure you don't do that yourself.

I was the only third class in the division because everybody reenlisted which made it...well, when the work came down, that was when the work came down. After a while they shipped over and they went to shore. Now I'm the head guy. I knew when you got assigned a job and you come back twenty minutes later and told me you were done, I know you didn't do it. So we'd go down and we'd look at it together. We would discuss what was going to get changed and how maybe we should do it better next time so that I didn't have to come down there and look at it.

I had a couple instances, I remember one a lot. The missile muzzle hatch on one of the closures wasn't passing the bubble test or the air test. We all came up with an idea of how to fix this thing. The boat was going to go underway the next day and if we weren't able to fix it we wouldn't be out underway. Somehow, the three of us, we got it open. We got it taken care of. You know how it was. Everybody worked together and we got that job done. It was amazing. Somehow out of it I got some kind of award from some Admiral somewhere. All I really wanted was that they needed to write a letter so the other guys could get up to MT2. They were stuck at MT3 just like I was. You needed something like that in your service record to get that boost and these guys were helping. Everybody helped. We just pulled it off really well. That was one of the better things that happened.

Working together for me is; what's the job, what do we got to do to get it done, what's the steps, what's the plan, and let's go get it done. When we had leaders on the boat usually it was the guys that wanted to get the job done, wanted to get the work done. I don't know where to put the leadership on some of that stuff. Everybody has a different drive wheel. Some of them don't turn as fast and some of them do but they're still good people. They still do lead in some way or fashion. Some guys might be really smart like super-duper smart but they, for want of a better word, they don't like to get their hands real dirty. So they'll tell you what to do. By doing that you pick up what they know but they unfortunately don't get to know what you know, which is what the fingers and hands can do.

I remember my first patrol, I was the lower-level missile two guy, which meant you had to get in, you had to open all the deck plates downstairs, get in and unpin every tube. All sixteen of them as if we were preparing to launch. The guys would be down at the other end. "We don't have to get in there. They won't know that." Well, I said "No, we're going to get in now. I'm going to do these eight and you're going to do those eight, and if you don't do those eight, I'm going to do those eight, and then you ain't going to be here no more." I probably got a lumpy head from how many times I hit my head on the bars coming out of there. They were right. You didn't have to unpin them. They would never know. But it was your job. You're supposed to do your job like it was your job, like it was the real thing.

I remember watching Stevie, he was the Casualty Control Technician. He has to sit there. If something went wrong, he had to think fast and get it done. I remember thinking; I want to do that so I took the books home during off-crew and I would memorize them and that's what I did. I memorized every relay, every front, backside contact, everything. I could draw it all. As soon as they gave me a shot at that, I didn't want to be an LOS [Launch Operations Supervisor]. I didn't want to work on the panels. I wanted to be a CAS control technician. I remember once when we launched we had one gauge stuck and Stevie showed me a little trick, give it a shot, comes back into line, missile goes back in the channel, we're fat, dumb, and happy. It was cool. I liked it.

When you had to know what the failures were and how to get there fast that's the part I really liked. That attitude was pervasive through what I did for Picker and Philips. It was, when you would walk in the room and there's a patient on the table you've got to be able to tell the tech if this is a five-minute fix or move the patient down the hall because I can't get this done today. It was something I worked on really hard to be able to do because later on in life I got a chance to sample that, unfortunately, with Sue [His wife]. How anxious some people can get when a test is going down. If you can get that thing done for them, that was what I wanted to do. The training I got on the boat definitely served me well back out here in the civilian world.

I did get to do a man overboard drill. Go figure, on a submarine, man overboard drill? When another MT reenlisted to go E5 he went to shore duty. I got all of his jobs on top of mine. Microfiche and all the parts guy and all of that. One of them was man overboard and I'm like, man overboard? He goes, relax, it's just a title; you'll never do it, you're a submariner. Third patrol, I'm getting woke up, c'mon man overboard. I go, "what?' You're the swimmer. They put me in this harness on top of the deck and just told me to run as fast as I can off the side, just be careful of the barnacles. You got to be kidding me. But there I was in my Navy-issue swimming trunks standing on the top of the deck in the gray skies and a guy standing there with a rifle. What's that for? Sharks. I'm feeling better already, thank you.

When Mac [the Division Chief] saw my writing, "Oh, you've got neat writing? You're in charge of all the pubs." The changes that come through, all the things that we had to put the line on the side whenever there was a change. That turned out to be a good job too because you had to read all that stuff. They told us that we had to read this and get it checked off. Well, I did actually read it because I had to make all these changes so some of the stuff I remembered. During one of our inspections the inspector wanted to know the lowest auto ignition temperature in the missile. To me, that was a trick question in that the answer he had was wrong. This guy went homicidal. I remember him slamming his hands down, saying "I'm going to be right back." He slammed the door and I remember Mac looking at me and saying "you better be right." I said, "I know I'm right. I can't tell you the page, but I know I'm right." The guy came back in, I was right and that was the end of it.

I remember some of the fire drills on the boat. I remember one in particular when we'd just got done doing a drill and then a real fire started. That was in the galley because we were coming up doing angles and there was grease or something in the galley and it started a fire. I remember standing by. I was ready right by the hatch with the fire hose. Put me in there. But the forward guys got it done before we could get in there. It was like, open the hatch, open the hatch, open the hatch.

I can't remember how many sub systems there were in the missile compartment, there might have been nine. I was in charge of seven. That's why I went to the yards or else they would have short-cycled me. When we were over in dry dock, we went in for refit, they sent us across the street in Norfolk for firefighting school. Basically, this firefighting school was more for surface fleet, definitely. Multi-layers, all these ladders and things, actual stairs, not ladders. I remember the drill was a runaway fire hose. The fire hose was in the casualty. The guy got hit with shrapnel and now the hose was flying around. They gave us a video on how to stop the hose and one of the guys, the trainers, would go out and show us how to stop the hose.

Now they step back they turn this thing on and I'm telling you, it's going bonkers out there. The brass handles on the end of it, I'm the second guy in line, and I'm behind Zeuss, this freaking guy is from Texas. He is amped. He was ready to go. He runs out there and that hose took a bounce, it clocked him right upside the forehead. Knocked him cold, right on the ground. This guy hits me on the back of the neck, "Go get him!" I'm running out there thinking oh man. I'm watching that hose, and somehow I got it down. I don't know how. This guy is on the ground, bleeding no and one's taking care of him. The guy goes, "Way to get the hose!" Dude! This guy is bleeding over here we better drag him out of here. Then they gave me some kind of award for that. I didn't even know what the hell I did.

But the best part was the last day of school. They would dress you up like you were serious firefighters. I was the lead hose guy and I had to go down and put the fires out. It was like a giant video game. They would sound this alarm and we'd start going down the stairs. They'd tell us the fire is on the lower level, lower level three, so as you're going down and they'd start another fire somewhere. We get all the way down to the bottom and the clock's counting. We got one minute left before this fire can't be put out and the ship is lost. We're standing down there at the last door and the rule of thumb was squirt the door and if you see steam off it you can't go in. So, I squirt the door, all the steam's coming off it. The officer there goes, "Well, we can't go in." The guy who's in control turns around and goes, "What are you going to do? The ship's going to sink. What are you going to do?" The guy goes, "Well, we can't go in." He [the instructor] looks at me and goes, "What are you going to do?" "I'm going in." He goes, "Go in" so I kick the door in and in we went. Man, I must have had God sitting with me that day, I'll tell you, because I aimed the hose right at the right spot, and boom, put the fire out like that. There were 35 or 37 seconds left. The instructor says, "This guy did what you're supposed to do."

At the end of my enlistment I had to have a job. We already had two kids. It didn't look like work was going to be easy to come by so I had a headhunter looking for me and I went on several job interviews. The night I was filling out the papers to reenlist the headhunter called me and told me I had a job in Rochester and I could start on Monday. I'm like, ah this is great.

I was sitting up in the control room, one of the welders, something fell into the frame bay. I'm sitting up there and I think I smell something so I wandered downstairs and I opened up the chief's room and it was pitch black in there. I couldn't see squat. I'm like, oh crap a fire started. I spread the word and stuff and everybody got off the boat and I managed to even put the fire out. How? I don't know. I go on auto sometimes. I got some kind of award for that too.

I don't know, they must have figured I was trying to get out. The Captain wanted me to extend for two months so he could meritoriously advance me. I hadn't been an E5 long enough. I had to ride the boat through the yards which wasn't a problem. I didn't mind doing any of that but I really wanted to go to college. Me and Sue, when I went in, we were going to go in for six years. I was going to get as much education as I could out of this use the GI Bill when I split and go from there. We had done that.

I ended up with an outfit called Picker International, later Marconi Medicine, and still later on, Philips Medical Systems. I got the job because they had hired a Navy guy previously and he flunked his physical and they wouldn't let him out. I left there on Friday and I started with Philips on Monday. I couldn't use the Navy GI Bill for the first year because they said learning the CAT scans at the time, that was the up-and-coming technology and they wanted you to concentrate on that totally, which I had to do.

One day I thought they'd hired a new guy and it turned out he'd been in our department for six years and I never met him because he was so busy. All I said is, "Hey, if you need a hand, let me know." Twenty-five years later, I was the only guy in that modality left. He needed a hand. He needed some help, and I didn't mind helping at all. That was nuclear medicine.

Nuclear submarines. Well, why didn't we see this right away? What the hell? Put him over there. That's how that worked. I finished my career with that company and here I sit.

Kevin Powers, my sea dad, he led by quiet example. He wasn't what I'd call a big ball of fire but when Kevin spoke he had the experience behind him. He usually wasn't wrong. He made good decisions. Somebody like that you look up to them. You follow what they're saying. Now, you might deviate and go your own path but you've got that input and from that you can make good decisions. Chief McCoy was intense. Whatever that guy wanted me to do I was going to do it.

Captain Gray; professionalism to the max, unbelievable. Oh my, where do you start? To start out with, between the two of these guys [Captain and XO], and I know we've said it to him and he's heard it, I felt like I was on the Starship Enterprise. I swear to God, you've got Kirk and you've got Spock. Between the two of those guys it was incredible. Captain Gray would come back and he could look at the logs and he could see something on that log and he would ask you a question about it. God dang it you better know that answer because he did. That was the impressive part. Front to back in that ship. He knew that thing. I had so much respect for him. He could take a joke, he could get serious when he had to, he also let us let our hair down when we had to. If you know how to read your crew that's how you get things done.

To me, a leader is someone that gets assigned a task, knows what the task at hand is, sets out the goals of how we're going to accomplish that task, and then goes about and meets those goals. If there's anything that comes up in-between that might stop you from hitting that goal, you adjust, you move on, you take input from the guys you're working with and you get it done. That's just how I was doing things. Even though NAVY stands for Never Again Volunteer Yourself it turned out to be a good idea. You know what, when the job's got to get done, I'm not one of them guys that leans on a shovel. Matter of fact, I don't think I could be. I want to get in there. I want to get it done.

Sometimes it's uncomfortable or the hours are long or the problem might be days long. I've had problems with the medical equipment that might run into a week as you chase these problems through the thing. It just requires focus, a lot of dedication, and you know who you're going to let down if you do. In my case, after I came out of the Navy, it was a lot of people; patients, the techs that work on the equipment, the people that schedule it. You know, the people back home who think maybe their test got delayed and now they get a little more anxious. In the Navy, it was totally different. It was national security. I took that very seriously. When it was time to play, I'm ready to play. But when it's time to work, I went to work. I think that came from Mom and Dad. Half the people I talk to don't even believe I was on a submarine. They're like, "You? You've got to be kidding me." I'm like, "Yeah, yeah, believe it or not."

Chapter 4

Silent Service

John Buffery
Petty Officer Radio Supervisor, RN

HMS Ganges Museum is dedicated to the 160,000 boys who went through the gates as boys and marched out as men, from its inception as a Royal Navy Training Establishment in 1905 to its closure in 1976. The training was tough, brutal at times, yet many of those who came through remember HMS Ganges, at Shotley Gate, with a certain fondness.
HMS Ganges Museum, https://www.hmsgangesmuseum.com

I had only just passed my 15th birthday when I left home and joined the Royal Navy. Probably unthinkable today but that was back in 1960 – a different time with different attitudes. I served for twelve years, 1960-1972, with the first 3 years classed as "boys" service (i.e., didn't qualify for pension). "Mans" service didn't kick in until my 18th birthday. Just about all the latter was spent in submarines. I was born in London in 1945 right at the end of WW2 when my dad was serving in the British army. My earliest childhood memories probably begin around 1949-1950 so I don't remember too much of

London apart from a lot of the buildings still showing signs of bomb damage.

When I was four my father was posted out of London to the county of Norfolk on the English east coast, it's the bit that bulges out towards Europe into the North Sea and it's very rural. It's agriculture. It's farming; wheat, corn, barley, sugar beets, a few cows but very agricultural so it was quite a change from big city life. Life there was better than in London but we were still suffering from war shortages. Meat and dairy products were still rationed so it was tough. The whole family was, I wouldn't say poor, but like everybody else my parents had taken a hit and they were coping the best they could. We had food on the table and warm clothes even if some were second-hand.

Educationally, it was probably a bad time for us. During the early 1950s most children in the UK started school at the age of five and finished at the age of fifteen. Country kids weren't really expected to go into further education; boys were expected to work on farms and girls in shops, that kind of thing. But, at the age of fifteen I rebelled, having decided working on a farm wasn't for me. I sort of liked the idea of going into the military because it was just after the war and there was still an awful lot of military around us, including a lot of American Air Force bases. In fact, both my sisters ended up marrying US servicemen and emigrating to the US. But that's another story. Anyway, I applied for the Royal Navy, was accepted and at fifteen years three months I left home and went to HMS Ganges. A boy's training establishment.

In today's woke society they would probably say it was a cruel brutal establishment, but it taught discipline, teamwork, and made you into a worthwhile person. Boxing (or milling as it was usually called) was mandatory. You got into a ring to fight an opponent but if you didn't hit each other hard enough a Royal Marine instructor got in and hit you both till you did. My nose has never fully recovered. There must have been 200-250 boys there from all over the country all aged about fifteen. We were split up into individual classes of about thirty. I applied for the communications branch as I didn't fancy being a seaman, gunner or mechanical engineer. I guess that influence came from my father who was involved in signals in the British Army. So I applied, passed the aptitude tests, and completed basic training to become a junior radio operator.

Boy's training at Ganges lasted for about a year. After that my class, most of us were now sixteen years old, was sent to HMS Mercury, which is on the south coast about fifteen miles inland from Portsmouth. This was the Royal Navy's communication training establishment. There we learnt naval communication procedures, improved our typing and Morse code speeds, and learned how to operate cryptographic equipment. After about six months of this I finished basic training (now nearing my seventeeth birthday) and received my first draft - to an old oil-fired minelayer, HMS Plover, running out of Portsmouth Harbour. We lived on the mine deck and slept in hammocks. We had what the British Navy called "mess desk catering," which basically meant the leading hand from the mess went to the galley, drew the vittles for the day and brought them to the mess where we had to prepare them. We then took the preps to the galley for the chef to cook. It was quite an education. Unusual. Occasionally, I go for a walk around HMS Victory (Lord Nelson's old Flag Ship, circa 1805), where life appeared to be no different – just like the Plover.

I served on Plover for six months; we cruised around the North Sea and did lots of visits to European ports. I seem to remember Amsterdam being a favorite – but then I was too young to really appreciate the benefits! After six months I was taken off Plover and posted to HMS Rooke, a naval shore base in Gibraltar where I was given 24-hour watchkeeping duties in the comcen. After that six-month tour everything changed. I was just coming up to my eigteenth birthday when I received a draft chit to HMS Dolphin for SM training. Not a clue. What was SM training? It was only when I got there and saw a row of submarines tied up on the trots that the penny dropped. I then realized that the past three years had been merely preparing me for my 18th birthday when, according to the Navy, I suddenly went from "boy" to "man" after which they could do whatever the hell they liked with me. I was not alone. There were dozens of us. No one had volunteered, the option of submarine service had never been discussed with any of us but being in the Navy that didn't matter - you did what you were told.

Bear in mind this was still 1963, and several things were happening in the Royal Navy. A lot of the old timers, the twenty-year men who had served in WW2 were coming up for retirement. They were leaving the Navy in droves. The British Navy still had about 30 operational diesel electric submarines so they needed crew for those. Plus we were entering the nuclear age. Beginning to develop, build, and run a nuclear fleet. I think HMS Dreadnought, our first nuclear submarine came into service in about 1962/3. So basically, the Navy needed a lot more submariners. Back in the 1700's the navy used press gangs – frankly, this didn't seem much different, but heck I was only eighteen, full of life and adventure so I thought "ok, I'll give it a go and see what it's like. Dad served in tanks in the army; if he could serve in a tank I could certainly serve in a submarine," so I did. Some of my mates though were really up in arms, they didn't want to serve in submarines. They deliberately failed their class exams without realizing that would make no difference. As far as the Navy was concerned, they were submariners but as they'd failed basic training they wouldn't qualify for submarine pay! Amazing what they could get away with in 1963. Can you imagine that happening today? I don't think so.

So, 1963, eighteen years of age, I found myself as a semi-qualified submariner but with no submarine experience. I'd passed all the basic exams and completed escape training but I now needed to get onto a submarine to fully qualify. Because so many of us were in a similar situation there was a bit of a lull in postings. Hanging around in HMS Dolphin was getting boring so a few of us started browsing through various training manuals looking for something to do when we spotted vacancies on a "Shallow Water Divers" course at HMS Drake in Plymouth. It didn't begin well. Our very first dive involved wearing leaded boots with UBA rebreathers incorporating a canister of soda lime to scrub CO_2. Problem was the sets were old, the rubber was perished and once water reached the soda lime it started to sherbet. Stuck thirty feet down with thick black mud up to your crotch, zero visibility, and foaming at the mouth was not a pleasant experience. Instructors described it as character building. Slipping on fins and a scuba tank after that was like winning the lottery.

We were taught to dive to 100', carry out hull searches, clear propellers, filters, grills etc.; all fairly simply straightforward jobs. Anything really serious was left for the professional clearance divers. As soon as the course finished I received news of my first boat. It was the one I wanted, dreamed about in fact, HMS Trump a T class diesel-electric submarine running out of Neutral Bay in Sydney Harbour, Australia. Gosh, in just three years from leaving home I'd travelled around Europe, lived in Gibraltar for six months, completed submarine basic training and a diving course, and now I was off to Australia for two years. Magic.

Oddly, back then in the mid 1960's, Australia didn't have any submarines of their own. Theirs were still being built in the UK so the RN stationed three diesel boats out there for the Aussies to exercise with. Another advantage was that the Aussies had a pretty laid-back attitude to it all. They seemed to operate on a Monday to Friday basis so most weekends we were back in port. As you can probably imagine it was a pretty good time for a nineteen-year-old. A lot of guys married Australian girls, some requested a transfer to the RAN, and one even went "on the run" disappearing into the outback never to be heard of again.

But I was fairly content. I'd become a competent radio operator with quite satisfactory reports, so I eventually returned to the UK (still single) to await another draft. This came very unexpectedly in the form of a pier head jump. HMS Artemis was about to sail on a six-week patrol when one of the radio ops went sick. I was given less than 24 hours to pack my kit and join the boat. Artemis was another old WW2 diesel-electric boat, so it was familiar territory, except this was Cold War running. Not swaning around Australia for a few days a week in crystal-clear warm water.

It's all in the history books now, so there's no secrets here. Basically, we were trying to seal off what we called the Iceland-Faroe's Gap. We would send boats up there, hanging around, trying to detect Russian submarines coming out of the Artic Sea passing through the gap into the North Atlantic. It wasn't a very enjoyable task. Boring mostly. Awful weather. Not particularly dangerous, although the Russians were notoriously unpredictable so I guess there was always the chance of a collision. We weren't there to stop them or anything, just to try and identify them then transmit a contact report. The early Russian Victors were big and fast but very noisy so we usually had plenty of notice.

It was whilst I was on Artemis that I met and married my wife. I was twenty-two, she was twenty, so we were both pretty young. It was only then that my life really began to change. There's not much I regret about my life, especially my time in the Navy, but looking back as a much older man I do regret not making the most of the opportunities the navy offered me.

We have this expression in the British Navy, "Jack the Lad." I was out with the boys, we were in the bars, we were playing sport or having a good party time. Not a lot of drive, not a lot of ambition. But when I got married that suddenly changed. I realized I did have responsibilities, I now cared about someone more than I cared about myself so I needed to buck my ideas up.

By this time I was a very experienced radio operator so I immediately applied for promotion to Leading Hand (a Killick in RN terminology). I passed the course, got promoted and found myself posted to HMS Tiptoe. My third WW2 diesel-electric boat. I think it was the last British submarine to fire a torpedo in anger towards the end of the war, so I think the drafting office was just having a bit of a laugh at my expense. We took the boat straight out of major refit up to Faslane for a general work-up. Long hard hours. Lots of sea time. Dozens of inspections but we got through it okay.

It was still Cold War running, same sort of stuff as Artemis only by now (1969-70) the IRA was very active in Northern Ireland so our replenishment trips up the river Foyle into Londonderry were greatly restricted. No shore leave and it was the first and only time in my nine years in the Navy that the trot sentry was actually given a gun. An old Sten gun of course, very fitting for the age of the boat but he only had the gun. The Officer of the Watch kept the magazine! We did other things as well. A trip over to the AUTEC range working with the USN in the Bahamas was great fun until on the way back we ran into a storm force 12. Surface running. All hatches shut, basically snorting on the surface. We lost half the casing, bits of the sonar dome, parts of the fin. On one occasion the boat went so far over one of the big heavy B40 HF receivers in the W/T office toppled out of the rack and crashed to the deck. I managed to jump out of the way otherwise it would have killed me. Before we made it back to the UK, I sent the longest encrypted signal by morse in my whole career. One hundred and twenty groups reporting storm damage. The boat spent three months in dry dock after that with diving depth limited to 150'. So we finished the commission as a local training boat. Tiptoe was the very last of the RN's T class diesel submarines. They've all been broken up now. A pity, they were good boats.

After Tiptoe I applied for a petty officer Radio Supervisors course at HMS Mercury. Three months of quite intense instruction and exams, a bit of a struggle for me as I had masses of experience in HF comms but not so much with the latest data/satellite equipment, which was the current thing. Nevertheless, I qualified and spent the last couple of years of service on Flag Officer Submarines (FOSM) staff at HMS Dolphin. Ironically, I was on duty in the comcen in 1971 when HMS Artemis sank alongside trot 1. Three men were trapped inside but escaped successfully using standard free ascent techniques that was part of our basic training. The only time, to my knowledge, that this has been done for real. It was an interesting evening. Unfortunately the boat was a write off.

Artemis sinking had no bearing on the fact that by now my nine years' service was coming to an end, so do I re-enlist and go for pension or leave the Navy and try my hand in civvy street? The deciding factor for me was probably Polaris. I knew my next boat would almost certainly be a Polaris boat running out of Faslane. If you're familiar with UK geography you'll know Faslane is right up north in Scotland, and I live just about as far south as you can get in the UK. My wife's family was down here. Everything I knew was down here. And I knew the Polaris boats were doing three-month 90-day patrols and frankly I didn't fancy doing that.

Fortunately, in 1972 jobs in the UK were plentiful. I applied for lots, got all kinds of interviews, got all kinds of offers, so a decision had to be made. Once again, the Navy helped me make it. In those days the RN had a policy that allowed you to return to service without loss of rank or seniority so long as you did so within six months of leaving. So it was a no brainer really. We'd try civvy street and re-enlist if it didn't work out.

I had a pretty good CV, good recommends with good security clearances so I spread the net far and wide. Of all the jobs I applied for one in particular intrigued me. A friend had left the Navy and joined a government department entitled Government Communications Bureau (GCB). He was a bit cagey on the phone, wouldn't say much about it except it was a good job, good pay, good prospects. So I sent off an application, filled in dozens of forms and attended a number of somewhat unusual interviews that cumulated in the offer of a job. It was only then that they told me I had actually joined the British Secret Intelligence Service (SIS) as a communications specialist.

One thing that made the transition from the Navy to civvy life fairly easy was the fact that a lot of the people I finished up working with in SIS were ex-military. You could pick them out; their manner, their bearing, their attitude, positivity, no nonsense stuff. Quite a few were submariners. I once asked someone if he was an ex-submariner but he said, "No such thing, once a submariner always a submariner." So that's where I spent the next thirty years.

We managed to get a few accompanied overseas postings but most of the time it was out and back. Once again Navy training came in handy for the family – once a Navy wife always a Navy wife. Independent and resourceful. I thoroughly enjoyed that part of my life but by 2000 technology was rapidly changing and I found myself trying to manage a group of whiz kids that were speaking a language I could hardly understand let alone comprehend so I decided to pack it in and try something new.

I went to work on a steam railway at a local zoo. Having spent most of my working life either in a submarine or a windowless office being out in the open all day long was bliss.

Whipsnade Zoo in Bedfordshire is a conservation park with a 2.5 mile looped narrow-gauge railway track. We ran two steam engines and one big old diesel. I worked with a small team of like-minded retired professionals taking the general public on rides around the park. It was brilliant. Best job I ever had.

Now I've gone full circle. I'm back in Hampshire, doing voluntary work as a guide at the RN Submarine Museum showing the public around HMS Alliance the only surviving A class diesel-electric submarine left intact. She's up on blocks so certainly not seaworthy but well worth a visit. Alliance is the same class as Artemis and very similar to Trump and Tiptoe so it's just like going back in time. As she is a WW2 boat I often get asked if I served on her during the war! I know I'm old, but not THAT old, so my usual reply is "which war are you talking about? There's been a few since 1945!"

If you're ever down this way come and see us. The submarine museum is located at Fort Blockhouse on the western side of Portsmouth Harbour. The RN took the site over in 1903 for use as a submarine base. It was renamed HMS Dolphin and remained a submarine base until 1998 when we finally phased out our remaining diesel boats. The museum has a number of galleries full of artifacts and memorabilia all pertaining to the submarine service from earliest conception to the modern day. In addition to Alliance we have X24, a four-man mini sub used in WW2 to attack targets in waters too shallow for normal sized boats; and Holland 1, the very first submarine designed and built in 1903 for use with the RN. Latest acquisitions include a full-sized Polaris missile and a full-sized Tomahawk. You can check it all out on our website if you're interested.

There are times when I wish I had stayed in the Navy and made it a full-time career, but I was lucky, I left at the right time and had a successful career with the Government. But memory fades with time – society and the Navy has changed considerably since the 1960's. Back then there was still quite a bit of British snobbishness. "Keep your place" or "Speak when you're spoken to." Little emphasis on progression or staff development particularly for junior rates. The RN had three classes: Officers, Senior Rates and Junior Rates. Officers gave the orders, Senior Rates made sure they were carried out, and Junior Rates did them. There was little other interaction between the groups, unlike today where personal development and progression are actively encouraged. I remember one disgruntled crew member complaining bitterly the only time his Divisional Officer spoke to him was when barking out an order. Fortunately, those days seem to have passed.

One officer I do remember with great fondness and respect was the First Lieutenant (second in command) on Tiptoe during our work-up in 1967. He was an Australian attached to the RN for submarine training. He was absolutely brilliant. He had a very calm, commanding but approachable manner. He worked us hard, but he had our trust and respect which in submarines is vitally important. I think he knew every man's Christian name and would always find time to explain things to you.

Looking back on my life I have a lot to be thankful for, and to the RN in particular. There's an advert for the RN running on UK TV at the moment. It shows a young lad going through basic training with the words "I was born in Newcastle but made in the Royal Navy." It could almost be my epitaph.

Chapter 5

Educators

Gregory C. (Greg) Kane
Topedoman Second Class, USN

More than 240 middle and high school students from across the state descended on Killingly High School on March 25, for the annual Technology Student Association Conference. The students came from 18 schools to compete in more than 15 technical competitions. Those events involved problem solving, mechanical, architectural, and structural engineering, robotics, dragster design, video game design, debates, and extemporaneous speeches. Connecticut Technology and Engineering Education Association Representative Greg Kane was one of the 40 people called in to judge the competitions. He is a retired state consultant for technology education for grades K-12 and is the current fiscal agent for TSA Connecticut. He coordinates CTEEA workshops and robotic championships that include underwater remotely-operated vehicles. He is also an adjunct professor in the school of Engineering, Science and Technology at Central Connecticut State University.

Hartford Courant, April 5, 2017

It started with my brother who was on a destroyer escort. I was always fascinated about that and thought that was really cool. He was part of the Fifth Fleet and when he came in from a training cruise the family went down to Newport and we watched the whole fleet come in. I thought, "Wow. This is cool." I liked what I saw. We went onboard his ship. It was the William R Rush and toured through it. All younger brothers look up to their big brother and I thought, "Wow, this is pretty good." He was a boatswain's mate, now in retrospect, submarine sailors we laugh at that but at the time I thought it was pretty cool. But what really turned me on to submarines was about the same time down in Groton fishing on the Thames River with my father, one of the diesel boats went by. When I saw it I said to my father, "I'm going to be on one of those someday." And I just knew instantly that was something that I was really so fascinated by and knew very little about submarines, but I knew that was something I always wanted to do.

I knew I didn't want to go to college right after high school. I was fed up with high school. I had enough. I liked using my hands and my head. I didn't like just sitting in a math class looking at a whiteboard and a chalkboard. Didn't make much sense to me but industrial arts classes did. So I knew I wanted to do something with my hands and it was during Vietnam. My draft number at the time was something like 160. So I knew that I would be drafted, there was no doubt about that because that was in 1966. I knew that I didn't want to go in the Army or the Marines. I wanted to go into the Navy and I wanted to be on submarines. So I enlisted in the Navy knowing that's how I wanted to go in. That's how I got into the Navy.

Remember the Arlo Guthrie story about Whitehall Street and they talked about what's going on there? I was inducted actually on Whitehall in the induction center in New York City. I took a train from Hartford and that was an interesting experience. I stayed at the Seaman's Inn, which were very small rooms, kind of a dumpy little place, but the Navy put me up there before I was sworn in.

During Vietnam when everybody seemed to want to get out of going into service, I wanted to go in so badly that when I was there going through the medical stuff, the checks, they found out that I'd had a concussion as a kid so they had me see a psychiatrist. I went, and I'll never forget this, when I went to the area to meet with the psychiatrist I was in this big room sitting with probably forty other people. Some of them were guys dressed as women, some of them were with their mothers crying and their mothers hanging onto them. When my turn came I went in and had to talk to a psychiatrist, not sure why. I explained what happened and he said, "Well, why do you want to get out?" I said, "I don't want to get out. I want to stay in. There's nothing wrong with me." I can remember to this day the guy looking at me said, "You're not here to get out of going in?" And I said, "No." And his next comment was, "Get the fuck out of here and go back where you came from." He was stunned that here I was wanting to go in.

I took the train to Chicago into boot camp and had the good fortune of spending from December 16th until late January, early February, at the Great Lakes Training Center in the dead of winter and all the goodness that comes along with that. Marching with our watch caps pulled over our head, only the first person in line could see where we're going, frozen clothes, getting up for your watches at night and shoveling outside, shoveling the road, shoveling the street.

When we went through the testing, the ASVABs and stuff, they said I did pretty well on that, and they said, "Well, what do you want to do?" I knew I wanted submarines, so the only thing I could think to say was I want to be a torpedoman, because I knew that torpedomen all went to submarines. That's how I ended up becoming a torpedoman. They said, "Okay. You're going to leave here and you're going to come back for A school, and then you'll leave after A school." I went through that and did fine. When I was getting near the end, I was near the top of my class, and I went to Key West, Florida.

So picture this. In February, I leave Great Lakes Training Center to go to Key West, Florida, to training school. Traveling in my winter blues, and when I got off the plane in Miami, they put me on a little puddle jumper to Key West and I got off in Key West and it must have been 90 degrees and I'm in my blues, my wool, heavy blues. I already looked sunburned because my face was so red, I guess, from being so hot. But I went through torpedoman school, which is kind of an unbelievable situation, because we did things like stood tank watches. There are big oil tanks along the shore there in the annex where the torpedoman school was and at night we'd go there. You could literally see the lights of Cuba. Cuba was close enough that you could see that.

I had a rude awakening. I went there, they said, "Okay, now you can look at duty assignments. So, we're not sure if we're going to have you on submarines or if you're going to be on a surface ship." I had absolutely no idea until I got to torpedoman school, that there were torpedoes on surface ships and I started to panic. I thought, "Oh my God. I'm going to end up on an aircraft carrier or something," which is the last thing in the world I wanted but fortunately enough my next assignment was submarine school. Went through submarine school back in Groton and then from there went to launcher school at Dam Neck, Virginia, and then I was assigned to the USS George C Marshall blue crew and reported aboard the Marshall. I didn't report right aboard the Marshall because I was in the offices. I reported to the office in Groton, not the Marshall, because it was our off-crew period.

As they were getting ready to leave, they told me I was going to a Mark 45 school. Guess where? Key West for a week. So they sent me back to Key West while they all flew to the Marshall, which was then located in Charleston. When I left Key West, I flew to Charleston and I went aboard, which was kind of scary because I was feeling pretty good about going there with the crew so we'd all be together. I reported all by myself to this submarine for the first time, which I didn't know what it was going to be like, or how it was going to happen, or how I'd be greeted. I knew nothing. I wasn't even sure how to get aboard. I had to go through a tender to get there. But anyhow, that got me to the Marshall.

When I first went aboard as a torpedoman there was either one of two things you did. Either you're up in the torpedo room, there were only three that were assigned to the torpedo room, or you were back in the missile compartment in the launcher area. At that point we would've been starting out as roving patrol where I was responsible every hour for going around checking different gauges and looking at different aspects from the bilges up to the third deck of the missile compartment; checking each one of the missile tubes for certain things and that's what I did. So I immediately started my qualifications.

The torpedo room had a three-person bunk area on the outboard side of the actual starboard outboard side. I was to live up there and stay up there and stand watches in the torpedo room but I had no idea what that meant. I had to very quickly get acclimated and qualified on everything I needed to do for the torpedo room. For the first patrol I stayed up there and for my six hour watches I just sat there walked around, looked at gauges, gave reports, and so forth. My other duty, my very exciting duty, was for the maneuvering watch, the anchor watch. Once again, I sat in the torpedo room, up by the release of the anchor in case they ever had to drop it in an emergency. So for my first patrol that's what I did.

Patrols after that, they moved me back to the missile compartment where I started on roving patrol and then I ended up as the launcher watch where I would sit in the launcher area for the entire time as I moved up from seaman apprentice to seaman. When I made Third Class I was in the missile compartment and as Second Class, I was in the missile compartment. So the rest of my time on the Marshall I was in the missile compartment until just before I got out, when I didn't have enough time for another patrol.

I thought I'd get out, but instead they transferred me to the Grampus, a diesel boat in Norfolk, Virginia where I spent four months on the Grampus as the leading torpedoman on a World War II diesel submarine; knowing squat about those diesel submarines and squat about torpedoes because I did missile compartment for two years. The Grampus was one of the last diesel boats in the United States submarine fleet. It was also assigned to NATO so they had to keep it active. It was stationed in Norfolk and it was set up to have a crew compliment of 75 guys. We had 45 on this submarine. We would go to sea with 45 guys because there were only 45. People had to stand starboard and port watches sometimes because there was nobody else to stand the watch. I was on that submarine for four months. I learned very quickly that the Captain had a piranha fish in the ward room that they used to feed hamburger and the forward capstan was brass and he was crazy about keeping it polished so he could see his face in it. So instantly I met some of the weirdest dudes I've ever met in my life.

Our job was two-fold. One was to go out on weekends to take submarine officers on shore duty out so they could collect sea pay. They had to spend so many hours a month at sea and our job was to take them out with us. The other was to go out and be a target for the fast attacks in Norfolk to practice torpedo shoots. We were tied up at a pier with fast attacks and this one diesel boat. The entire time I was on that submarine it never once dove without emergency surfacing because someone forgot to shut a hatch, someone forgot to shut a valve; every single time that submarine dove it had the emergency. I swore to God I was going to die. I didn't think I was ever going to make it back.

When I reported they said, "Oh, you're a Second Class torpedoman." I said, "Yes." They said, "You want the forward room or the after room?" I said, "What's the after room?" Of course, I knew what it was, but it set things up to start with. They said, "Well, you're our leading torpedoman now so you can pick which room you want to be in charge of and here are your qual cards." I said, "Two things. One," and by then I'm a Second Class with four months to go, "I don't know shit about torpedoes, and I am not going to qualify in this submarine. I'm not going to be here long enough. I'll do what I need to do to help you and everybody else stay alive." I slept on a bunk that was on one of the torpedo skids so the torpedo's next to you. I'd see it banging back and forth. I'm leaning up against a Mark 14 torpedo when I slept. It was the most God awful thing I've ever seen.

In the chow hall they had a main vent over one of the tables that would drip oil onto the table while you're trying to eat. And this is not a sea story. We had a bowl of mashed potatoes, and one of the guys sitting at the table said, "Hey, some oil dripped in the mashed potatoes." He called the cook over and said, "Hey, Cookie. There's oil in our mashed potatoes. We can't eat these." He said, "Yes, you can. He took a spoon and stirred it and said, "Here. You won't even taste it." It was like that all the time. I have no clothes left over from when I was in the Navy because everything I owned smelled so poorly of diesel smoke, I got rid of them when I left. It was so bad that we were pulling in one day after going out on the Chesapeake Bay to be a target for the fast attack, we lost hydraulic power and we rammed into the stern planes of one of the fast attack submarines tied up in front of us.

One time we had one of our machinist mates standing on the pier, and it's like, "Okay, we're going to bring the brow over. Come on, Smith, get on board." "Nah, I don't think I'm going to go." And we're all standing there listening to this. The Officer of the Deck up in the conning tower says, "Smith get your ass on board. We've got to go." "Nah. I don't think I'm going to go. I got a bad feeling about this trip." He wouldn't get on that submarine. We had a machinist mate that would refuse to wear shoes when we were at sea. Did not wear shoes when he was on watch at sea. He was assigned up in control because he was watching the manifolds and stuff. He wasn't back in the engine room, but he was up in the control room doing that. That is what it was like. But what I did learn in that four months is an unbelievable respect for World War II submariners.

If you had never gone to sea on a diesel submarine, if you've never rode out a storm on a diesel submarine, or had someone shoot a dummy torpedo on a diesel submarine, or see what it's like to snorkel when you had to, or see what it's like when your batteries are running low and you have to surface, then without that you could never fully appreciate these brave, brave men that went to sea on submarines during World War II. It was absolutely remarkable. I'll never regret that experience because of that. Many of the guys on the Marshall, at least the younger guys, I don't think anybody I ever knew, some of the older chiefs might have or first class but most never rode on a diesel submarine. So I don't regret it because of that. I get out of the Navy one day shy of my full four years. One day. They let me out one day early. That was it. But that was my USS Grampus experience. Remarkable. Absolutely. But I also met some very interesting people there, too, some decent people on that submarine, but you talked about F Troop. Remember that TV show F Troop? That's exactly what that was.

When I got out of the Navy I knew what I wanted. A couple of my friends worked for a phone company. What I decided I wanted to do was install telephones in people's houses. I applied for the job, and lo and behold, they said I was overqualified to do that because of my electronics experience with the Navy. What I was qualified to do was to work inside a building on their big circuit boards, which to me would've been a kiss of death because I still didn't like the idea of just being inside when I wanted to go out and move from place to place and meet people and do that kind of stuff.

I ended up going back to what I did when I was in high school and got a job from a very gracious man who did not need me and told me that when I asked him if he had any openings. But he called me back later that day to say yes he did need me, which turned out to be absolutely ridiculous. He just hired me out of loyalty and I made soap for a company that's now become Simoniz. I was his first employee ever when I was in high school, worked just weekends. He hired me and I was there until I decided that I wanted to move on. I applied and for three years I was a parts man and then a service advisor and then a mechanic at a Volkswagen dealership and then I decided I was too smart for that and I wanted to go to college.

I started off at a community college. An old industrial arts teacher helped me get in because I knew if I did go to college I wanted to become an industrial arts or Tech-Ed [Technology Education] teacher and the semester had started but he was friends with the registrar and he got me in. I went through three years of community college and four years at Central Connecticut State University and I became a Tech Ed teacher at a middle school. I taught industrial arts, Tech Ed, and earth science at the middle school.

Then they asked me to move to the high school and rebuild a program that a young teacher had started but died early. I did that and then a friend suggested that I apply for the job to be the state supervisor for Tech Ed for the state of Connecticut. Never thought I'd ever get it, but I thought it's good experience to try and I applied, and they hired me as the third ever state consultant for the state of Connecticut for Technology Education, Grades K through 12. That's what I did until I retired, and now I teach part-time at a university, Technology Ed teachers, full circle. I'm back teaching teachers now to become what I was when I got out of the Navy.

I want to talk a little bit about lessons learned, what the Navy did for me because this is the reason I'm still involved. I shouldn't say still involved. This is the reason I got reacquainted with and involved with the Navy. When I went in I thought, I was like most teenage males, I was smarter than everybody, stronger than everybody, better looking that everybody, but that was true. But I realized that there's some things that I just would not put up with. For instance, and what's really scary is that during my high school years, I dated the woman I'm still married to. She knew me when I was in high school, she knew me when I was in the Navy, she knew me when I went through college, and we're still together all these years later. So when we would go to the movies if there were three people waiting in line outside I'd keep going because I have no patience for that. I'm not going to wait in line. If someone cut me off, I got mad and I'd yell at them and call them names, and say things like, "Old man," which people do to me now or, "baldy," which they also to do me now.

When I was in the Navy I found out very, very quickly that that didn't work. That you had to as they say, "Hurry up and wait," but that was the truth. That impatience would get you absolutely nowhere. I also learned very quickly something that I kind of knew all along that the people that were telling you what to do were not always smarter than you were. Now that was a lesson that I picked up in boot camp because we had a company commander that was literally a drunk and sometimes we'd find him passed out in the bunk early in the morning and stuff like that. He was the chief. I realized he wasn't very smart if this is what he was doing with his life and his career but I also learned that in order to survive; it didn't really matter if you were smarter than they were. If they outranked you, if you're going to survive you had to respect that and you had to at least attempt to do what it is that they requested or told you to do. I also knew that was essential because they may not be academically smarter but their life experience in the Navy was such that maybe what they were telling you to do you weren't smart enough to know that will save your life if you do it that way.

It didn't take me long to learn that. That was real valuable lesson because I think for the rest of my life I always questioned twice. "Okay. I don't think you're very smart, but let me see. Maybe you are, I'm just not looking at it the right way." I've been more patient with people and try to be understanding, and look for that part that was like that. That was a lesson that I really learned early on and I think if anything, that's one of the biggest things I brought from the Navy.

The other was my father always owned his own businesses. He was the kind of guy that would say, "You get paid for eight hours, damn it you work for eight hours. If it takes you longer to do the job, you stay until it's finished." I was brought up in that environment and that really helps in the Navy. I found, especially on submarines, that it really helped. When I first got on board I met somebody named Delbert Hayden who became our leading torpedoman, who I'm still friends with and he didn't seem that smart because he kind of had garbled-y talk and slow talk. I learned that he was brilliant when it came to like, well first of all he was the best poker player I ever saw in my life, but he was brilliant in lots of other ways and I learned how important it was to be part of a team because when Hayden would say to do something and you did it, it paid off at the other end. You didn't question why, because there was always a rainbow at the end of it if you listened to him. I found out that sometimes you have to do stuff you're not really wild about, that you don't want to do, but you don't have much of an option at this point.

I also learned to trust people. That was something that, as a young person, there weren't a lot of people that I trusted. You always think what's behind us? Why are you saying that? Why are you doing that? But I learned very quickly that if you're going to survive on a submarine, as I started to go through qualifications, what a dangerous place it really is and if you don't trust the person in the job that that person's doing, that they're doing it right, your life's in jeopardy. You start to build up trust but that also goes two ways. If you're assigned to do something, I learned, you better damn well do it and do it well because their lives could be impacted by a mistake that you might make.

I remember one time, and this I can vividly remember, is how important this is when you go through qualifications and why qualifications were so important. Hayden and I were talking in the missile compartment about something and there's a very small valve located in the missile compartment that controlled pressure sensing that actually calculated the depth of the submarine. And I realized, and I didn't know until I went through the qualifications with him, that if you open that at the wrong time you can sink the damn submarine. As simple and little as that was a really valuable lesson to me that when everybody does what you're expected to do, how important it is that you do it right and you know what you're doing.

I also learned that leadership was a lot more than just your rank because of someone like Del that I trusted. There was another guy named William Macpherson. He was our gun boss. Lieutenant JG at the time, and once enlisted guy. You'd be down in the bilges and next thing you know he's down there in the bilges next to you asking you questions, looking at something. If something went wrong he's picking up a wrench, he's doing things. He was one of the few people that I stayed friends with, officers, after I got out of the Navy because I felt like he cared about you as a person and you would do anything for him. I also saw the rest of our weapons department felt the same way and anything that man needed we did. Anything he said we should do, whether we liked it or not, we did because of that.

I started to formulate then that this is what leaders are all about. They're people that people trust, they're people that others don't always look up to, but they don't ever underestimate. They understand exactly what they're capable of and there are people that others aren't questioning. You've seen that too, I'm sure. All of a sudden here somebody says something and nobody questions it and you think it's kind of a little bit weird. It doesn't take you long to realize, they don't question it because they've seen that this person knows what they're talking about, they've been right. That's what leaders are all about and I saw that, and learned that in the Navy. It also helped me as a teacher, not always having the answers, and not always knowing everything's right and sometimes admitting you don't know the answers. That's when people start to look up to you rather than think you're full of shit and don't pay any attention to you. So I think in a roundabout way those were some of the things that I learned when I was in the Navy and how they impacted me for the rest of my life.

I got into Subvets because of my buddy, Harry Baker, who was an auto shop teacher that I met in my early days working for the State Department of Ed when the guy that I worked with said to me at a meeting, "Kane, you ought to talk to this guy Baker. He was a submarine sailor, too." You know what happens with two people that didn't know that. We became very good friends. It wasn't until after Harry retired from teaching, and I had retired from the state where I was working, that one day he said to me, "You told me joined the Subvets in Groton." I said, "Yeah. I saw that online somewhere and I did join. It's not expensive." He said, "I see they have a club house. Have you ever been there?" I said, "No." He said, "Well, I met this guy at a Francis Scott Key reunion named Bud Atkins." He said, "He was a Master Chief Torpedoman. He's a pretty cool guy. I'm going down to have lunch with him in Groton at their club house. Do you want to go?" I said, "I've never been there, but sure. Let's go down."

After about 10 minutes of sitting, talking to Bud, I thought, "Oh my God. This is like back when I met Hayden," the gun boss, and I said, "God, this guy's just like him." And the more we talked, the more I thought I really like this guy and all of a sudden a lot of the Navy stuff that I liked, because at the time, and you've heard this because of one of our reunions, this chief torpedoman, Chief Benson, said to me at one of our re-unions, "Kane, I remember you," and I thought oh, that's pretty cool. He remembers me, because I'm getting old and don't re-member everybody. He says, "Yeah. I remember three things about you. One is you hated to get your hair cut, two is you hated lifers, and three, all you wanted to do was get the hell out of the Navy." I thought oh shit that's what people remember of me? Oh my God and I realized that was true. But when I met Bud it brought back, sitting in the Subvets down in Groton, it brought back all the stuff I liked about when I was in the Navy.

I loved sitting around at launcher talking to guys hearing about their families and telling stories about being in high school and crazy stuff. I liked hearing about what their fathers and their mothers did. I liked talking to Macpherson hearing about how he went from being an enlisted guy to an officer. I liked being in the chow hall and just watching people push buttons, and laughing, and watching movies. I liked people qualifying coming and asking me questions. I started to think about the stuff I really liked. And I said, you know what? I'm going to stay friends with these guys. After that, it wasn't long, and Bud said something one time, "Hey, you're coming back down for lunch?" I said, "Yeah." After Harry went back, he actually spends winters in Florida and summers up here, and I went down to meet him. We talked a little bit about what I do and so forth, and he's the kind of guy that says, "You know what? I need your help." He said, "I run this thing called the Holland Club where guys that are qualified 50 years or more in submarines, we induct them and we have this thing on this stage. You're a teacher, you like to talk, why don't you come volunteer and help me set that up? We'll do that." So I immediately said yes.

I said, "Okay, I'll give you a hand." And we did the Holland Club, and I helped set up the stage, and I stood on the stage and helped pass out the stuff to the people that were bringing it out to hand to the presenters and so forth. And after, Bud and I went for lunch and he said to me, "You know what, you're a pretty good speaker. We're always looking for people to speak at sub school graduations and TM graduations. How'd you like to do that?" I said, "Yeah. Obviously I don't have a problem with speaking. Sure. That would be fun." So I ended up getting involved with speaking as one of the Subvet reps at basic submarine school graduations. I spoke at a couple of officer graduations. You speak at torpedoman graduations and sonar graduations and radioman graduations.

Then I saw they were looking for docents at the Submarine Museum and I thought this was a good way to get me from Manchester, fifty miles away from Groton, to at least come down once in a while. So I started volunteering to be a docent at the Submarine Museum and of course when I went down there I'd meet Bud for lunch and started to meet some other guys around there. I ended up deciding one day in talking to him that maybe I ought to see if we can put together a reunion for the submarine I was on, because I was in the museum one day when some guys came in from another crew that were there for a reunion. I thought this looks pretty cool.

I don't know how I got hooked up with Neal Santangelo, a guy that was on the Marshall but on the gold crew at a different time, and the two of us put together the first real organized reunion. I started doing that and really enjoyed that, with the 100% guidance of Bud. Because Bud Atkins was a major mentor in my life when it comes to the Navy and the submarine volunteering stuff and what that's all about, to the point where I say this with all truth, if I had met Bud when I was in the Navy, I would've stayed in the Navy for twenty years. He was the kind of person that would impress me enough that I'd say, "Boy, I want to be like him when I grow up." It just took me a long time to get there to meet him.

Along the way he got me to go to some conventions, to the World War II memorial down in King's Bay for World War II submariners, got me to speak once again. One day they said, "You know what you ought to do is run the scholarship committee for the Subvets." So being a good teacher like you and I are, I said, "Oh, yeah. I can do that, too." So I volunteered to do that too, not knowing what that meant. At that time we had to get volunteers and man a golf tournament and do all kinds of other stuff. What that's done is really reconnected me with all the important stuff that impacted me as a young person, and impacted me in many ways as I grew older.

It also gave me a chance to recognize and understand the importance of these young people that are going in the service now. To meet with their families and to be able to thank their families, tell their families how great it is, what a great thing they're doing. To tell their families how they're going to be part of this big family of submarine sailors. They'll be protected, they'll be watched after, they'll be taken care of, and they've got a group of people that will watch out for them for their entire life and make friends that will be friends forever. I also share with them that there are people I was with in the Navy that I started to realize after a couple of patrols, I knew more about some of these guys in the submarine that I had only been with for a year, than people I grew up with my entire life. A lot of it was sitting around launcher telling stories, and talking about their families. A lot of that has made me become more patriotic, it's made me want to give back in any way that I can. I love being able to speak at these graduations. Tell them how great they are and what a wonderful career they have ahead of them. What opportunities are out there and also how smart they are for doing what they're doing. That's the one thing I really recognized and appreciated on submarines, that some of the smartest people in the armed services are submarine sailors, enlisted or officers, doesn't matter.

I think that the friends that you make are really lifelong friends. I've learned, once again, how to trust people. And I didn't realize it. It took me a long time to realize that it was my experience in the Navy that did it. I learned to appreciate the things that other people have given me. The friendship, the advice, the help, the direction, all those kinds of things I realized a ton of that has come from one of my experiences being in the armed forces, being in the Navy. I just wish that we could get more young people to see that, experience it, and do it, and understand the importance of it.

I also realize more now than ever, because I've had the good fortune at different things at the Sub Base or in the Holland Club listening to these leaders, the current, modern day leaders of the Navy Submarine Service, how important the Submarine Service is to the security of the United States. What those young men and women are doing now out there on patrol, or going out to sea in their fast boats, what they're doing, how that is keeping us safe. That is the number one deterrent and when you talk to high-ranking Naval officials you hear that they understand exactly what it is. The Navy is our foremost weapon. Our submarines are absolutely important to everything we do in our well-being. And I'm very happy, and I'm very proud to be part of that.

The other thing I didn't mention and I do want to mention, is that there's milestones in people's lives. One of the proudest moments of my life, and I've got quite a few, when my children were born, that's probably top of everything. Getting married, that's another and graduating from school, that's cool but it's not that high up. The day that my dolphins were pinned on was one of the proudest moments of my life, that being part of the Submarine Service, and being part of this brotherhood of the Phin, is so much more than just symbolic, there's something about it that's in your gut.

It's not something you say, it's not something you put on a t-shirt, it's not something you just put on a hat or you say in a text message; it's real. It's palatable, that submarine sailors, whether they're modern submarine sailors or old guys like me, there's a connection. When you meet them, you feel something, and you know they feel something about you and I think that's really important that that's noted. That pinning those dolphins on is more than a symbol. That is a life changing experience as is what you did to earn those. Dolphins are never given. Those are earned and what it means when you see somebody with the dolphins on you learned on your submarine that's someone you can trust. You learned after that, that's someone you're going to probably like and that's someone you've got a lot in common with. That's a life changing experience and I just wanted to mention that. That it's important to note that. Qualifying in submarines is one of my proudest moments in my life. Maybe it sounds simplistic, but that's okay. That's what it is for me. We're both qualified in submarines my friend. That's what it's all about.

Harrison H. (Harry) Baker
Topedoman Third Class, USN

The highest recognition for professional commitment and dedication bestowed by the Connecticut Technology Engineering Education Association is the Harrison H. Baker award. Its namesake, Harry Baker, was the first recipient of the award.

In high school, I wasn't in any college program. I was a shop hands-on guy and I graduated at seventeen years old and the day I graduated from high school I went down and tried to enlist in the Navy. As sad as that is in the Summer of '68 it's probably the first time I realized that there was a war going on, which is shameful to say but the more I think back about it I think at seventeen the only thing I was worried about was how my girlfriend was and if my car had gas in it.

They took me in on a program. They wouldn't enlist me right away because I was only seventeen. I had to wait until I was eighteen, so I went through the summer there and on November fourth of 1968 I went down to New York and stayed on Whitehall Street and got on a train the next morning. I went to see the Merv Griffin Show too then got on the train the next morning and took an eighteen-hour Pullman first class train ride all the way out to Great Lakes. I used to hassle my father about it. I said, "You could've told me not to go to Great Lakes in November." My dad was a twenty-year man, '38 to '58 on heavy cruisers in the South Pacific. People always ask me if was he was the reason that I joined the Navy and I'm not sure it was although it was fascinating because I was young when he got out.

I was fascinated for whatever reason with submarines. I had books that my father later found at the house taken out of junior high school on Bushnell's Turtle and all about different submarines so for some reason I was always fascinated with them. When I joined I volunteered for submarine service as well. I got out there in November and the more I thought about it for the last couple of days but when I got out there it was all backed up. Everybody was, for one reason or the other, whether it was avoid Vietnam or just in love with the Navy, they were all backed up there. They had tons of people joining at the time.

They put us in Camp Moffett. We got there that night, as I said, off the train and over to the barracks. They gave us two gray blankets, one of which I had to stick in a window that was broken and the snow and the cold air was coming in and the other one, I slept on it. It was a pretty messed up facility at that particular time. It was one of those days where you hit the rack and you say to yourself, what was I thinking, what am I doing? Because it was backed up for the whole time, it took forever to start the basic training, boot camp and that got split and I think there was some kind of bad flu season or something going on because they let us go home for Christmas, which is kind of unbelievable from boot camp to being there a couple weeks and then wind up going home for Christmas and coming back again. I remember that the drill instructor, I can't remember what they even called him, the fella at the boot camp, he came in with a huge bag of cough drops for everybody.

From there I went to basic electrical and electronics school right there in Great Lakes and had to wait for those classes to start. After that I flew to Key West for advanced undersea weapons school and we had to wait for that. I think I was the last class to go through undersea weapons school down there before it moved up to Orlando. I got down there and was in a transit company or holding company until that school started and got through that one and went up to Dam Neck Virginia for missile school, launcher school and from launcher school I went to sub school and got through that.

My first boat was the George Bancroft. I went down to the Cooper River refit site in Carolina. It was the same time that I guess the 640 classes were all getting ready to go in for their missile conversion. I did one run on that and then I got off of that one and they put me on the Key. Francis Scott Key was the boat I qualified on and the boat I finally made third class on and all my evaluations were onboard in less than 90 days so nothing was evaluated at all these different places I was at. It was nice getting to the Key. The Key was a very different boat than the Bancroft and again, the needs of the Navy and getting the crews together to go in for yard periods I think was a lot of the reason that I experienced some of the things I did. As soon as I said I was not going to reenlist to go through the yards it seems like I had an awful lot of the messy jobs to do but that's in the needs of the Navy.

They were getting people qualified to go into the yard so fortunately I was lucky enough to bring the Bancroft back into New London and that was a time I'll always remember because my dad got on. He went down to the missile compartment and looked at where I was staying and he said, "I had to make chief before I had a mattress that thick." It was a time I'll always remember. Then as I said, I did two runs on the Key, got back, I made second class but again I couldn't accept that because I wasn't going to be in the Navy that much longer. I was probably in schools for just a little shy of two years before I ever saw a submarine on a four-year enlistment, which was kind of strange.

I got there and they said, "Would you mind staying onboard for a few more weeks and take the boat over to Bremerton?" It was going through the first missile conversion from Polaris to Poseidon at the time and they wanted to get the families out west because they were going to be there for three or four years. That was probably the biggest, my only real Navy story. You sit with these fellas like Bud Atkins, Lenny Robbins, some of these master chiefs that have been around, seems like forever, my stories pale compared to that and the things that they did.

Going out of New London just trying to get over to Bremerton. We had a new Captain, he wound up making admiral but we hit a buoy going out of New London and that triggered the collision alarm and all that stuff. Get down to Exuma Sound and we chopped up a multi-million dollar piece of sonar on our way out there that was doing some kind of calibration or testing. We went into the Panama Canal and the after bullnose hooked up to the camel there and it just ripped away from the boat. Never did get a good explanation why that happened but we went through the canal and it was very fortunate for me that I had the topside watch through the whole transit. I won't tell you how sunburned I got but it was quite an experience. Had a nice cookout on missile deck and some of the higher ups from Panama came out and joined us.

Got through on the Pacific side and forgot to come up and rendezvous with, I'm not sure if it was a Navy or Air Force craft, but they were a little irate and just about ready to report us overdue going from the Atlantic into the Pacific. There were a lot of communication problems so they couldn't raise anybody on the radio for whatever reason. The joke was why don't we put somebody in a small boat and send them ashore to use a payphone to let them know where we were.

We wound up in San Diego in the shipping lanes and I was just getting into my rack and this I will never forget. I hear reactor scram full scram and I said, "That's not right. I don't think we're supposed to do that one when we're underway" and then my light started to flicker and finally went out. I found out later after it all happened that the nukes were having a drill and scrammed the reactor and the snorkel valve was pinned open and we had the full scram. We lost depth and flooded out a couple of thousand pounds of water dropped down into

LEADERSHIP FROM BELOW ~ 71

the snake pit, the scope wells down there and the water spilled over from the snake pit into the fan room and the fan started pumping water aft, which took out missile control center and they tried the emergency propulsion but we just kept losing depth. They tried a normal blow and that didn't work and finally somebody hit the chicken switches and we came up out of the water with an emergency blow like a cork.

I think that was about the same time that Chief Baptiste, one of the missile tech chiefs, asked me if I was sure I didn't want to reenlist and I said, I think I was pretty sure at that time. Finally, we get up to Bremerton and coming into Puget Sound, it was explained to me later that, you have to test your anchor before you go into dry dock so we dropped the anchor and of course couldn't get it back in and dragged it along the bottom. We cut off some phone cables going from Seattle to Puget Sound and they put divers over the side late that night and hooked the crane to it and finally lifted it up and put it on the pier next to where the boat was. That was quite an experience for a transit after a couple patrols where really not much happened other than burned out light bulbs. It was a memorable experience.

A side story with Greg. Greg Kane called me one Christmas Eve day. He says, "Hey listen, the George Marshall just pulled in, I just talked to the topside watch and the officer in charge said I could come visit. Do you want to come with me?" I said, "Oh sure." Went up with him and I told the story I just told you there about the little trip we had, the disastrous trip through the canal and the topside officer in charge there after hearing this story he says, "You know, I think we read about that in school," which immediately made us look at each other, feel a little older than we wanted to feel. It's very possible there's a reference to that whole spiel at the Academy.

I had gotten a letter from the Dean of Central Connecticut State College and that released me, I figured it was 30 or 60 day early out program and from there I went into New Britain, Central Connecticut and I started my work in becoming a teacher. I just happened to be there on the night that a lieutenant commander, a retired lieutenant commander was working. He was the Dean. He brought me into his office because I was in dress blues so we talked about the Navy for about two and a half hours and we talked about college for about fifteen minutes but he took me right under his wing and it was pretty smooth sailing after that.

I started college older. You have a little more experience under your belt. I think that helped me. I was able to give a lot of students throughout my teaching career guidance and suggesting the Navy and to not give up on themselves. A lot of them came in to sign up, so it was the guidance counselor who said you'll never go to college or you're not this and that so I used to clarify that for them that you can go to college and you can change and you can do anything you want inside of your life.

The Navy, the schools, the organizational skills I think would be the number one thing. The importance of having a plan and going forward and through with that plan until you achieve what you want. Just the label as a former veteran in the Submarine Service I think has opened so, so many doors for me and it's been great. I gained a lot of confidence. After some years of teaching I became a department head and then wound up taking on the alternative school responsibility, which was a big step. I met another former Navy gentleman that was in the district that I was working at in Naugatuck. He was an AG2 and he flew in the plane that followed the Nautilus under the ice. He did all the ice observations for that whole business there and we talked for a long time. He pushed me a little bit to step up to the plate and take on a Principal's job at an alternative school where the kids really needed some help. I wound up as the Assistant Superintendent for a little while and we did about 28 years of that and bought four of my years in the military, retired as a teacher in 2004, which was pretty good. Not a lot of people get to retire at 54 years old.

Greg and I didn't know each other when we were in the service, but I met him at a ITEA [International Technology Educations Association] conference in New Hampshire and that's when we started talking about the USSVI [United States Submarine Veterans Incorporated]. I said, "Yeah, let's go down and do it." We joined up. One of my first meetings at a boat reunion down in Virginia I ran into Bud Atkins and I introduced Greg to Bud Atkins. It's been history since then.

The naval experience and being on a submarine I think is different from the surface crafts from all the stories you hear. The guidance you get from senior members of the crew and the way the blend is of new crew and old experienced crews is a remarkable learning experience. It's got so much structure and so much foundation to it. The confidence building is remarkable. There's not as much rank and difference between officers and chiefs. Of course it's there but it's more of a family experience and I think that helps in a lot of ways to comfort you and put you at a state of mind where you're more able to learn, it's easier to absorb things, and not feeling challenged by some hierarchy, I guess I would say.

There was a vast difference between a missile tech chief and the torpedoman chief. I was a torpedoman but the torpedoman chief was prim and proper. If there was any kind of work activity going on he'd disappear. The MT chief, if you had an all hands loading party or whatever, he'd have his chief cap on backwards, his sleeves rolled up and he'd be right in there with you all the time. Two different experiences. Two just entirely different people. His friendliness encouraged me to move on and try different things more than the torpedoman chief. It was just their behaviors, their styles as individual people.

There was this first class, Clyde Lewis, and again he was a missile tech but I was struggling with LOS watch I guess it was and the launching panel. He was trying to explain it to me and he always had the big smile on his face and he was a first class. He said, "Just think of it like it works like a scoreboard." He was explaining relays and how different electronics work and again, a first class taking the time to help me go through the learning experience of how the missile part of it was working. He was a great help.

Some of the people were grumpy. We had COB, he was the full bird. I think his name was Hall and I remember when I got qualified he hit me so hard my Dolphins bent around his knuckle. They were U shaped when he got done whacking me in the chest. Yeah, that was an interesting time. He happened to be on watch when I went up to qualify on the planes as helmsman/planesman. I spent a couple of seconds in each seat. It was can I get signed off on it and he just kind of looked at me. He says, "Baker, all right, you can sit there but if you take me five feet off depth or five degrees off course, I'm going to rip off your head and shit in your windpipe."

I'm sitting there in the left seat, which I can't even remember, must have been the stern planes and of course I'm as nervous as a cat in a room full of rocking chairs and I'm just moving that thing up and down trying not to get off depth. I hear the phone ring behind me and it was someone from the engine room and they call up and they said, "Who the hell's driving this thing? I feel like I'm in the ass end of a whale." I could hear the hydraulics under me, they're flashing and they're moving back and forth. The old chief said, "All right, you're done. Get out of here." That was my driving experience.

I was told everybody goes mess cooking and they were harassing me as they did everybody about different things and they asked me to go find some coffee cans, the round coffee cans, fill them with water, put a string in it and put them in the freezer. I thought it was another one of these go get a can of checkered paint or bucket of steam or whatever. I said, "I'm not going to do that." He says, "We need them. We need them." There was somebody else in the galley there, it was one of the officers who overheard. He said, "Well, let me explain it to you." You may already know about the ice cube that they drop down the garbage disposal before they put the metal cans in so you don't scar the ball out as it rotates on the ice rather the wrapped up metal can that we shoot the garbage over with. It was a legit thing. These were ice cubes, they had to be made and actually even went to affect the whole integrity of the boat. It could take on water through that if that wall would become scarred. It was one of those things that you think they're pulling your leg and then you find out that it is something important.

The other thing that I found a couple of times and won't mention any names but they did have me as a third class watching over a second class at one time just to keep an eye on him. Rank wasn't always the total concern of who got jobs or was going to do what. So many different variables pop in your head during a disaster, during a drill, not a disaster. Everybody looking to see who was around, who's the senior there in the group that happens to be there at the disaster with you, who was going to say, "I'm in charge," and take it over. As I alluded to before the whole way it was conducted, the way it is structured pushes, not pushes, but sometimes leadership qualities float to the top of the heap when they're needed. That comradery; I'm not sure submarines could live without it but it certainly sounds different than other military experiences I hear from people.

Teaching, the biggest thing is the organizational skills. I think doing lesson plans and preparation and of course the hands-on experiences, using tools on the submarine led to better understanding of mechanics and how to put things together and take things apart, which I was always pretty good at anyway but I would have to give credit for that to the Navy too as well. Just basically having a plan, organization, neatness, the reason things are done the way they are. Some of the seniors, they'd probably be put in jail for it nowadays, but some of the seniors used to say, "Why do we have to clean these tools when they're going to get dirty again?" I said, "Well, let me ask you this, why do you wipe your butt after you poop because you're just going to poop again?" That clarified their thoughts a little bit.

Yeah, and even with the tools, a place for everything and everything in its place. That definitely helped run an auto shop where you're working with high school seniors that are coming and going every forty minutes and trying to get something done in a shop that holds seven cars with seven different things going on. You get a little crazy, frazzled at times. I think all of that, and again the age, just being a little older going into a lot of stuff. It was always helpful. That delay being in the Navy. It was four years I would never trade, that's for certain. Met all kinds of people, some good, some not so good, but mostly good.

I went to a Key reunion in Virginia and I got on one of the tour buses and a person was sitting next to the window all by himself. I said, "Would you mind if I sat there?" He said, "No, go." I sat down and we just started chewing the fat. I didn't know him from Santa Claus. He didn't know me, but Bud Atkins is your leadership type person, I'll tell you that. He started telling me some of his stories. I got to know him a little better and of course, Bud, he's ready to put the bite on you, trying to carry on some of the traditions and how would you like to do this or help out here? He certainly got Greg for docent and scholarship chairman and a lot of other things to do there and I'm, probably because of him, definitely because of him and Lenny, I'm the Secretary at the Weeki Wachee USSVI down in Florida.

That was it. It was just a chance meeting during the reunion and I palled around with him going here and there to different establishments. We can call them establishments. Trying to keep up drinking beer with him, which is not always a good thing to do. We became friends. Again, it was just a fortunate meeting. Then Greg and I've been going back and forth about joining USSVI and like two little kids. Okay, I'll hold your hand. If you're going to join I'll join. We both joined at the same time and as I said, I introduced him to Bud and that was it.

Another thing I got for a moment and it goes back to the Navy too. When I took on the Principalship you wander around through the school and the one day somebody along the line had told me one of the leadership things is don't sit in your office all day. Get out, tell people that they're doing a good job, that you're aware they're there. One time I went down to the other end of the building and the football coach was at the far end in the gym. I went down just to say hi. He looked at me and said, "What are you lost?" because they had never seen a Principal wander down that far before, I guess, away from the office. It was funny. The amount of mileage you get out of an individual by just stopping and having a couple words or giving them a pat on the back when they do something is more important than any pay increase or trophy or anything else one time at the end of the year. Just being in plain sight and encouraging people on a daily basis for the job they're doing. I think that's important. That's a big part of leadership.

I was working in an older building. I was working up in the attic when I first started as a principal and this fella came over and started asking me, "What are you doing up there?" I said, "I'm just cleaning up." He said, "Don't hurt yourself." Later he found out that I was the new Principal of the school and he came back and he was like, I don't know if he was worried he was going to get fired or what but he was apologizing, "Oh, I didn't know you were the Principal." "Hey, relax, take it easy." One thing I try to encourage with everybody in a school is that everybody is important. There's nobody that's more important than anybody else. We need everybody there and everybody rowing in the same direction. I don't care if he's a custodian, a cafeteria worker or whatever. Show them the respect, show them that their job's important and you know they're there. I think that's all good stuff. It worked for me.

Put the time in. Be there. It's like the chief sitting up on the missile deck working with us at an all hands party or we used to have some teachers and department heads that used to be following the last school bus out of the lot as it was leaving in the afternoon. Put the time in you want them to put in. Lead by example I guess is key. You can't be telling them one thing and doing something different. People have told me that they, maybe it's because they're getting away with murder I don't know, but they told me that I did a good job in the different positions I was in and they never had anybody pay as much attention to what they were doing as I did. Again, it's that presence. Be out there in the hallways or offices or wherever asking "What's going on? How are you? What's going on at home? Everything good? Anything I can do for you?" Just your presence is important.

The interesting thing is every job I've had I have been hired before I filled out the application which is, thinking back, kind of strange. A lot of it was because you would go on an interview in a school system. Well, at least the ones I'm acquainted with, most of the superintendents, assistant superintendents of schools were all former military people. A lot of them were former military people so they'd look and they'd say, "Oh he screams military. Hire him." That says something for military leadership because everything else, when you're classified or grouped into people of that kind, veterans or military folks, it gives you a heads up and gives them a heads up as interviewing candidates that there's an expectation that you're going to be coming with certain things already in you. I guess right away it helps with the screening process.

Another thought that I had when I was in the alternative school. Even after teaching for twenty-plus years, when I took on the principal role there, I think listening skills were either improved or heightened or whatever. I'll try make a long story short. I had a lady that came in. She wasn't a teacher. She was a paraprofessional who came in, used to run that cafeteria duty for us. It was a smaller building. Very religious. One of the first things she asked me when I came in, she said, "Would it be okay if I take my lunch hour in the morning?" because she goes to church every morning at a Catholic church. Well she came in all upset one morning and had seen a couple of the kids the night before with a BB gun shooting up a statue of Mary. She was just out of her mind.

To get to the point, when I brought the kids in and it still shocks me to this day that it can even happen in New England and Connecticut, these two kids, neither one of them had any idea what they were shooting at. We know the Virgin Mary statue. She knows the Virgin Mary as one thing; to them it was just something to shoot at. You have to listen to that and hear both sides of the story before rushing to judgment about things. I had a kid that was sleeping in a garbage truck every night. He was sleeping in the cab of a garbage truck before he came to school each day. Kids that had good attendance I used to take to breakfast and at one of the times we ordered the breakfast and it came and the kid did not know how to use a knife and fork. This is a high school kid and what amazed me was the kid sitting next to him said, "Don't worry, I'll show you." Here's a kid who's either eaten fast food all his life, not eaten or whatever but he had no idea. They all ordered steak and eggs when the Principal was going to buy them breakfast.

That word got out pretty quick. I guess it was a leadership thing. Be sure you have the whole story. Listen to what people's needs and concerns. You've got to be a good listener. You can't rush to judgment about things just because you hear one person's point of view.

It's a great place to start. Some of the stories are a little scary nowadays about how it is now but boy it was absolutely great for me. That's for sure. There are people that are discouraged about the military. I don't even know what it is now but the GI Bill, oh my God. That paid for my bachelor's, my master's and my sixth year, all of the administrative certificates. I tell people when I went to college it cost me 75 dollars and 50 cents a semester. That was the fee to go to college at the time. It certainly was very lucrative for me because I probably would've wound up being an electrician with one of my uncles somewhere. He told my father somewhere along the line if I didn't want to go in the service he could get me an apprenticeship as an electrician. It wasn't until years later I found out he was a submarine sailor during World War II. I said, "You got to be kidding." He was quite a guy. I wish I'd known about it earlier. Would've had some interesting conversations with him.

The Navy's been very, very good to the people I know. It's just an experience you can't really explain it to people too much but it's just the comradery and what did the chief once say to me? We were up there waiting for a missile to be loaded next to the tender. This is that chief, Chief Baptiste. He was a character and he'd be on one of those styrofoam things they put around the nosecone and you got the missile hatch open, half around type of thing. He was sitting in one of those like it was a lawn chair and he'd say to me, "Baker, what more could you want? You're on a multi-million dollar yacht in the Mediterranean?" I said, "Yeah, well that is true."

Chapter 6

Keeping the Lights On

Doug Ackley
Machinist Mate Nuclear First Class, USN

Navy nuclear power and civilian application have been closely aligned from the beginning. The first nuclear submarine, the Nautilus, and the world's first full-scale commercial nuclear power plant at Shippingport Pennsylvania both claim Admiral Hyman G. Rickover as their "Father." Rickover was famous for his incredibly high standards and grueling and unusual interview techniques like cutting several inches off the front legs of the chairs of candidates or ordering them to stand in the closet for a few hours to think about their answers. He also personally drove the standards, selection and performance of the Navy's nuclear fleet including all nuclear submarines. Those standards for both enlisted and officers in the Nuclear power program make it among the most demanding careers in the Navy. It also creates significant opportunity for civilian employment and leadership in commercial nuclear power.

In high school I started working for our local town recreation commission. In the summer I was lining softball fields, football fields, and in the winter I was driving the Zamboni in the hockey rink. My best friend was a year behind me in high school. Probably midway through his senior year, he was still working part time, we kind of got this illusion of joining the Navy and we'd be visiting all these foreign ports and all those exotic things together. The two of us went to a recruiting station and took the test. We knew what we wanted to do; we wanted to be in the Seabees. We both had an interest in construction and the things that the Seabees do but the Seabees were full. Our recruiter convinced us about this nuclear program and how wonderful it would be. We thought about it. The only catch was it was a six-year commitment right off the bat, but again, with that you come out of boot camp as an E3, you come out of A school as an E4, and then normal progression after that. We talked about it and decided that we would go in the delayed entry program. We went ahead and signed up, probably in April or May, for active duty in September.

We enjoyed our last summer, we kept working right up until the time that we left and off we went. We went to boot camp together, which is part of the guarantee of the buddy program. After boot camp we went to A school together, which was right there in Great Lakes. Then you had to wait for your position to open at nuke school and that could take anywhere from three to six months. Well, here's where my best friend and I went separate ways, he went to a reserve Navy ship down in Philadelphia and I stayed at the A school to be an instructor at the school that I had just gone through. When he got to his reserve ship he was talked out of the nuclear program. So that was the end of our career together and we weren't going to end up seeing all these foreign ports and all those activities that you kind of think will be glamorous.

I went to nuke school down in Orlando and after that it was to prototype, which is a mockup submarine or destroyer of various types. That was another three months and after prototype when I was qualified they asked me to stay. I was a Machinist Mate and I was asked if I wanted to become an engineering laboratory technician, or an ELT. I just thought it was three more months of not going to a submarine or a surface vessel so of course I said yes, and that's when Nancy and I were married. While I was there, this was all at prototype at Saratoga Springs, New York, I filled out my dream sheet or wish list of where I wanted to go, what type of vessel I wanted to be on, and I said that I want to be on a submarine and I wanted East Coast. Having just gotten married the idea of a boomer and the relatively set schedule was much more appealing than the fast attack where you don't really know. I felt very fortunate that I got exactly what I asked for, a boomer out of New London, that being the Marshall.

We moved to Groton and the boat was on patrol, but they were pulling into Roosevelt Rhodes. They decided in April of '78 they would fly me down to Puerto Rico and I would join the boys there and have like five weeks before we pulled back in. That's where I went. For me it was a lot of anxiety between leaving my wife back in Connecticut although she went home. Not knowing anything about the boat or anyone on it, I walked down the pier at Rosey Roads and a guy that I had met in nuke school, a reactor operator, was walking off the boat. Automatically I knew somebody right away.

I did five patrols on the Marshall. We were operating from Rota Spain and Holy Loch Scotland and we did the one refit in March of '79 in Kings Bay, Georgia. It was just a continuous motion of qualification. First qualified on the engine room, lower level. Soon I could stand watches and then you'd move around to different watch stations and had to qualify ELT. I think one of the things that I really took away from the Marshall was that everybody had a job. Even though the military has chiefs and lieutenant JG's, commanders, and seamen, I came to believe, especially on the submarine, everybody's job was as important as everybody else's.

It stayed with me forever, even after the Navy that when I would introduce somebody in a social setting that worked for me, I always introduced them as somebody that I work with. Whether it was the engineer on the sub or somebody else, I always felt that I worked with them. We had different jobs, and their job, part of it was to make sure I was doing my job, but I just kind of took that away from the Navy very strongly. That's just a reflection of Mike Gray. It wasn't really the Navy way. The Navy way many times is very different.

I got to be about my four-year point in my six-year term when they had the STAR program. The deal was you dropped your two-year extension and re-enlisted for four, giving you a total of eight. If you were qualified you could pick the duty that you wanted. I could pick a different boat, I could pick shore duty, with the understanding that if I was accepted to go back to prototype in Saratoga Springs to be an instructor that I would drop my two-year extension and re-enlist for four. That's what we did, and got a small bonus for doing it. I think it was like $15,000 back then in 1980.

I left the Marshall in August of 1980 and went back to prototype to be an instructor for four years and three months to finish out my time in the Navy. I left the Marshall as a second class and very quickly when I got to prototype was advanced to first class. But I knew that by now we had two young kids and I didn't really want the thought of going back to a submarine where if I got a fast attack I could be gone for months and months. Even with a boomer, three months is hard with two small children. We made the decision that at that point in time we would get out. The family separation would just be too hard. Didn't regret any of the time in the Navy. Obviously, the family separation was very difficult.

Out of the Navy I looked all around the country and I kind of made my mind up that everybody's going to need electricity so I'm going to see if I can get a job in the nuclear utility industry and continue my career in the nuke field that way. We interviewed a few places in New England and I was offered a job north of Syracuse, New York, at a commercial nuclear power plant. The James A Fitzpatrick plant of the New York Power Authority, and I accepted the job as a Radiological and Chemistry Technician. I went out of the Navy as an ELT and went right into work in the commercial industry doing radiation protection and chemistry.

I liked the job but I was on shift work, so I did about a year of shift work and then I had the opportunity to leave the bargaining unit as a technician and go into management as an instructor. I took that opportunity and went into management. First, I was an instructor in the general employee training, which is the entrance exam for anybody coming to work in the nuke plant. I did general employee training, which everybody had to redo every year and it was the basic knowledge of the plant, radiation protection. Everybody who goes on the site with a badge has to take that training.

After about nine months on that a job came open to do the emergency planning training. I would train the entire plant staff in emergency preparedness, what to do in an emergency. Everyone from the plant manager, the operators, mechanics; everybody had a job during an emergency. I also had people from accounting that attended that training to have a better understanding of what we would be doing during an emergency. Did that for about a year, year and a half and applied for and was promoted to the technical training supervisor.

I had all of the technical training programs under my responsibility; the mechanics, electricians, instrument control technicians, chemistry, radiation protection, and general employee training. I had those instructors who worked for me providing the training. In a commercial nuke plant you're in training every six weeks. Enjoyed training very much. My goal was at that time I wanted to become the training manager, but the person that was there I didn't see as leaving very quickly based on age. He was doing a good job.

An opportunity came up and I was asked to take a job in operations as the operations review group manager. I asked the superintendent who was doing the hiring if I had a better chance to become the training manager if I stayed where I was, or if I became a department head in a different department. He felt that it would be easier for me to do a lateral to training manager, plus they really needed somebody to do the operations review group. I took on that challenge and went to operations. The operations review group's responsibilities were the corrective action program; all the root-cause analysis and everything any time an accident occurs. It was human performance so it was looking for trends and opportunities to improve the human performance of the staff. We also did a quarterly trend report that showed the trend of just about every metric you can imagine. We could try and predict where problems were going to occur and do something, put something in place, or make training or procedure or supervision changes to avoid those problems.

I was then on a committee as a collateral duty around 1999. They were looking at the possibility of either selling the nuke plant that I worked at, or forming a New York State Nuclear Operating Committee to operate all the nuke plants in New York. It became evident to me that the power authority was going to sell the nuke plant. I didn't want to leave the power authority because of the retirement system and if we went to a different company my time and service credit in that retirement system wouldn't continue to grow. In the power authority I searched very hard at their hydro facilities and found an opportunity to jump ship from nuclear to the hydro.

I interviewed at three different stations that have hydro and fortunately a gentleman hired me to go work at Niagara Falls in their big hydro project as a first line supervisor for the general maintenance department. General maintenance has all the civil structural, everything concrete, which in a dam there's a lot. And then all of the support systems and everything for running facilities including the fleet maintenance, all the vehicles, even ice breakers. I did that for a year and the gentleman who hired me took the plant manager job at a smaller hydro up in Massena, New York, the St. Lawrence project. He had a department head that was moving on. He asked me if I would be interested in interviewing then he subsequently offered me the job as a department head at the St. Lawrence project, which happens to be in the hometown where both my wife and I grew up.

We were really fortunate to be able, at the time her mother was aging, and my mother was aging, for us to be able to go back home to Massena. But it also then took me back to department head level within the authority. I was the general maintenance superintendent. The hydro facilities have licenses that last 50 years, and they were in the negotiation phase of the relicensing effort. Our corporate office for the power authority was down in White Plains, New York, and it was hard for them to, in my opinion, do an adequate job because they didn't live up there. After that agreement was reached it became evident that they needed someone to be in charge of the licensing activities at the site. The plant manager asked if I would accept those responsibilities along with the responsibilities I already had as general maintenance superintendent.

After review and turnover, I accepted those responsibilities. I was the general maintenance superintendent/licensing man-

ager for the projects. Really that was the job, as a general maintenance superintendent I had about 65 people working for me;
carpenters, painters, welders, fitters, mechanics, auto mechanics, equipment operators, planners, engineers, a couple of supervisors. I thought I had the best job in the power authority.
Outside, inside, all around the grounds of the dam and everything.

I got to the point where I was eligible to retire, but there
were three projects that I wanted to finish. Well, two projects
and I wanted to make sure a guy that I hired got my job, so I
ended up staying probably six or seven months longer than I
would have. I just wanted to see those projects through as they
were very high-dollar. Of course my replacement, to me, was
very important. Then in 2013 we retired and I've been enjoying
retirement and chasing our granddaughters, and now we have
a new grandson, around. We split time between Massena in the
summer and Annapolis, Maryland in the winter.

I think the first thing was, as I mentioned earlier, we all have
a job in an organization, whether it's military or out in the civilian world. Although there's different pay grades and different
responsibilities, I'd like to think that everybody's job was important otherwise we wouldn't have created that job. In the
Navy under Captain Gray and the lieutenants that I worked for,
whether it was Tommy Stewart or Jim Ellis, the engineers, Jim
Sullivan, I felt like they were just a part of the team and that I
was part of that team. I was an important part of that team.

I never thought I was looked down upon because I was a
second class or a third class or a first class petty officer. They
respected the job that I had to do. They made me feel that
way so I wanted to do a good job. I always felt that it was a
very important lesson and I wanted to take that when I left
the Navy. When I got into a supervisory role I wanted to make
sure that I made the people who worked for me know that they
have an important job to do and I'm going to ask them to do

it. Don't ask me not to do my job and I won't ask you not to do your job. I'll never ask you to cut a corner. I'll never ask you to take a safety risk or violate something. Never ask me to look the other way when you're doing that or if something's not right. We were part of a team where everybody respects what the other person is doing. But sometimes you don't like it and there are many times in the civilian world people are like, "Why are you being such a hard ass, Doug?" I'm like, "Well that's what's expected of us working in the nuclear industry." I carried that to hydro as well. There just isn't a lot of room for error at a nuke plant and the better you can prepare the people the better off they're going to be.

I always thought to do a job correctly was like a three-legged stool and this was something I got from a committee that I was on years and years ago. It's like a three-legged stool you're sitting on and the training was one leg of that stool. You took training away, you're not going to be successful, the stool's going to fall. Supervision, the appropriate amount of supervision or for a new person or a new task you need more supervision, obviously. But if you take the supervision away that stool's going to fall. The last was procedures. It's a combination of those three things. In a simple task a procedure might be very, very simple and supervision might be simple, but you had to train the people depending on their level of expertise. Every job that we're going to do, or every job that we are assigned, I ask myself those three things. Do we have the right level of supervision? Are the people adequately trained? Is there a procedure in place, and is it adequate for the task they're doing? I carry those things from the Navy in my early days in the nuke industry throughout my career.

I think the wardroom takes on the personality of your commanding officer. I have been in other commands, maybe not on a submarine or a ship, but in prototype and in training facilities, and I think that the commanding officer's personality can really shape the crew. Starting with the officers in the wardroom down to the seaman who reports aboard who's undeclared yet on what they want to do. I think the stronger the choices the Navy makes for commanding officers really shapes how people under them are going to do. Look how far the engineer under Captain Gray went on to be ComSubPac. I think it's a tribute to their selection process and I think a lot of it is individual credit also, in our case, to Captain Gray.

I just think on a submarine you get to know each other as you are all in that tube together. I think you learn a lot about each other and a lot about yourself when you're there. Trying to reflect a little bit more. It's funny, when I first started working at the nuke plant, everybody knew I came from the Navy because of the position I got hired at and I got hired as a journeyman not as an apprentice. They all knew I was a Navy nuke as most of my department was. It was probably the only department along with maybe some engineering that were Navy nukes. Nobody really told sea stories. Yeah, you might have heard once or twice what boat they came from or what ship they came from but you didn't talk about it very much.

It wasn't until I got to the hydro world where people were interested in it, wanted to know more about it, what it was like. Then since retirement after seeing some of our old brothers from the boat and Facebook reconnecting with people that we had lost contact with it's much more obvious to people now that I was in the Navy and that I was on a submarine; by a t-shirt or a hat or a glass that I'm drinking out of, or something. It gives me a great sense of pride to have served but especially to have served in such a small group on a submarine. It's still a pretty small brotherhood.

The other thing I noticed about sailors, they seem to walk with a purpose. They don't strut, but we walk with pace, we get to the next place we're going to do whatever that task is. Where a lot of times when I'm walking with a group when I was working outside of the Navy, the people were just kind of meandering down the hall getting to the meeting; the two guys who are going to be there first are the guys that were in the Navy. They'll just get there, let's get this baby going, let's find out what the job is and let's get it done. I think that's all from the Navy. Maybe it was the constant drilling, the need to make fast decisions. But I think that's something else that I carry was get to the point, tell me what you need to do, tell me what you need done and I'll do it right now.

I've been very fortunate. It was hard at the time, but I look back very fondly. It's good reconnecting with people from the Marshall. Another thing that I think about as a bonus is being able to think on your feet very quickly. No matter where you were on the boat, if something went wrong you were expected to be able to help out. I think that that was pretty important too, being able to think fast on your feet. Again, that wasn't so much your competition, but for staying alive. That's how we had to be or what I think we learned as well. Don't panic. Do what you're trained for.

Robert (Rob) Davis
Senior Chief Petty Officer Machinist Mate Nuclear, USN
(Ret.)

I got out of the Navy in '86. I went to work at Millstone, I stayed in the area. I didn't even know there was a Submarine Veterans Organization. I was in a bag pipe band, we did a parade in Groton. We ended up at Subvets for some reason, invited us in to play the pipes and stuff, we're all downstairs in the bar area. I said, "This is quite the organization." They said, "You have dolphins, you can join." I said, "Really, I didn't know that." I joined and I liked what they were doing, I liked being able to go into a place where I could sit down and have a beer with people I know and even people I didn't know, but we could still have a conversation because the majority of us had the same background. We might have had different boats, different commands, but we had the same background.

I graduated high school in '65. That was like the height of the Vietnam war and I hadn't planned on going to college. For some reason I decided college just wasn't for me because I didn't want to put up with all the extra stuff that you got to go through in college to get your degree. I had uncles in the Navy. My older brother was on a fast attack out of San Diego and thought the nuclear power program would be a good fit for me. My intention was, when I joined the Navy, to make it a career. Do 20, get out and get another job and then retire from that job and then a life of ease. I enlisted in the delayed entry program in November of '65 and went through recruit training in San Diego in March of '66. My specialty was Machinist Mate, which meant that I was working on a propulsion system; engine room, turbines and pumps and valves and stuff, mechanical stuff that I like to do.

Got out of boot camp, went to Machinist Mate A School and Basic Propulsion Engineering school that taught me the basics of what I was going to do. After that, I went to Basic Nuclear Power school because Mr. Rickover thought that if we were going to push a button in the engine room of a nuclear ship, that we should know what that button did. There was a lot of theoretical stuff, reactor plant knowledge, physics, we got some electrical theory, reactor theory. They said it was equivalent to getting your Associate's Degree in six months because we went to school eight hours a day, five days a week. After I got out of Basic school, I went to Prototype in Idaho Falls, Idaho and that was another six months of actually running a nuclear power plant that was out in the desert. I was at the A1W Prototype, which was a mock-up of one of the engine rooms on USS Enterprise, an aircraft carrier. After six months there I graduated and I went to Engineering Laboratory School. I became a Water Chemistry Technician.

I was an instructor out there for a while and then I got orders for submarine school. Finished submarine school and then got orders to go to USS Skate. I was on Skate for a couple of years as a Machinist Mate in the engine room and then from there I went to the USS Tunny new construction. I was on her for a number of years. Again, Machinist Mate, I made chief on the Tunny. From there I went to recruiting duty for three years and I went back to submarine force on USS Groton out of New London for five years and then finished up my career at the Naval Submarine Support Facility in New London, working on repair and maintenance on board the nuclear submarines that were based out of New London. After that I went to work at Millstone Nuclear Power Station, I was there for 25 years using my experience in the Navy to get a job there and I retired in 2010.

My career choices worked out exactly as I'd hoped. I did my 20 years in the Navy and got out, a retirement check going. Did another 25 at Millstone. Strangely enough I did water chemistry, the same thing I did in the Navy except what I did in the Navy compared to what we were doing at Millstone would be like going from a '57 Ford to a 1986 Ferrari.

The chemistry, the apparatus out there, the civilian nuclear power plants are equipped to do so much more with water chemistry and chemistry control then we were on the boats. I went into the lab at Millstone unit three and looked around at stuff, I recognized the Ph meter and conductivity bridge. The other machines were all just bells and whistles that I had never seen before. I didn't even know existed. One of the guys looked at me, he was an ex nuke sailor, and he says, "Don't worry about it, they have a procedure for everything and they're going to send you to training and so by a year from now when you're qualified shift technician you'll know how to run all this stuff, so don't sweat it." I was fortunate enough that I was able to get a pension from there because at the time I went to work there you could still have a pension. Everything worked out exactly as I planned.

As far as the leadership role, it's funny, I never considered myself a good Chief Petty Officer until I'd been out of the Navy a number of years. I thought, "Okay, if you were to go back in now you'd probably make a good Chief." But when I was in the Navy I never thought of myself as a Chief, although I was supposed to because I was one. When I took my first Chief's exam while on the Tunny, I wasn't going to take the exam because I just didn't feel I was ready for that step up on the leadership ladder. I was a First Class Machinist Mate at the time, qualified engine room supervisor and I thought, "This is exactly where I want to be."

I was working for a Master Chief Engineman named Herbert F. Gay, we called him Ben Gay, think about that. He came down to the 18 man bunk room and he yanked me out of my bunk and he said, "Why aren't you up in the crew's mess taking the chief's exam?" I said, "Well, I don't think I'm ready for it." He said, "Well, you better get ready for it in the next ten minutes because if you don't I'm going to kick your ass." I said, "Well, okay." I went up to the crew's mess, took the chief's exam for the first time and that was the exam I made chief on. After that, I had to learn how to be more a leader than I was as a First Class because once you make Chief you can be acquaintances with the guys that are working for you, but you can't be really good buddies. In that case, I kind of failed because we always had the guys in the division for beers and stuff like that.

One thing I learned to be a leader is that you got to think about, when you're gone, who's going to replace you? If they can replace you do they have the ability? By the time I left the Groton the guys in my division pretty much ran the division. I just hung around and supervised and made sure everything was going right but I was sure that had I dropped over dead at any time during that time period when I was on board the boat my First Class Petty Officers were all equally capable of taking over and running that division. That was one of the things I learned about leadership and the other thing I learned was, you got people working for you, you got to take care of them because if you don't take care of them they won't take care of you.

One guy that comes to mind at the top of the list would be Archie Clemins. When I got on board the Tunny Archie had just become the Engineer and he was a Lieutenant at the time and he was just sharp as a razor. We'd go up into the stateroom to get something signed for maintenance and he'd be at his desk with his reactor plant manual open reading, learning about the plant and he did that all the time he was on board. He made Lieutenant Commander as Engineer and of course he's still officer of the deck and he performed all the duties that officers are required to perform onboard submarines. He was always fair, he treated everybody that way. We respected him for it.

It was not, "I'm an officer, you're an enlisted guy and you got to do what I say and you can't have any questions." You could always have a question, you could always say, "You know Eng, maybe this would be a better way to do that." He would give it thought and if your idea happened to be better he'd say, "Well, go ahead and do it. That's a good idea." And then he'd give you credit for it. One of my other examples was Herbert F. Gay, Ben, he had been on the Sculpin with my brother so he saw me coming up as the new generation. He qualified as Engineering Officer of the Watch on the Tunny. Most guys normally didn't stand that watch. It was usually a Commission Officer's watch station but he took that over and excelled at it. He was a good EOW. I guess I picked up some of his leadership traits. Maybe I just thought the way they thought and it turned out because the way I thought seemed to work pretty good for me and it seemed to work pretty good for the guys that worked for me.

Those two guys are probably right at the top of my list. If I ever grow up, I'd probably like to grow up to be like both of them. Archie, by the way, I went to a ship's reunion a number of years ago down in Mobile, Alabama, first time I'd seen Archie since I'd left the ship and that had been a long time. Found out that he got up to be Commander in Chief of the Pacific Fleet. I told him when I saw him that if I would have known he was going to be such a lofty Admiral, I would have treated him with more respect when I knew him. He became quite the guy. Those two guys were probably at the top of my list. No, there was one more I should mention, one of my favorite Skippers, well I had two favorite Skippers. One was Denny Sloan, Denny retired as a Captain and the other one was George Emery, he was Commander Atlantic Fleet Submarines when he retired, he was a Vice-Admiral.

Denny Sloan was the Skipper on the Tunny and we called him Big Red because he was a big guy and had red hair. He also was one of those officers that treated you like a member of the crew. It was none of these, "I'm the Captain, you're the enlisted guy, do what I say or else." He was the same as Archie, you got an idea of how to do something and it's better than my idea then go for it. He was a personable guy, a very good leader and he had a good personality. We were leaving the tender, we'd been in La Maddalena, a six-month med deployment and Denny always liked that he had this big Stetson cowboy hat that he wore underway and Ben Gay made a hat band for him out of orange shot line. He was wearing it on the bridge on the boat, getting underway one day and the Commodore was up on the 0-1 level of the Tender and asked him about the hat, he says, "Why are you wearing that unmilitary type hat, you should be wearing your regular Officer's hat." Denny Sloan just looks at him and says, "Well, Commodore, it's my submarine and I'll wear any freaking hat I want to wear on board." and then off we went.

One of the things we did on the Tunny was on the med run. Our job was to find Russian fast attacks and follow them around because their job was to find our fleet ballistic missiles submarines on patrol in the Mediterranean and follow them around. If the war ever started they were supposed to be able to take out the ballistic missile submarine before it could get their missiles off while we followed the fast attacks around and our job was to take them out before they took the boomer out. We followed one for 72 days, they never knew we were behind them, when our time was up we turned them over to another fast attack and then we exited the Mediterranean.

George Emery was the second Skipper I had on the Groton. He and his first XO, Terry Jones, they made a perfect team. You could tell Denny Sloan and George Emery were probably the least political captains of submarines I'd ever seen. These two guys were sailors first and politicians afterwards. As sailors, they always got everything done, we never missed a deployment on either ship and George Emery and Denny Sloan, they knew how to run a submarine. They knew how to take care of all their people. They were smart and if we had to go to war, I'm sure we would have been successful in any combat operation.

When George was Skipper of the Groton we did two runs to the Persian Gulf and we did surveillance on any surface warship that happened to be above us, most of the time it was the Russians. We did a lot of surveillance stuff underneath them and they had no idea we were underneath looking at them and taping their engine signatures and photos of their hulls and stuff like that. Their leadership abilities, their knowledge and the way they treat personnel, that's what made them effective leaders. I try to be like that. I still have guys from both boats and even the Skate, that's 50 years ago, that I still know.

I think the best thing that any leader can do is know the people that are working for them and be fair to them. Everybody's got to pull their weight and if they can't pull their weight then maybe they should go somewhere else and not pull their weight. My next piece of advice is don't make a snap decision if you don't have to. If you've got time, step back from a situation and look from another point of view. If you aren't sure about a decision, call in one of your peers and say, "Hey, this is what I've got going on, this is what I think I should do to correct it or to make it better, what do you think?" Use all the resources you have at your disposal to do things. That would probably be my advice and like I said, everybody will say this year at graduation speeches all over the country, "Take care of your people and they will take care of you." I've always been a firm believer in that.

2

COBs and Mustangs

Chapter 7

Chief of the Boat

Edwin "Bud" Atkins
Master Chief Torpedoman, USN (Ret.)

Chiefs of the Boat serve as command-level senior enlisted leaders aboard fast attack, ballistic missile, and guided missile submarines. They have a significant role in every aspect of command-wide readiness and mission accomplishment.

Chief of the Boat Ratings Description US Navy

Edwin Atkins was an inspirational leader with 40 combined years of experience and leadership in the Wisconsin National Guard and the U.S. Navy. Atkins was a key element in establishing ties between USSVI, and the Staff and Students of the Naval Submarine School. He is a key link in this very important relationship. Atkins provides mentorship to the young Students, as well as passing on History and Traditions. Through Atkins, the close ties with Naval Submarine School leadership, SUBVETS are continually invited to participate in graduations for Basic Submarine School and other technical training courses.

Connecticut Veterans Hall of Fame induction, Class of 2014

I stayed in the National Guard for four years [he joined at age 15] and as soon as I transferred out of school I got my draft notice. So I joined the Navy. I was a Recruit Company Commander in in Boot Camp because I had four years in the National Guard. Our company commander, First Class Boatswain Mate, he said, "Well we'll pick you to be our Company Commander," and away I went. From there on, I was a leader. I was out in front. In whatever we would do, I would get on the recreation committee. I was Seaman Third Class right out in front. Every boat I was on, I always organized. If it was a volleyball tournament, whatever, I was always on there. Raising funds, you name it, I did it.

Out of Boot Camp I went to sub school and then went on to Wahoo where I qualified. I was Second Class by the time I got off of Wahoo. Most of the crew when I went on, three quarters of the crew were all WWII sub vets and they had been on patrols. We really never talked about their experience. They never talked to us about their experience and so we didn't question them. They kept pretty quiet. But they taught us how to run the boat and how to qualify.

I got out of the Navy for about a year, and went back to school. I went back in the Navy and did a few tours on some fleet boats and then I went to put the Sculpin in commission. I made First Class and I was the lead TM on the Sculpin. Then I went to the Webster, put that in commission and was the lead TM on the Webster. From the Webster I went to the Key, put that in commission and was the lead TM. Then they sent me to sub school. I was a leading instructor at sub school in advanced nuclear weapons. From there I went to being COB aboard the Kamehameha. I had a lot of leadership on the Kamehameha as the Chief of the Boat and from there they pulled me off and I went to Squadron and was weapons readiness and training where I did most of the weapons stuff at Group at Groton.

I went back to sea on the Michigan, Chief of the Boat on the Michigan. From there I went back to new construction, Chief of the Boat, Command Master Chief on the Alabama and then I went to Group Nine where I was Command Master Chief. So that's basically my career. I went to work at Electric Boat up in engineering working on the overhaul of Trident submarines and spent three years up in engineering. Then I went SDO ship-board testing and spent another three years testing all the systems. Then went to the casino and tended bar for fifteen years.

I was a TM in the Navy, and at that time, most of the Chief of the Boats were TM's. So they kind of groomed us younger TM's to be Chief of the Boats and instilled in us the leadership that we needed. From day one they said, "Take care of your people." My whole career was taking care of my people. I didn't care what happened to myself, I just took care of my people and I did that for over 35 years. Looked out for them, whatever they needed, I took care of them. At sea your life depended on a lot of your decisions and on shore it doesn't really matter. If you made a mistake on shore you weren't going to die but at sea you were. That's the big difference because you could make mistakes ashore but you couldn't make them at sea as you know.

Leroy Engles was the first Chief of the Boat on the Nautilus. He was our Chief of the Boat on Wahoo and he was a great leader and he taught me a lot. One of my XO's on Kamehameha was Admiral Konetzni. He retired as a Vice Admiral and he was a great XO and he went on to be a great leader in the Navy. Big Al, the sailor's pal is what they called him. He went on to be SubPac and Vice CNO. One of his books he wrote while he was at the Naval Academy was "Command at Sea." In there, he wrote about all kinds of leadership for all these midshipmen coming out, what they should learn and do for their people.

They were right out in front. They didn't wishy wash the leadership roles. They stood right out and said, "This is what we're going to do," and we did it. And they didn't tell you one thing and then go behind your back and do something else. They were right up front which is good leadership. So, what I learned is you've got to be up front with them. Honesty with your people, you've got to have honesty with them. If you don't, you're not going to be a good leader. And integrity, integrity is the big thing. If you tell them something you should mean it.

A good leader will go out and relax and have a drink with his people. You're going to find that some of the bad leaders won't go out and sit and relax with their guys every so often. I had one, George Washington Davis, didn't want the Chiefs and Officers to associate with each other. He didn't want it but Konetzni says, "I'll have a dinner with the Chiefs," and he invited the CO. I've had good CO's, bad CO's, bad XO's, good XO's. But I tell these younger guys when I do the officer graduations, "Get with your Chiefs and have integrity with them because they're going to teach you and train you. But you've got to have integrity with them and if you don't, your career in the Navy is not going to be that good."

As Chief of the Boat, you come on as Chief of Boat and your senior Chiefs are sitting around in the Chief's quarters and you ask them what they're doing, "You're holding a field day or something?" Well they said, "I got a First Class." I kicked them out of the Chief's quarters, told them, "Go back to your spaces and supervise it." Some fought you, didn't want to do it, but in the end you won out. You had to be careful how you did it. You treated each guy a little different. That's good leadership too. You know what the guy needs whether he needs a kick in the seam of the pants or a pat on the back. That's leadership. You got to learn that and that's pretty hard. They don't teach that in schools.

I never went to the Senior Enlisted Academy. I always call that touchy feely cause you got to learn it by yourself. They can't teach you leadership. Nowadays, they try to teach you leadership but you can't. You're either a leader or you're not. Some are leaders, others never will be leaders. All my brothers were in the military. My father was in the military. The same with going up through the Boy Scouts, Cub Scouts, Brownies, the same way; If you're a leader there you just get going. If you're a leader in athletics you just kept on leading. Leadership is not taught really. Follow me. See what I do. You got certain examples you can tell them, show them certain examples of leaders, of leadership because it's all around you. You say, "You want to be this kind of leader or do you want to be this kind of leader?" It's up to you.

Chief of the Boat, he worked for the CO. That's your only guy that you answer to. You work with the XO but we tried to instill on all the Command Master Chiefs, "You work for the CO, you don't work for the XO." They brought us in when a CO was going to school to be a CO, they'd bring the COBs in and we'd sit down and talk the same way we'd sit down and talk with the XO's and tell them how we did it and they either could take their advice or not. It was up to them and the ones that took our advice did a good job, others didn't. A lot of them take it as important, some of them don't. They say, "I can do it on my own. I don't need the Chief telling me what to do or teaching me."

I joined Subvets when they first started in about '65 and carried on. About '90, I went to be Vice Commander for eight years and then I went into, right now, I'm a Chairman for the Holland Club. We put in about 450 people a year qualifying submarines for 50 years. I enjoy it. I'll do it for about another two years and then give her up. The Holland Club is anybody that's qualified for 50 years in submarines. At Groton, we have a ceremony where we usually have about 50 guys a year going into Holland Club and we do it at Subvets and Dealey Center on base on the stage and that's a good program. They usually have an Admiral or somebody and we bring them in on Friday noon. The Chiefs invite us to Chief's Club, we introduce them. Saturday morning we do the induction. Then we go to the clubhouse and have lunch. We have Sub School students, there's about 900 of them, come to the inductions. We also do graduations. We're guest speaker at graduations. We do tolling of the boats where we read off each submarine that was lost during WWII. We also have an Honors Detail. We go to the funeral and do an Honor Detail for our lost submariners.

We are their heritage and they are our heritage. We try to pass down what we learned to these younger sailors that are so much smarter than we are. We try to rub off our experiences with them and they try to honor us as we honor the WWII guys that we lost. One thing they're doing now is the USS Colorado has got my Command Master Chief pennant and they're passing it from COB to COB. If the new COB comes and he's the Master Chief, he gets the pennant. Otherwise it's on the plaque up on the wall. I passed one of my set of dolphins down to a Third Class Torpedoman the other day when they came back. They pinned him, his Dolphin's on and they're starting to do that, the newer boats, they're getting the Command Master Chief pennant from one of the retired guys with your active duty guys and they're passing that along from COB to COB. That's heritage too.

Jack Gallimore
Master Chief Electrician Mate, USN (Ret.)

"Underway Diesel Power" is a fictional tale about a U.S. Navy diesel-powered submarine during one of her intelligence-gathering missions. The book is based on several facts, and quite a bit of fiction, in the year of 1958 during the Cold War. The story is dedicated to those who have served in our submarine service throughout the years. Always in harm's way, braving the pressure of the sea; they did their jobs.

Underway Diesel Power by Jack Gallimore

I joined the Navy in September of '56. I went to Naval Air Station Miramar, California for temporary duty and then I went to "A" School, Electrician's Mate. And so that's where I had my first encounter with submarines. The officer in charge was a World War II submarine sailor and I can remember making the decision when I graduated as Honor Man [first in his class]. I went up to his office because he wanted to see me and he said I have my choice of orders but before I made a decision, he said, "let me tell you what I have for you." And it was in special weapons at White Sands, New Mexico, nukes. I remember specifying to him, "No, I want submarines." And he said "I can guarantee you submarine school, but I can't guarantee you'll make it through."

So I went to submarine school and raked a lot of leaves. I graduated in December 1957. I went home on leave to Massachusetts and I went to my first boat, which was the Sablefish. I put three years on her. I can remember talking to the Engineer, he put the word out that some of the people would be taking the exam for Electrician Mate 3rd class and my name wasn't mentioned, the same excuse as "A" School and Submarine School, I hadn't been there long enough to receive a recommendation. I remember talking to the Lieutenant Engineer, saying that, "I have been screwed over twice and I don't intend to be screwed over this time. So I will request an interview." And so he yelled up to the chief, who was a World War II sailor. He said, "Set up an interview with Gallimore and recommend him for taking the E-4 exam." So I did that and I was recommended and I made E-4 and then I made E-5 on the boat and then I went to E-6.

I went to "B" School and I received orders to the Sabalo or whatever boat and I remember mentioning to my wife, "I've got to call the detailer to get the orders changed back to New London." Because the boat was out of Norfolk and so I called the detailer and he said "tough titty", if you will, "you're going to such-and-such a boat." I wrote to the skipper of the Sablefish and I didn't hear back from him and went to my mom's and dad's house in Massachusetts. Then Western Union showed up at the door, got a telegram, your orders are canceled. Proceed USS Sablefish. So, there is a God. I went to the Sablefish for another few years and saw four skippers on Sablefish.

I was at a place called Vality's, a store at Gales Ferry and I can remember meeting one of my old skippers and he said, "If there's anything I can do for you, come up to my office." It didn't take a rocket scientist to figure that out. So, I went up there and I said, "I'm due for shore duty and I would like to work for you at sub school." I went to sub school staff at that point in time and put five years at sub school and I put it in for a sixth year and the Lieutenant said, "it would be cheaper to let him stay here for a sixth year instead of repaving the tile."

I had orders to an oiler, and I called the detailer, same thing. He said, "they're leaving for the Mediterranean." I called squadron and talked to my old yeoman, he was a squadron secretary at the time. I said, "I don't want to go to Norfolk again" and so he said, "I'll call you back." He did call me back and he said there was only one boat on the waterfront, diesel boat, that has a Mk-19 on it and so it was the Hardhead.

I went onboard her, the Hardhead in 1968 until '72. I took over as Chief of the Boat in 69.' We put the boat out of commission in 1972. We were turning the submarine over to the Greeks. We ended up transferring it to the Greek Navy and we were still back up crew but the Greeks had most of it and so we go to sea. I remember looking at the compensating water, the pressure gauge in the after battery. It was compensating water but it was sea pressure. It kept going up, up, up and the bow was down and I can remember thinking, "After all these dives, why now?" I think I thought that, but I guess I said it out loud because a Torpedoman 3rd Class walked up to me said, "COB, I wasn't scared until I heard you say, "After all these dives, why now?'" So what I learned from that is to keep my thoughts to myself.

I went to the guided missile cruiser Yarnell DLG-17, super skipper, super XO. I started growing my beard back then, and the XO was a full commander and he asked me, "what is that on your face?" All he needed to hear was "a beard and hunting season's coming," as he was a duck hunter and I was a duck hunter and we became friends. I never let a friendship interfere with a skipper or XO, if you will. The skipper was a full four-striper, very, very senior. He was selected for Admiral if I remember correctly.

So I went to the yard and I was on deployment until '74. On the Yarnell, we were at battle stations and we intercepted an aircraft. We were off the coast of Lebanon, Israel, whatever. We were running traffic, aircraft going into Israel. But I remember we had gone to battle stations because one of the aircraft coming out of Iran wasn't identifying itself and I heard the missiles run out on to the launchers and "this is not a drill" was passed over the One MC. "Battle stations, battle stations. This is not a drill." And so we held fire and they finally turned on the IFF, Identification Friend or Foe and we were within seconds of shooting a missile at the aircraft. Fortunately, it wasn't a fighter aircraft. It was a commercial aircraft but it came out of Iran. So I guess, same thing I learned. I can remember one of the guys saying, "I don't want to die" And I said, "You won't." And that's leadership skills, I guess.

Then I went to sub school, Naval Submarine Support Facility and two years there. The CO asked me what I could do to stay because I put my papers in. That was my 20th anniversary, so I put my papers in. The skipper came down to the ship yard. Not the ship yard, the office, if you will and he asked what I could do to stay one more year. And I said, "I don't want to push holes in the ocean anymore." He said, "I'm talking about staying here as Electrical Officer for one more year." That's my submarine career and I went to work for myself for three, four years, went to Stone & Webster Engineering Corporation out of Boston for 15 years at a nuclear power quality control supervisor.

Know the crew, know the crew. I think that was the most important thing I did on the Yarnell as well as the Hardhead. I learned that from the skipper and the Chief of the Boat on Sablefish. I learned it and I applied it on the Hardhead and the Yarnell. I was Chief of the Boat on Yarnell. Excuse me, Senior Enlisted Advisor. They changed that to Command Master Chief years after I left there.

I learned a lot from my second skipper, he would go through the boat almost daily just to check and see how the crew was doing. I learned a lot from the World War II chief of the boat when I was on Sablefish along with Captain Blum. I learned a lot from them attitude-wise and I knew most of the crew by name. They were very, very important to me and I learned that from John Hansley, who was Chief of the Boat and a World War II sailor. I learned a lot from the skipper and the XO on the Yarnell as well and I learned a lot from a skipper on the Hardhead. He was my second skipper on there as well. They were super, super guys that were interested in the crew, as all of them were but they were more specifically interested in the crew.

They had indicated I should join Subvets for years. They being my shipmates, if you will. I didn't join until 2001, I think. But I wasn't interested and Tom Russell, who was the Chaplain before me, he inspired me to be his right-hand person, if you will. So I got involved. John Carcioppolo was the Base Commander at the time and he had asked me to take over Sub School from him and so I did. Chaplain duties I took over in 2014 after Tom had retired from that responsibility and honors detail. So Subvets has been very, very important to me.

For Sub School I took care of the speakers determining which people could go to Basic Enlisted Submarine School, Torpedoman School, Senior Officer, Submarine Officers Basic Course, Submarine Officers Advanced Course and FCCF submarine electronic computer, radar, radio people. We started giving out challenge coins and recognizing the honor man and the most improved sailor of the class. We did the tolling of the boat where they read off the 52 boats lost during the war but they stopped those because it was just disheartening for the parents who were there.

I wrote two books, one of them is Underway Diesel Power. It's a fictitious sort of one up North of the Arctic Circle, roughly 60 days. My grandchildren had asked me what I did in the Navy all their life and so I said, I got to write another book. I put together the chapters including childhood years, the Navy years. The Navy years were the interesting ones and the years I put in the nuclear industry were also rewarding. Now my grandson is a First class machinist mate on the New Mexico, Virginia class fast attack boat. Chief of the boat and Senior Enlisted Advisor were two of the most rewarding experiences in my life. Quite frankly, they were. Some of the laughs, some of the hard times and making deployments were just rewarding.

Chapter 8

Coxswain

Steve Thorpe, MBE
Warrant Officer First Class, RN

Warrant Officer Thorpe was recognized with a place in the 2020 New Year's Honours List being awarded the MBE (Member of the British Empire). He was recognized as "one of the Silent Service's most experienced submariners with 34 years under his belt in almost every class of submarine operating since the mid-80s, and as a key member of a team sent to Argentina in late 2017 to help the international search effort looking for the missing submarine ARA San Juan."

"There's a fundamental pride in being a submariner – it's a unique job in a unique environment. I am immensely proud to be receiving the MBE," said Warrant Officer Thorpe. "Despite the sad outcome and the loss of 44 submariners in the San Juan, it was an unforgettable experience. "The Argentine military and people were welcome – and appreciative of the assistance offered. There's a mutual respect between submariners whatever the nation, a common bond so you understand what your counterparts or their families are going through."

-Royal Navy News, 27 December 2019

I joined the Navy in 1985. My dad was in the merchant navy and loved listening to his adventures but there was a recession in the UK at the time so they weren't recruiting to the merchant navy so I decided to give the Royal Navy a try. I was successful in my application and was recruited as an ordinary seaman in general service; skimmers as you might call them. I got on to HMS Raleigh and completed my training. A number of my entry were selected to fly and join a ship in the Falklands returning via the Caribbean. I was lucky enough to be selected. Unfortunately, the trip was cancelled and as compensation we went to Bovington to visit the Tank Regiment. On reflection I am unsure this came to fruition, as a young sailor being sent to an Army camp you can appreciate there was some banter.

Upon returning to HMS Raleigh, submarines had always interested me, so I volunteered. So, the beginning of '86 I joined HMS Dolphin and began my training at the submarine school. I really liked the idea of diesel submarines but got assigned to a bomber, HMS Repulse was in refit and my instructor at the time said, "If you're going to join the Repulse in refit, the first trip you will do will be 24 days in America." So my first ever foreign trip in the Navy was to Cocoa Beach in Florida for 24 days during Spring Break in 1987 as a young sailor meeting people who I am still in contact with through social media. That was an impressive introduction to jollies in the Royal Navy, the first of many.

While on Repulse as a junior sailor, I'd qualified as a submariner, but I didn't really like the idea of just being at sea and not seeing anywhere doing deterrent patrols as I joined the Navy to try and see the world. So just before we sailed to America I decided to volunteer for diesel submarines and when we arrived in America I was assigned to HMS Oracle and subsequently got loaned to HMS Otter (where I experienced my second jolly in Liverpool UK). I got qualified on a diesel submarine, which was a complete culture change from bomber with showers to a diesel submarine with no water, so no showering, but I loved it. You did what I joined the Navy to do and that was to see a bit of the world, work hard/play hard type ethos and meet different people.

I went back to Oracle, did another two and half years on her and during this time I was promoted to Leading Hand within my core job, Tactical Systems. I was required to return to the submarine school to complete the Leading Hand's course. Upon successful completion I was assigned to a build submarine called HMS Ursula, which was a 2400 diesel submarine in Birkenhead. After just over two years the UK made the controversial decision to cease operating diesel submarines so the four Upholder class submarines were decommissioned and sold to Canada. So I was drafted to the headquarters in Northwood for about a year, but this was my first shore job except courses since joining up and it wasn't for me at that time so volunteered for more sea time.

Joined HMS Trenchant in 96, which is a Trafalgar-class submarine hunter-killer. I looked at what all the programs were for all the boats and decided that Trenchant was the boat of choice as it was going on an around the world trip in '97, Ocean Wave 97, which was the best trip I have had in the RN. I joined her in Easter '96, immediately sailing for an exercise then another trip to the states. We came back into Plymouth for Christmas then Trenchant sailed on a nine-month deployment from the UK, Gibraltar, Crete, Hong Kong, Singapore, Philippines, Australia, Diego Garcia, Gibraltar and back to the UK along with HMS Triumph and numerous UK skimmers in a task group. One of the lads bought a new video camera and decided to video the whole trip, so starting in Plymouth he would video events at sea and alongside. At the time it was annoying every time you turned your head he was there videoing proceedings, however over 20 years later it is good to have a memento. On numerous occasions a select few have got together to reminisce and amuse ourselves of the memories of Ocean Wave 97. After having spent long periods away during this draft I left Trenchant in '98 and joined the submarine escape training tank in Gosport. For two years, I was a swim boy teaching submarine escape training and undertaking a parachute qualification to form part of the Submarine Parachute Assistance Group (SPAG). It's unusual for submariners to be parachute trained; it is still a talking point when in uniform trying to explain the rationale behind it.

In 2000 my time had come to return to sea, returning to the bomber fraternity, HMS Vanguard back in Faslane. Shortly after joining I was called forward, in fact 20 years yesterday, I got put on standby to go and help with the *Kursk* rescue, the Russian submarine that suffered an explosion. So I went probably 20 years ago today I was on a plane to go to Norway to join the Normand Pioneer to go and help the unfortunate Russians. We were in the vicinity of the *Kursk* with the rescue vehicle off the Norway coast so potentially we could have assisted and rescued some submariners. It was a heart-wrenching experience. We had the impression the Russians just didn't want us there and didn't want any survivors for whatever reason. The Russians have a saying; may all your surfaces equal the number of your dives, relevant for all submariners worldwide. Unfortunately this wasn't the case for the *Kursk*. Rest in Peace.

After the *Kursk* I returned to HMS Vanguard. During my draft on her I was offered the chance to qualify as a Ship Control Officer of the Watch, a position normally a senior rate or Officer position. I was only a Leading Hand but as I was offered the opportunity I invested a lot of time and effort to gain my qualification. I believe I was the first Leading Hand to be qualified on a UK SSBN. Also, while onboard I was selected to be promoted to Petty Officer. On completion of the qualifying course I was assigned to be an instructor, both in the Submarine school and in Phase 1 instructing initial trainees, a really satisfying role watching civilians slowly convert into junior sailors.

During my time there I conducted the cardinal sin and volunteered to go to sea, the offer was to fly to the Seychelles, join a submarine, and conduct a five-day transit to Diego Garcia. Unfortunately, upon arrival in DG my relief was unable to get a flight to join the submarine, so what was meant to be a two-week trip away, three months later I returned home. There is the proof don't volunteer.

As I had passed my ship control qualification I met the criteria to undertake the selection to transfer to Submarine Coxswain at a relatively junior stage in my career. I was successful but was required to return to sea for some more experience. Early 2004 joined HMS Vigilant for a year to re-qualify ship control and to understudy the coxswain to prepare for going on course. In 2005 I again joined HMS Raleigh to undertake Coxswain course; Chief of the Boat in US speak. The course is made up of various modules, five of us were on course and we all supported each other to ensure we were all successful and pass the course. On completion of the course I returned to HMS Vanguard and took her to the States again to complete a DASO [missile firing test]. During this time there were some serious discipline issues so it was a baptism of fire in my first role as a Coxswain.

In 2008 joined the Flag Officer Sea Training; instructing in a simulator and undertaking some sea riding. This was a different challenge to my previous instructional roles. HMS Astute was the UK's new hunter killer submarine and she was preparing to sail on initial sea trials. The new simulator was still being trialed and a select team was dispatched to Montreal Canada to ensure the simulator reacted as we expected the submarine to behave. In additional to the simulator work much of the Emergency Operating Procedures (EOPs) and Standard Operating Procedures (SOPs) required developing. In 2008 the opportunity arose to join a build submarine HMS Ambush in Barrow-in-Furness and experience the changes of training and preparing a crew to sail, and as HMS Astute was still in Barrow I was utilized to assist with their training for sailing. During this build process we were delayed so had the spare capacity to be the first Submarine crew to enter the Royal Navy Field Gun competition in 2010. This competition sees crews from all areas of the Armed forces compete in HMS Collingwood conducting a series of drills with a gun and limber weighing in excess of 1.5 tonnes. Over twenty crews competed with each crew having eighteen members with their own specific job with the kit on the track. It is billed as the most challenging team sport in the world as one mistake can ruin a crew's chances. The average run lasted approximately one minute thirty seconds and there is little room for error. This event covers all the Royal Navy's core values; commitment, courage, discipline, respect, integrity and loyalty. Despite the expectation, HMS Ambush Field Gun Crew did amazingly well by winning our final and receiving three trophies for our endeavors. This event most certainly had a positive impact on the cohesion of the ship's company.

Towards the end of my assignment I was in the privileged position to get promoted to Warrant Officer. In 2011 I went back to Sea Training as sea rider, training all different classes of UK submarines. In 2014 I was offered the opportunity and took up the Executive Warrant Officer position onboard HMS Portland, which is an anti-submarine warfare frigate; poacher turned game keeper. This position requires looking after welfare, manpower and involvement with whole ship co-ordination. I joined it in Cape Town, went to the Falklands, through the Panama Canal, around the Caribbean, Lisbon, and back to the UK. That was a great experience; very different to jollies on submarines mainly, no hotels.

Whilst in this role we changed some routines and attempted to empower Leading Hands offering them more responsibility. The engineering cadre had already done this to some degree by the implementation of the Faraday model, which passed levels of responsibility down the rank structure. We attempted to implement empowerment by giving individuals areas of responsibility, assigning some senior rate responsibilities to Leading Hands, which in principle worked however in many parts of the RN and society the attitude of 'that's the way it has always been' prevails. We did make positive steps and the moves were generally well received, however changing the mindset is difficult and I believe once I left the post things would have reverted back to source, which is unfortunate as the changes would have been retention positive in the longer term.

Following a successful assignment on Portland I once again joined the submarine escape training tank in 2016 as the Senior Instructor as it was preparing to relocate to Faslane. This relocation was significantly delayed so while the preparations continued the team re-invigorated the training at SETT in Gosport resulting in positive feedback and the unit was awarded a Flag Officer Sea Training commendation for the most improved training with minimal financial cost.

In 2017 I was asked to cover the position of Coxswain onboard HMS Vigilant. I was to fly to the states again and conduct the transit back to the UK. After agreeing to do this task it came to light that the Captain and XO had been removed. This was a challenging period, but we eventually sailed and successfully transited the submarine back to the UK.

Upon arrival back in the UK the news had broken about *San Juan*, an Argentine submarine that had been reported missing. So two days later I was told to prepare to potentially deploy to assist in my core role within submarine rescue. We boarded an RAF flight and flew to the Falkland Islands, a team of eight of us. Four parachuters stayed in the Falklands in case they were required to join one of the searching ships or assist any escapees. Under difficult conditions we managed to get three onto HMS Protector that was assisting with the search. Myself, an RN officer, and an army interpreter flew into Argentina to go to their search headquarters, Puerto Belgrano to help the Argentinians and Americans to investigate and figure out what had happened, this was November 2017. Unfortunately, the search efforts proved fruitless. Evidence came to light that it was likely *San Juan* had suffered an explosion. If this was the case it was a different scenario to the *Kursk* where a few of them suffered for a few days. A year to the day since *San Juan* went missing Ocean Infinity found the remains of the submarine in 940 meters of water. This at least brought some closure to the families.

I spent nearly two weeks there and mostly a really hospitable reception from the Argentinians. I am still in touch with some Argentinians and Americans from that unfortunate event. It's mutual respect, everybody knows that you go underwater. It's a dangerous game and people respect that, don't they? And understand the dangers that are involved. The Russians saying is a really poignant statement and I have used that at mess dinners as a toast at the end of mess dinners because I believe that is so true for submariners, unfortunately that didn't happen for the *Kursk* or *San Juan*.

Submariners do a lot of sea time and ultimately you need that good balance between fairness and good leadership to keep morale up and that's where the submarine service I believe gets it right a lot of the time. Not perfect, obviously, but right a lot of the time. I think general service can learn a lot from the Submarine Service when it comes to empowerment of Able Rates and Leading Rates because they don't seem to do it as well and then you get quite junior Leading Hands or Petty Officers that have got to learn responsibility and leadership and it's quite a lot for some people to take on if they redefine the model and give responsibility earlier. I think that that would be a lot smoother transition into a leadership role.

I had one lad when I joined the submarine force, I was a Junior Able Seaman, and I had a Senior Able Seaman called Shiner Wright onboard HMS Repulse. He taught me the skills that were required but it was a completely different mindset in society and in the Navy then as well. It was quite a hard robust style that was employed back in the 80s. It was quite difficult. You had to hold your own and he taught me the rules or the ways if you like. When I subsequently went to Oracle he joined as a Leading Hand because he liked what he saw and how he developed me. I continued to develop underneath him, and then he went to the HMS Ursula in build and he was a Petty Officer on there and he requested me again to be a Leading Hand on his submarine. So that was quite nice that he took me under his wing and he developed me into the sort of person that could be trusted and was pretty good at your job. I developed and he recognized that and he trusted to ask for me on two separate occasions to be underneath him onboard that platform which was good because he had empowered me as I said and trusted me and saw me develop.

Being at Flag Officer Sea Training, either in the simulators or when sea riding, what's really good to see is how you impact on the development of the individuals and crews. At the start of the training phase they may not have the teamwork and spirit. Obviously underwater you've got to have that reliance on other people and everybody has to know their core role. So a team would go onboard and put emergencies on for the crew to push and test the crew. What was rewarding was that you would go onboard, the crew would be nervous and apprehensive. The team would guide them, coach them, and mentor them and after a few days the development of the crew was noticeably more competent and safer.

I've developed quite a lot of people over my time. One really good example, one lad now that's a Coxswain, he was my assistant on Ambush. We were on a non-sea going platform at the time. He always expressed a desire to be a Coxswain. I recognized that he could potentially be a good candidate in the role. I booked him on a ship control course, which is normally a senior rate or officer course. He passed the course with ease. He ran the office, obviously, what he was allowed to do. That responsibility and delegation allowed him to thrive and demonstrate his potential. He got a recommendation to go at the earliest opportunity to Coxswain. He is now fully qualified and he's doing a really good job. By allowing him that responsibility under supervision he was allowed to demonstrate his potential and develop to fulfil his aspirations.

I think leadership is acknowledging your team, giving praise when deserved, offer guidance when required and understanding the limits of the people in your team. You can only do that by knowing them individually. Get as much as a personal relationship as you can to ensure that you understand their limits so that they remain approachable. So if they are struggling with any tasks that are given to them they feel comfortable that they can come and speak to you about it to get guidance from you so you don't ostracize yourself from your team. I think there's many people at officer level that don't understand that concept and I think that the general service, in particular, could learn a lot from that team ethic and team ethos. I think teamwork is paramount on a submarine and teamwork goes hand in hand with leadership.

The people are key; I believe that if you treat people right and you give them the responsibility but don't overburden them with responsibility, the majority of people will thrive on a little bit of responsibility, especially if they are recognized and they are praised accordingly. We delegate a lot of tasks to quite junior people and give them an area of responsibility and the majority of people thrive on that. So by the time that they're ready to get promoted to Leading Hand they're already used to responsibility from learning the leadership elements of it. I think we do a lot better than general service, having experienced both sides of the ocean if you like.

From a Chief of the Boat point of view though, I think that's an interesting one, I keep saying Chief of the Boat, but obviously it's Coxswain in our world. The selection process has to be robust to make sure that the individual has got the right criteria. Doing the Chief of the Boat from a leadership point of view comes down to having ground rules and not moving those sets of rules to make sure that everybody understands what the requirement is. Once you start changing the expectation of people it then becomes a very confused environment because people don't know where the boundaries are. You can still be fair, but you can be hard and fair and people respect that more than changing the boundaries.

The Coxswain is the Captain's right-hand man. You have got to be 100% trustworthy to have the confidence of the Captain. The minute that you betray trust then that's when your relationship breaks down and it's noticed by the ship's company. If you haven't got a good relationship with the XO and the Captain, then it's very difficult for the ship's company to understand. So if there is bad leadership and plans are not clearly defined then you very quickly see that that teamwork suffers. I think submarines in general are good at doing this. The Captain's selection process is still robust with the Perisher qualification in addition the XOs have to pass Perisher. Every department has a head and a department coordinator (DEPCO), but the CO, XO and Coxswain are three key figures and are a fundamental part of the submarine crew and the leadership style can dictate how the submarine crew will perform.

I am formally the Head of the Coxswain Branch because I am pretty much the longest-serving Warrant Officer Coxswain now. It was previously undertaken by the Submarine Command Warrant Officer, but they've changed all the structure so we had to look at who was going to take it on. The figurehead of the branch is held in high regard but council is taken from two other Warrant Officers that are on the waterfront. I will make the ultimate decisions but we collectively discuss prior to any changes being implemented.

The Coxswain's course is administered by another Warrant Officer who is based at the Royal Navy Submarine School in Torpoint. We liaise on a regular basis to discuss who the candidates are, when the selection board will take place and when the course will be required to take place. We do scrutinize the volunteers harshly but quite rightly and justifiably so I believe. The people will be nominated by the Coxswain in the fleet as potential candidates that will be recorded as declaring an interest. There is a list of criteria that includes ship control, Captain's recommend, and do they meet the criteria to be promoted to chief.

Once the candidate meets all the criteria and has manning clearance to transfer, a selection board will be conducted. The board will normally consist of myself and normally another Warrant Officer Coxswain, a command qualified officer and another submarine officer. In the first instance the candidates will compose an essay stating the reason why they wish to become a Coxswain and what the individual can bring to the branch. They will be required to give a presentation on a service-related matter and be open for question from the board on completion. Usually in the afternoon of the board they will have an interview about their beliefs on how a Coxswain should run a submarine. There's no real right or wrong answers. It will check they understand the guidelines. The board will explore certain avenues on how they've answered questions; really testing the integrity of that individual and whether they're willing to stick to their answers because as a Coxswain they will make un-popular decisions that won't be liked by the ship's company and they've got that resolve to stick to that decision and ultimately support the Captain. That's what we're looking for. On successful completion of the board they are required to complete the course and join a sea going submarine to ultimately test the individual. After receiving another captain's recommendation, completion of a task-book whilst continually receiving mentoring and completing an administration inspection they will be confirmed as a submarine Coxswain. This is a new routine on completion of course as some individuals have not had the correct attitude and have been required to return to the source branch and bring embarrassment to the individual and the branch.

We have made it a robust process to make sure that we do get the right caliber of person to go into that vitally important role onboard a submarine where you are a cog for everything that happens. Everything from manpower to morale onboard, discipline, watch keeping standards, cleanliness standards, every aspect of life onboard a submarine Coxswain is involved in. It's a really challenging job but it's a really rewarding and when people come to you and say, "Thanks, Coxswain for all you've done onboard." It's a really rewarding position to hold if you do the job correctly. As someone once said to me at the start of my coxswain training, there are more astronauts in the world than there are submarine coxswains, which I think is a unique fact.

I've loved my time in the Navy, finding it challenging and rewarding. I think it's a great model for people to grow up and mature. I think even if you do a few years in the Navy like I see quite a lot of lads that join and lasses that join get to leave and walk into jobs because they know that they've got that discipline. Just by turning up smart on time every day speaks volumes for the individual and I think that's what the armed forces, and in particular my experience in the Submarine Service, teaches you to let you realize your potential.

I'm immensely proud to call myself a submariner and wear dolphins on my chest. I think it's still quite envied in the British Armed Forces and beyond. The Submarine Service is manned by very capable, professional individuals. It takes a special attitude to proceed to sea in a steel tube. A lot of people still don't know what we do. I think it's still viewed as a secret service, which I think is a positive. I've achieved more than what I ever imagined when I first joined up as a junior seaman. I only intended staying in for five years and here I am 35 years later. I have been developed by the RN, educated myself and took my opportunities, met some great people and visited some amazing places, to unexpectedly receive the MBE has been the icing on the cake to a very rewarding career.

Chapter 9

Mustangs

Howard Patrick (Pat) Urello
Lieutenant Commander, USN (Ret.)

Mustang is a slang term for a former enlisted officer. It refers to the wild horses who tend to be smart, strong, tough and maybe a little unpredictable. While the exact origin of the term is unknown it may also highlight the difference between these former enlisted sailors and the thoroughbreds or Naval Academy graduates. There are multiple programs that enable individuals to complete this journey. Similarly, although not called Mustangs, there are also paths to commissioning of ratings sailors to officer ranks in the Royal Navy. Mustangs are typically technically adept and older than their peers in rank.

Throughout my thirty-year Naval career, I was extremely fortunate to have exceptional leaders and mentors from the beginning of my career to the end. And just to throw out some names, when I started my career after boot camp in Great Lakes and Yeoman "A" school, I was assigned to Naval Nuclear Power School, Bainbridge, Maryland. As a yeoman, a brand new YNSN, I was advanced to third class petty officer. The commanding officer at that time was Lieutenant Commander Frank B. Kelso, who became the Chief of Naval Operations and the Acting Secretary of the Navy. I remember him coming out of his office and congratulating me on third class by tacking on my crow. That is frowned upon in today's Navy, a form of harassment. So that is the caliber of leader that I began my Navy career with. Fast forward thirty years later to my final tour in the Navy and I had the pleasure of working for another four-star admiral, Rich Mies. His final assignment in the Navy was as the Commander, U.S. Strategic Command in Omaha, Nebraska. In between I had similar leaders and mentors that I counted myself blessed to be among.

During my time at Nuclear Power School, Captain Kelso asked "Have you considered going into submarines?" I said, "No, I don't know anything about submarines, other than all these pictures I see on the wall." He said, "Well, you know, I think it would be a great career for you. You ought to give it a shot." So I did. I completed my tour there and was transferred to my first submarine, USS Simon Bolivar (SSBN 641), out of Charleston, South Carolina. I completed three patrols on her. I was advanced to first class petty officer and was transferred to my second submarine, USS George Bancroft (SSBN 643), where I completed three additional strategic deterrent patrols.

Following that, I was assigned to shore duty at Submarine Group Two at the Naval Submarine Base, Groton, Connecticut, where I was the SSBN personnel monitor. Our job there was to assign the right types of personnel on each one of the submarines assigned to Submarine Group Two. By the right types of personnel, I mean the correct number of nuclear trained personnel, quartermasters, electronics technicians, radioman, machinist mates, etc. We tried to balance experience levels and things of that nature. We worked directly with the Executive Officers of each one the submarines, which made it a fascinating job for, at the time, a first class petty officer. I was subsequently promoted to chief yeoman.

I liked the job. I enjoyed the work I was doing, but I thought there had to be more to what I did on submarines and I didn't want to do that for the rest of my career. I did that. I liked that, but there has to be more of a challenge. So I looked into the limited duty officer program, and I was successful in applying and being accepted for that program while at Group Two. I was subsequently commissioned as an ensign in 1980-1981 timeframe. And from there all my tours in the Navy were submarine support or submarine staff related. My first officer assignment was as the Squadron Secretary at Submarine Squadron 2 in Groton, Connecticut. It was another great job with a great group of people from the Commodore on down.

As a LDO administrative type I could not be assigned to a submarine because there were no billets for those type of people on submarines. So I went to a submarine tender, USS Frank Cable (AS 40), out of Charleston, South Carolina. That was one of the greatest tours that I had. I served as both the Administrative and Personnel Officer. But I was a department head and I thoroughly enjoyed the working relationships I had with fellow department heads, the Chief Engineer, Weapons Officer, and Executive Officer.

I said all my tours were related to submarines. That's not entirely true. This two-year tour was at the Shore Intermediate Maintenance Activity in Newport, Rhode Island. The only thing that appealed to me about that job, when the detailer brought it up to me, was Newport, Rhode Island. So I thought it would be a great place to raise a family, and it was. We enjoyed that tour immensely, made lifelong friends who we continue to see periodically.

From Newport, I was assigned to the Portsmouth Naval Shipyard in Kittery, Maine as Officer-in-Charge of the Personnel Support Activity. Another great job working with great people. What I liked about that job was my commanding officer was geographically separated by about 150 miles from me. So I did not see him or her on a daily basis. I only saw them at our quarterly meetings. I was assigned additional duty to the shipyard commander for all matters affecting shipyard personnel. After that tour, I was assigned to another submarine tender, USS Hunley (AS 31) in Norfolk, Virginia. During my entire naval career, I made a point of staying away from two geographical areas: Washington, DC and Norfolk, Virginia, because I heard such horror stories about both of them. I was wrong.

So I received an ultimatum from my detailer, "You retire, or you go to Norfolk." I opted to go to Norfolk, to the USS Hunley. I was on her for three and a half years and decommissioned her in 1994. I would like to point out that during this tour I had the distinct pleasure of working with one of the finest Naval Officers during my career, Captain Bill Helfen. Not only was he an exceptional mentor for me, he was a leader that everyone respected because of the way he treated people. On this particular submarine tender we had a crew of approximately fourteen hundred Sailors, seven hundred male and seven hundred female. This was during a challenging time for the Navy when women were being assigned to ships. With Captain Helfen this was a seamless integration. His genuine concern for the welfare of all his Sailors was remarkable. To this day, he and I remain close friends.

As an aside, over twenty years after I left Hunley, I purchased a home in Connecticut. During the course of getting settled I needed some home repairs. I contacted a repairman. When he showed up at my house he noticed I was wearing a submarine ball cap. He asked if I served on submarines and I said, "I did." He said, "So did I, I was on the USS Phoenix." I said, "I have a good friend who was the commanding officer of USS Phoenix, Bill Helfen, did you serve with him?" He responded, "I did and Captain Helfen took me to Captain's Mast for a relatively minor violation and Captain Helfen was kind enough to give me a second chance, I will never forget it."

I think first and foremost was integrity. We all learned that early on in our submarine careers. We count on each other. We depend on each other for our, basically, for our own lives while underway, and knowing the systems on the submarine we are all required to know and to operate. I had a chief petty officer tell me early in my career, it's doing the right thing when nobody is watching. I believe that and I tried to live up to that. Teamwork is another. I don't think there is anything more important than working as a team. You know, obviously, I think it's a cliché, but the strength of the team is kind of impacted by its weakest link. And I think teamwork was probably the key in both my time in the submarine force and as an officer.

There are some that have this perception that if you are an officer you know everything and you are the one that provides all the direction. Well, that is not true at all. You learn so much from the people that you're surrounded with. And that leads me to your peers, subordinates and superiors. I always tried to surround myself with great people. And that's not hard to do in the submarine force because most people are great people in the submarine force. So it's easy to surround yourself with stellar individuals and it makes your job so much easier.

One of the things that I found interesting in the submarine force, particularly with the nuclear trained officers, is that they are not all alike. Although they have the same training, Naval Academy, college, nuclear power school, prototype, on to a submarine to become division officers to hopefully motivate and inspire their subordinates. Some have the right attitude when they come aboard, that they do not know everything and they're here to learn and to lead. Sometimes they forget that, or never learned that, and they go their entire career up through the ranks to commanding officer and beyond and think that they are better than the people that helped them get there. Sometimes they carry that attitude with them throughout life. It can be rare that you will find the leader that understands they're where they are because of the people behind them. I think a good example of those great leaders is Master Chief Bud Atkins and Admiral Al Konetzni. I put those together because I first met both of them when Bud was serving as Chief of the Boat on USS Kamehameha and Admiral Konetzni was his XO.

On that subject, Admiral Konetzni is one of those transformational leaders who inspired everyone he came in contact with. He was one of those individuals that everyone loved. When I say everyone, the enlisted folks absolutely loved him, and some of the officers loved him too. The rest of the officers though, he was too much of a friend of the enlisted personnel and he didn't maintain the appropriate professional decorum that he should have. I do not know anyone that I met in my career that knew how to take care of people better than Admiral Konetzni. I met him in 1975. To this day we are friends and see each other at various events throughout the year.

I can go on and on about the great leaders I served with during my career but I will just highlight a couple more. Admiral John Richardson was our most recent Chief of Naval Operations, Director of Naval Reactors and Commander of Submarine Forces. I served with him while he was the Commander of Submarine Forces. In this capacity I had observed, during two significant events, his leadership skills to bring them to successful conclusion. The first was the Fukushima Nuclear Power Plant disaster in Japan in 2011, following a major earthquake where a tsunami caused multiple cores to melt. This was a massive effort by many entities and Admiral Richardson made his submarine force, with obvious nuclear power expertise, available to assist. The second event was the fire onboard USS Miami (SSN 755) in 2012 while undergoing major overhaul at the Portsmouth Naval Shipyard. The fire was caused by a disgruntled shipyard worker and subsequently resulted in the decommissioning of the submarine. Again, there were multiple entities involved in extinguishing a major fire in an industrial environment that burned throughout the night.

Vice Admiral John Grossenbacher was Commander of Submarine Forces during the early 2000's. In 2001 the Russian Submarine Kursk was lost with over one hundred Sailors onboard. During the period of time the submarine went missing and when it was located, Admiral Grossenbacher had repeatedly offered to provide assistance to possibly rescue any survivors. Although his staff and submarine rescue personnel were prepared to assist they were never requested. Another Commander of Submarine Forces during my time on the staff was Vice Admiral Chuck Munns. What I remember about his time as Commander, among many memories, was when he invited and escorted former President Jimmy Carter on an underway onboard USS Jimmy Carter (SSN 23). He relayed to his staff after the event how excited President Carter had been to be underway on a submarine named in his honor and how he related his own grooming as a junior nuclear trained officer while he was in the Navy. To be sitting around the wardroom table in conversation with a former President of the United States was one of the highlights of his 30 plus year naval career. All of these former Commanders of Submarine Forces imparted something of their leadership style with me and I am indebted to each of them.

I think, and as I alluded to earlier, treating people with respect and dignity is very important. You know, and you hear so many times, often because you are wearing the uniform with a particular rank on it, that automatically you think that you are superior, and a lot of your young Sailors, whether they be Sailor or civilian personnel, think the same. But when you are able to show those people that you truly care, care about them as individuals, their families, their careers, it goes a long way.

They know that you are not out for yourself; you are out to help them be successful in their careers.

When I was commissioned an ensign there was a period where I thought I was being treated as a second class citizen. I went from being a Chief Petty Officer, where I supposedly knew everything, to a lowly ensign, where you know very little. There were times initially where I enjoyed my time more as a chief than an ensign. It took me a while to recognize that I had some work to do to mature as an officer.

I know most people say nice things about you when you get ready to retire. I have this large picture of a submarine in my den. It is inscribed with congratulatory notes by many on the SubLant staff. Some of them I can feel they are genuine and that they appreciated my contributions to the submarine force. I do love submarines and I do love the submarine force. It has been good to me.

When I retired from the Navy in Norfolk, Virginia, I don't know exactly how I got into this, but someone, I think it was retired Navy Captain Merrill Dorman, asked me if I wanted to join the Naval Submarine League. I said, "Well, what do they do? I thought that was an officer group, and the Subvets was an enlisted organization. He said, "Yeah, well, there are a lot more officers than there are enlisted and we're working on that. We think that you would be a good person to help us work on that since you were both." So I said, "Okay." Merrill Dorman was the Vice President of the Naval Submarine League in Hampton Roads, Virginia. So, I joined, and about eight months later, he said, "Pat, I have too much on my plate, and I need to give up this role as vice president. I'd like you to move into that slot." I said, "Oh, I don't feel at all comfortable doing that, you know, because the members are much more senior than I was. Most are Captains and retired Admirals, and executives at Newport News Shipyard in Virginia." "No, no, no, You'll be fine. You'll be fine" he said. I did that and a year later I was the President of the Naval Submarine League in Hampton Roads. I enjoyed the periodic meetings I had to attend as president in Washington, DC. And if you remember I said I wanted to stay away from Washington, DC? Once I retired, and spent some time there, I began to really enjoy all that Washington, DC had to offer and said to myself, "Boy, was I fool in trying to avoid Washington."

When I began my career being around these magnificent people with such character, integrity and leadership qualities, I just felt very fortunate. Months prior to my retirement I asked Admiral Mies, my current boss, and a former boss, Captain Helfen if they would be my guest speakers. They both agreed and they both said great things about me, some of which was true. Seriously though, they both made my family very proud.

I met Tim Oliver, Executive Director of the Naval Submarine League, through his brother, Dave Oliver, a retired Rear Admiral. His brother wrote a leadership book called *A Practical Approach to Leadership, Lead On*. Well, I ran across Dave Oliver at one of our Submarine Veterans Conventions, where he was the guest speaker at a Holland Club breakfast. It was the first time that I sat with both Dave and Tim Oliver. An interesting morning of conversation with two great submarine leaders.

Remember in the beginning I said my first commanding officer was Frank Kelso, who became the CNO and Acting SEC-NAV? He, at the time I was President of the Submarine League Hampton Roads Chapter, was Chairman of the Board of Directors for the Naval Submarine League. We had communicated periodically over the years via Christmas cards and such but I had not seen him since our days at Nuclear Power School in 1970. When we met again during one of our meetings in Washington, he said, "You have come a long way Mr. Urello since third class petty officer and our days in Bainbridge." I responded, "Not nearly as far as you have come, Admiral!"

Stanley (Stan) Mathis
Lieutenant Commander, USN (Ret.)

"How I got in the Navy, I was born that way. No, seriously, my dad was in the Navy. He joined the Navy in September of 1939, and he retired in 1969. He was in the Navy, and I was born here in Portland, Maine. He just happened to be up here and my mother ended up coming all the way across country to be with him because he was going to the Brooklyn Navy Yard. When you're born into the Navy, you stay with it. It was good tasking for him, so it was a good tasking for me. His friends were in the Navy, so my parents' friends were in the Navy, so I got a chance to meet all these people. Actually, my cousins and relatives, god-parents and stuff like that, they were in the service one way or the other. I figured, well, I'll join the Navy, and I'll make admiral in four years and I won't have to worry about it. Hey, you got to set goals."

I did end up getting a commission, but when I joined the Navy, I just joined the Navy because I got tired of going to school. I was in a year of college at the junior college in San Pedro, California. I lived in LA, and it was a twenty mile drive every day. That wasn't what bothered me. It's just that I got tired of studying. One day, when I really got fed up, I went down to the recruiter and signed up. Well, my dad didn't know about it and neither did my mother. They knew about it the day before when I said, "I need to get a ride downtown to go to AFFEES Los Angeles." He said, "What for?" I said, "Well, I'm supposed to go into the Navy tomorrow, and I'm supposed to get my induction physical and stuff there." Well, after the whining and the crying and stuff, my dad took me down there. This was an early morning thing. We (the recruits) got our physicals and all this other stuff and running around in our skivvies all over the place. We finally got dressed and went down to San Diego, because that's where I went to boot camp.

We got there at, I don't know, it was dark but it was September, so it was after 9:00 PM. We hit the rack in the dark. They got us up at 4:00 AM in the morning. Here we are, marching out on the grinder. It was a lot of fun, especially in boot camp. You meet a lot of people. I had a couple of guys that were from Texas and stuff like that. I'm just sitting around looking, and it's, oh, you guys are from this, this, this. Most of them were from east of the Mississippi River, and I'm thinking, really? They sent you all the way out here? Well, I was fortunate enough that I did not have to go to boot camp at Great Lakes. At the time they didn't have Orlando. That was fine with me, I was close to home. A two-hour drive and I'd have been home. Besides that, we lived in San Diego before my dad retired; they bought a house in San Diego, sold the house in LA. Then his last tour of duty was in Key West, Florida. Oh, he wasn't going to retire in Key West, Florida and that's 3500 miles from where we lived. That was fine and dandy, we went with him, we had a good time. We came back to LA, because my grandmother had passed away, and so we stayed with my grandfather to take care of him, so that was great.

My brother and sisters and I went to S. M. Dorsey High School and we all graduated from there. That's spread out over eight years. Then I got into college at L.A. Harbor College in San Pedro, and that was great, but it was time for a change. The Navy served my dad well, it served us well as a family so what other choice did I have? I didn't get into the manufacturing business like my grandfather and my uncle, but if I had, I might not have gone into the Navy.

I went in the Navy and they said, "We need submariners." I signed up right away. My dad was on surface ships on the West Coast, I said, "I'll be on submarines on the East Coast." As you noticed, I'm still on the East Coast. Come out here [New

London, Connecticut] and you go to sub school. You stay out here and fortunate enough you get orders to the submarine out of New London. Actually, my first real assignment after Basic Enlisted Submarine School (BESS) was to go to, let's see, to Quincy, MA, for a boat in new construction, PCU Garyling (SSN 646). At the time they were a little bit slow, so I got assigned to Submarine Flotilla Two at Naval Submarine Base New London (SUBASE), and we were assigned to assist with the battery job on Grouper. I had an electrical background, so I was designated as an IC striker for interior communication. I went down there with a bunch of First and Second Class electricians, and we put together the battery boxes because they were going somewhere for refurbishment. Then, I got picked up to go on, USS Henry L. Stimson (SSBN 655) Gold Crew as an IC man. Actually, Fireman, because we had engineering, and deck rates and stuff like that at the time. I went aboard Stimson, qualified there on the boat, and then qualified as an IC electrician forward.

Now, all this time it's not unusual to not have a lot of blacks, or Puerto Ricans, or Filipinos on the boat. There were only like four blacks on Stimson and we used to tease each other that, well there's four of us, and we can take it over. We just chuckled about it because it was funny. Then, I read a book on it and that someone had written, and I can't remember the author, but it was interesting that six people hijacked a submarine out of Rota. After you get qualified you realize, not six people, you have to have more than six people to get this nuclear-powered submarine underway, period. I don't care if you go up there and chop all the lines and play the silly games with the screws and stuff, there is no way six people are getting it underway. I thought it was really funny after I read the book and thought about it for about two seconds.

Anyway, I went to Stimson, we were operating out of Rota, Spain, and it was very nice. I just enjoyed myself. One of the five guys I went on board with said, "Well, they've got this program to become officers." All five of us put in for it. I think two of us were machinists, two were IC men, one of them was a quartermaster. We all signed up and sent it through our division officers, department heads, and the CO signed them all and put his recommendation in for it because we worked damn hard at getting qualified in submarines. We did a pretty good job. Out of the five of us, I think three of us got a commission. One didn't the first year that he applied for the NESEP program, Navy Enlisted Scientific Education Program. I think he qualified the second year. I went to Miami of Ohio University, a buddy of mine went to North Carolina State, and we got a commission.

After that I got transferred to USS Pargo (SSN 650) being low man in the division. I ended up riding and going to sea on five submarines, and I was assigned to one that was in the shipyard for conversion but because someone on USS Kamehameha (SSBN 642) Blue Crew decided to become a conscientious objector I was assigned as the AWEPS on Kamehameha. I went from Kamehameha to USS Darter (SS 576), and then I came back and went to USS Sam Rayburn (SSBN 635) Blue Crew. All this time, with exception of Darter, I was here. When I went to Darter she was homeported in San Diego; we took her over to Sasebo, Japan, for overseas residency program assignment. That was interesting. It was my first time to Japan. Now, my dad, he was a West Coast sailor, so he had hit all these places. He brought back a couple of bicycles, one for me, one for my brother. He got both of them in Hong Kong. One was a Chinese bike, and one was an English bike. We enjoyed that.

I spent four years out there. Two on Darter, and two at Fleet ASW Training Center Pacific teaching naval control of shipping and convoy commodore courses. Then I came back here on Sam Rayburn as the NavOps. Another good tour. The whole time I was in, I never had any conflict with anyone. It's not like what's going on now. I'm part Native American, part African, part Dutch or something like that, because we hadn't figured it out yet. It was a good ride, I enjoyed myself through the years. That's just the way it is. That's how I got into the service and my track through the service.

Now that I'm out, I've been working for Electric Boat for 33 years. Doing that, I'm still in submarines. I'm like, what can I say? That's just the way it is. I've stayed in submarine the whole time, from day one up until I retired. I work in Integrated Logistics Support (ILS) specializing in maintenance planning, configuration management and ILS coordination for ILS elements; Configuration management development, maintenance planning analysis and development, supply support and provisioning coordination with ILS elements, logistics support technical documentation (LTD) products, integration with engineering and design development of submarine construction.

Same things that are in the book in your glove compartment of your vehicle are done with submarines. Now you have to maintain it, so you have to say, oh, you have to do these things, and here are the parts that you need to do the maintenance that we as civilians can do. Then I moved up a step and started looking at the big picture for integrated logistics support for them. I've pretty much been in that role for a long time, but I also did the configuration management.

Most of my principles tend toward, you think about what our goals are, and you really look at it like, oh this is what Rickover thought. Oh, this is what someone else thought. When I look at it, I think the same way. The biggest thing you have to learn is how to manage people and that's hard because everyone's different. You have to learn how to manage them, lead them, and they have to follow your example as much as possible. If you don't do your job right, of course no one's going to pay any attention to you.

I've had a couple of COs and XOs that really knew how to take care of people and how to get them to do the job that they were supposed to on the boat and follow directions. Sometimes you think, well the CO, yeah he's new, or something like that, and he's not really the smartest guy in the world, or something like that. Well that's hogwash. He's so far ahead of you; you don't realize that he really has his act together. Some COs have it together such that no matter what you say, if you think about it for a half a second you know he's on the right track. If you follow that track, we're going to get there; we're going to do our job the right way.

I've had like, two, three of them specifically like that but I've also had a couple of them that had change of commands while I was on board. I'm sitting there watching them, and you can see the difference. It's the way the crew reacts to that CO. Hey, if they'll follow him into a meat grinder because he knows how to get through it; you know he's got his act together. I've seen it when I've gone to reunions. The COs are really on top of it. They know how to manage people; they know how to talk to people. The only thing that you find different, you don't know what the CO says to the XO to get the XO to be the bad guy. Sometimes, that really does happen, and the XO seems to be the hard ass all the time. Well, maybe he is, or maybe he's not and it's actually the CO that's trying to get him to get other people to do the right thing. It's just the way things are. I've been in the wardroom longer than I was down there in crew's berthing.

I skipped over Chief. My dad was a Chief (SDC) and I knew what he wanted. It was relatively easy. He'd say, "Paint the bedroom." Well, I'd thin out the paint because I knew he was a cheapo, and then he'd say, "You know, you could have put some paint on the wall." I said, "I did." He said, "No, it's not quite enough. You want to try again?" That's what you need, and you can really see it in a lot of Chief Petty Officers because you learn from them. The officers learn from the Chief Petty Officers that really have leadership skill. If you're going around yelling at everybody, kicking them in the dirt, and stuff like that, that's not the skill that you want. What you want is to encourage them to do it right the first time so that when liberty call comes down we're not there waiting two hours so we can get out of there. We want to get it done, and you need the maturity of those people that are actually doing the job to do it.

Yeah, I've had a number of chiefs and officers that are really right on top of it. Some of them, I wasn't thinking along the same lines, but I had to think about it, am I really that wrong or something? You don't know. Even as you mature, you're ready to retire, you still don't know. I think you always make a list and you try to follow the list and you try to do the things that you need to do to make it happen. It's like when you're thinking about game planning, you've got to have a focus on what you're trying to accomplish. If you don't accomplish a particular task the way you think it should happen maybe you should take the opinion of one of your subordinates, or leaders, and try to fit that into the game plan that you've got established.

I think all of them are pretty decent guys out there on the front line. You see it today, but you've got to follow the rules. You can't let yourself get caught up in stupidity. My advice is, listen to your superiors, but don't forget your subordinates are also there to help you. You got to listen to what they're saying because what's in your head, and what you're doing may take longer, and they have already figured out a shortcut for you. That's why they're working for you, instead of you working for them. You just got to pay attention to your people, and listen to them, analyze it and come back.

When I came back here, I had a number of submariners that were in our departments, on that same floor and of course they twist your arm. Why don't you come over to Subvets? So I did.

What they were trying to do with Subvets is spread out the tasking. You have a board of trustees and you have a bunch of committee chairs. I was doing brunches, dinners, calendars and stuff like that, and you become fairly proficient in trying to schedule the activities for the organization while someone else is scheduling the activities of the clubhouse. I took on that role, I'm still doing it. I was sitting here doing this morning, looking at the calendar because I've got to plan for next year. I'm trying to figure out what we're going to do for Thanksgiving. We usually do a Thanksgiving celebration that takes the youngsters that we have over in sub school in its entirety, whether they're officer sub school, or enlisted sub school, and bring them down to the clubhouse to sit with our families and just talk and be away from sub school. Here's what you're going to join, and trying to show them that we're still a bunch of good guys. Yeah, we spend our time at sea, yeah that's our job, but we still have time to relax.

I think it's important to realize that the submarine force is a pretty good part of the Navy. As I was talking to my brother-in-law, he's an airdale, he's doing stuff for the naval air community. My other brother-in-law was in the Marine Corps and he is doing work down in Florida with the disabled veterans. He works with the crew on the Wall South. This is a great part of my life to know that my brother-in-laws are in it with me. I've got a sister-in-law in the Marine Corps too. We rounded it out. I think yeah, I got a nephew that retired from the Coast Guard. Yeah, and a cousin that was in the Air Force. We hit them all.

Ron Gordon
Lieutenant Commander, RN (Ret.)

"I think most people are not self-aware. I would tell you that that's a difference, too, because you know what you told me, I've heard this too, that people actually talked about what they wanted to do when they became a leader. Not from schools, not from programs, they thought about it. They looked at their experience. They remembered what went well, they remembered what didn't and did it on purpose."

I was brought up in a little village near Faslane, the submarine base, on the Gare Loch. I had no interest in submarines at the time. I was desperate to get away from the village because I couldn't see myself spending the rest of my life there. When I completed my education, I was offered a job at a garage in the local village, but I said, "No, I'm sorry. I've got to get away." I went up to the recruiting office for the Navy. Now, the reason I went to the recruiting office was, I was down on the shore one day when I saw HMS Vanguard, which was a battleship. It was coming up the Clyde and into the Gare Loch to go up to the breaker's yard. I was just so impressed by that. I thought, "That's what I want to do. I want to join the Navy."

I went straight up to the recruiting office in Glasgow and they asked me what qualifications I had. I'd done well at school. They said, "Well, you can go through Upper Yardman to be an officer." I said, "No. I'm from a council house background. My mum won't be able to afford me to go through for officer training. What else is there?" They were talking through the options, and one of them was Artificer training, but because I was just over seventeen and a half, I was too old for that, but I was lucky enough to get into an adult entry apprentice scheme called electrical mechanician apprentice, so I went for that. I joined in December '64 to HMS Raleigh, and that's where you do the parade training and all the other military training. Then I went to HMS Collingwood for my initial electrical training, and I joined my first ship, a Commando carrier, HMS Bulwark.

Now, when you're talking about leadership, my first introduction to the petty officer I was going to work for, for the initial four months on the Bulwark, didn't impress me one little bit. As me and my three mates walked into the heavy electrical workshop in HMS Bulwark in refit, his exact words were, "I hate mech apps." That gives you a really good feeling, doesn't it? That's not leadership, telling them you hate them. You should be there to encourage people, especially youngsters. Well, we weren't youngsters. We were seventeen and a half. One of my mates was twenty because we're adult entry. I spent my sea training on the Bulwark. From having been in this quiet little village in Scotland, before I knew it I was out in Singapore, Australia, Hong Kong, everywhere. It was brilliant.

I went from there back to Collingwood, did my two years and passed through that. Then I was drafted to another aircraft carrier, which I was quite happy about because I played football for the ship's team. The aircraft carrier, Hermes, was doing the trials of the Harrier jump jets, so it was really quite interesting. I joined there as a leading hand and I left there as a petty officer. I was then drafted up to HMS Neptune in Scotland, which is where I came from, next to the village I'd left to join the Navy. I spent a year there working alongside submariners still being a skimmer.

In the end, I volunteered for submarines. I volunteered for conventional submarines, diesel electric, but their Lordships in their wisdom gave me Polaris submarines running out of Faslane. I was a bit gutted when that happened. My first submarine was HMS Renown. I was working in the missile compartment. I did my part three on there, and I also had to do some work on getting ready for my exam and interview for

Chief Petty Officer. I was only away on patrol for four weeks, so it was an extremely busy time, keeping down a job watch, keeping and doing my part three and, in my off-time, learning how to pass the exam to be a chief petty officer.

I left there and then I joined HMS Resolution. I stayed with Resolution for six years. Two of those were in refit in Rosyth, and it also included a trip to America for the firings, the DASO trip. Most of the time I was on Resolution, I kept saying to my boss, "How can I get out of the Polaris system?" He said, "Well, even when you're a warrant officer, you'll still be in the Polaris system. The only job available is down in Bath, and it's who you know to get that." He says, "You know, Ron, I've been trying to get you to go through for officer for a long time." He says, "That's the only way you'll get out of this," so that's what I eventually did.

I went through for officer, and I was lucky enough to get selected for a course at Greenwich. I did the engineer's course at Manadon. Then I joined my first submarine, it was a diesel electric, as the electrical officer. Unfortunately, it was running out of Faslane, so I was still stuck in that little village. That's where I met my first bad leader. It was my first Captain.

When I joined my first Captain was a nice guy who was well-loved by the crew, he was very reasonable. Then this other guy came on. He just used to shout at people. I said, "I'm never, ever going to be like that," because he was ruthless. He just didn't seem to understand that you can't shout at people to get things done. The whole crew hated him, but he was a good seaman officer. After a year he was relieved by a Lieutenant who had just passed Perisher and his Perisher course had been on our submarine. The crew wanted him to join us as our Captain because we knew the previous Captain was leaving. We wanted him there and when he joined the whole atmosphere, the whole submarine changed. We were very professional about everything but the atmosphere on board was completely different. He to me was inspirational and he must've been inspirational because he got to Rear Admiral [Niall Kilgour, Chapter 14] and he was in charge of the whole of the submarine fleet, the Flotilla.

When I was finished with my first diesel boat in the middle of '82, we paid off down at HMS Dolphin in Gosport, which was where I'd been trying to get to for much of my career. So, eighteen years of trying to get from Scotland down to the south of England, and finally I was sent there. I got a phone call from the appointer who used to be my first Captain on the diesel boat and he said, "Ron, we need an engineer to go into the submarine escape training tank (SETT) to take it through a refit." I said, "What's that involve?" He says, "Ron, get off your arse and walk up there and just ask the question yourself." So I did.

Now, having spent two years on a seagoing diesel submarine, I'd put on a lot of weight, and as soon as I walked in, the guy in charge says, "Ron, if you want this job, you're going to have to lose a lot of weight and get fit." I did that. I was at the SETT for three years and it's the best job I ever had in the Navy. It was nothing to do with my engineering qualification, but it was something I loved, because I love to keep fit and it was a really challenging new environment.

I qualified as a ship-diving officer. I completed escapes from HMS Sealion at depths of down to 300 feet. I completed sea acceptance trials of exit and re-entry on one of our diesel submarines using its new chamber. I trained the SBS on exit and re-entry on HMS Ocelot that included U.S. Seals. I completed 20 parachute jumps as part of the submarine parachute assistance group, including some night jumps. I completed two dives on the US Navy's deep submersion rescue vehicle Avalon down to the depths of 430 feet where we transferred personnel from an SSBN to a diesel electric. I was a bit reluctant to leave the SETT but I had to go because they had somebody to replace me.

Then I went up to refit HMS Ocelot, which was a diesel electric submarine in Rosyth. That was a two-year job up there. Then I came back down to Dolphin for a short spell in a job that I didn't particularly like, which was a Trident training and design officer. Then I went to another job, which was my second best job in the Navy. I was a sonar trials officer for harbour trials. I just loved that because you managed a small team of four, but you made decisions on whether you'd accept these weapons into service or not. You had the backing of the Captain of the weapon trials and assessment team.

Following that I went back to Greenwich where I'd done my SD's course. I did a Lieutenant Staff course. I didn't particularly want to be there because I'd been doing a degree with open university, but then because of the amount of work I had to do for the Lieutenant Staff course, I had to give up the degree course. Whilst there I did a presentation on submarine escape. The Admiral was there and he said, "Thank you, Ron that's you showing the youngsters how to do it" because I was the oldest person there. It was all young lieutenants.

Then I spent my last six years in the Navy at submarine school at HMS Dolphin, Gosport, working as Development Projects Officer. That was a brilliant job as well because I got to visit all the IT seminars including Orlando, I got to visit Groton, I got to visit the submarine school in San Diego. It was just picking up all this because the USA, as far as technology was concerned, was way ahead of us. We were trying to catch up on all that technology. Then in March '98 I retired.

I left the RN but before I left a funny incident happened. At the submarine school in Dolphin their support services were getting transferred to a private company that was taking over many services in Portsmouth RN training establishments that didn't have to necessarily be done by Navy personnel. The company came around with the Admiral in charge at the time to do a presentation at the submarine school. They did a good presentation. Then they asked for questions. There was this silence in the submarine school audience because they didn't really know what to ask, and so I just stood up and said, "Excuse me, Admiral, very good presentation but for years Marconi have been stuffing the RN, ripping us off, right, left, and center. Now they're going to be providing our support services. What are you going to do to stop them stuffing us again?"

The Admiral just looked at me; this Lieutenant Commander stood there who had nothing to lose. I was just giving him my thoughts. I didn't know any better, and then the managing director of Flagship stood up and says, "What's your name?" I said, "It's Ron Gordon," and he said, "Right Ron, we are a joint organization not just Marconi and we're working together with the RN. We will not rip you off. We're going to make savings for you, the RN, and we are going to deliver the same services." A couple of weeks later I was sitting in my office when I got a phone call from my appointer saying that he couldn't give me an extension in my job because he had somebody to replace me. I said, "Okay, fine." Then this young lady walks into my office, "Ron, can I have a word?" "Would you like to come and work for us?" She was from the company that was going to deliver the support services. That worked out for me. I left then, knowing that I was coming back to a job. Then I spent the rest of my time until 2011 working for this company. I ended up manager for the whole Portsmouth area. That's my career in a nutshell.

There's a big difference in submarines, the way the hierarchy react to their subordinates. When I was on aircraft carriers, when I was only an apprentice, a lead apprentice and petty officer on the ships, I thoroughly enjoyed it but it was us and them. You just did exactly what you were told. There was no explanation of why you had to do it, nothing. When I got into the submarine service it was different. People explained to you that you were part of a big team; your one mistake can make the submarine sink, so you're extremely important to the team. That's a big difference. You're an important cog in the wheel. That gives you a bit of a lift, I'm part of a good team here. I have to do my best. I can't let the team down. That was one of the big things, probably the biggest thing.

One thing I remember is when I was a Chief Petty Officer and I was in submarines and I'd been managing my team for quite some time and then I had to go to Royal Arthur, which is the Royal Navy leadership school. I was aghast at how they were trying to teach us to be leaders. Firstly, we had to do practical leadership tests. We had to say well this is the situation, you've got to do this and do this and this, and you've got your team to do this. One of these things would get a tire over a big pole and I had three seamen Chief Petty Officers, very experienced in my team, so I said, "Chief Brown, what do think is the best way of doing this?" The Chief Petty Officer who was the instructor said, "No, he's dead." I went to Chief Petty Officer Smith, "You're a seaman Chief Petty Officer, what do you think is the best way to do this?" "No, he's dead, as well." To me it wasn't teamwork. They just wanted somebody to be somebody that comes up with the answers, whether they be right or wrong.

Another example of bad leadership was the guy who was our officer in charge of our course at petty officer leadership course, a submariner officer, Lieutenant Commander. Obviously not very successful because he'd been sent to Royal Arthur, which is not the best place to be sent to if you want to get promotion. He came up with what I thought was a great idea. There were four submariners in my leadership course. One from Polaris, two from fleet fast attack nuclear submarines, and one from diesel electric. He said, "I think it would be a good idea if you put together a presentation on submarines for the rest of the class." We thought, "Oh that's good," but it wasn't to be part of the curriculum.

We worked hard on that and then we were given a date to present. It was after we'd done the whole day's syllabus and we'd done our dog watch sports, and then we had to go into this hall and present to the rest of our class. Those two didn't turn up. The Lieutenant Commander and the Chief Petty Officer in charge of the course. That sent me a message, don't ever disrespect your teams. Set an example and show interest in what they're doing. He said it's not going to change your markings in the course, but he'd asked us to do it. Not asked us, he told us to do it.

The final thing that really peeved me off on that leadership course was that each of the guys in the course were given a task where they became team leader. I became leader of the mountains team, which is the last weekend of the course. We go up the Black Mountains and take your team. You spend overnight in the mountains. You have to get to certain points on a time scale and arrive back at the base camp within a two-hour slot, which I did. I had two of the most unfit guys I'd ever known. One of them was a fleet submariner, but I cajoled them through it and got them to the end, just got them through with five minutes to spare and we had the highest score of the teams competing. He queried it and in the end he said, "Well it's a low score, you won't win the prize." The next day at the presentation we won the prize but the worst thing about it was when I went for my write-up, it didn't include my leadership on the mountain. I said, "Why is that, sir?" He said, "Because I had written up your report before you went on the mountains."

I'd just been selected for special duty's officer at Greenwich when I was on Resolution and I went to do the leadership course at Royal Arthur. I told my divisional officer, "Please don't tell them I was selected for officer, because that will put a different pressure on me." I said, "I just want to go there as just a normal guy." So they didn't. I arrived there and just went through the whole course. When I got back to my submarine in Rosyth and I gave them my report, my divisional officer said, "That's not you. That is definitely not you. They have not gathered what you're all about." That was really enlightening. At the time I was really concerned about it because although it wasn't a bad report, it wasn't a good report. If you go through for special duty's officer, you should be getting a glowing report on leadership skills, so I was really concerned about it. He said, "Ron, don't you worry about that. That's not going any further because that is not you." That just shows you what leadership at that school was all about.

My feeling about leadership is it's all about the attention to detail, what you want to achieve from your team. I mean you need to earn respect as a leader, that's one of the biggest things you've got to do. It's not about shouting or screaming at people, it's not about telling them exactly, well you tell them exactly what you want them to do as a team, but you need to set an example. One of the things that's worse is when some of the leaders shout at somebody in front of others. To me, I've never, ever done that. I've never run down anyone in front of others. If I've got anything bad to say to somebody, I won't say it in front of others. I'll take them aside and have a quiet word. You need to set high standards of behavior. Set a good example. If you want them to behave exemplary, you need to do exactly the same, behave exemplary. The other thing is you need to praise them when they've achieved something. It's all very well the people that shout to them and say, "You bloody idiot, you've done the thing wrong," but if they've done something good, praise them.

One of the key things I think, I find so amazing about senior officers, is they remember their people that were on their submarines. They remember their names, they remember their background, they remember their family, and that is a big plus. If you're a leader and you remember that sort of detail, all right, you might not be able to remember but if you know you're going to be meeting them again, you just look back in your records and see what notes you kept. It means so much to the teams when they meet them, "He remembered me, he remembered my wife, he remembered my son," all that sort of stuff.

When I went into civvy street, I was a manager of support services for the whole Portsmouth area RN training establishments. I regularly took out my management team. We finished work at 13:00 on a Friday afternoon and I'd take them down to the pub. I'd say, "Okay guys, tell me what you think. Nothing goes outside these walls, Chatham House rules, just tell me what you think. It was good. They'd tell me. I'd say, "Right guys, okay, that's good, point taken. That's a very good point," Then at the end of the year I'd take them out for a big meal to thank them. It's just all a matter of making sure they understand they're part of a team, they're valued, it's not all about the man at the top. It's all about the whole team.

My way of leadership, especially in the Royal Navy, you probably won't believe the next thing I'm going to say, but in my 33 years I never charged anyone. On a few occasions I had to lecture a few of them and give them a choice of my punishment or report to the Commander, and every time they took my punishment because it didn't go in the records but they knew they'd done something wrong. I knew they were good guys so I didn't want to blot their records.

That was through thirty-three years in the Navy, you change probably your appointments every two years. I wasn't a leader at the start but after about six years I became a leading hand, so I had a little team underneath me. You have to work with that team to try and make sure that they deliver what's expected of them. You have to understand the team, what their foibles are, what their likes are. When I got promoted to officer I knew exactly how the mindset of the lower ranks worked. I just manipulated that to my good effect. The one final thing you need, you need good diplomatic skills. You never say what you think, especially in some circumstances. You just try and make sure that you give them enough support as you can.

To me, you set an example, lead by example, discuss things with your team, then you make a decision. Somebody has to make a decision. To me it was just like a family. You know every one of them, you know their thoughts and you know how they behave. You know what their likes and dislikes are, you've just got to know your team inside out and you've got to spend the time to do that as far as I'm concerned. The other thing about leadership is being truthful in the assessments. Never butter them up, just tell him/her as it is. You've got to have evidence but never surprise them with anything new. You must've mentioned something through the year or the previous six months or whatever it is, give them a chance to rectify them. There's no point in not saying anything and then saying in the interview at the assessment, "Oh, you've been crap at this," but they've not had a chance to improve it. That's leadership, as well, is giving people a chance to improve their performance.

At submarine school in that last job I was doing lots of procurement. I was thinking I need to get myself set up for when I leave the Navy, and I did that, a Prince Project Management Course. I did the course and then the exam. When I sat for the board it was with three civilians. I passed the written exam, but got really nervous about the oral exam when they interviewed me. However, what they were most impressed about was when I informed them that in the Navy you can't choose your team. It's the team you're given. Whereas in civvy street, you can recruit people and choose the best candidates, can't you? In the submarine service you've got no choice. They're just given to you and you have to make the best of that. They were absolutely amazed by that. That's what makes you good leaders, being able to manage people you haven't chosen, they come in, they might have some backgrounds or some ideas that are not your ideas, but you have to manage that.

3

In Command

Chapter 10

Blue and Gold

William F. (Bill) McGonegal,
Captain, USN (Ret.)

SSBN's have two separate identical crews called "blue" and "gold" for the Navy colors who alternate manning the boat [called Port and Starboard in the Royal Navy]. This arrangement allows for maximum utilization of the ship at sea while managing to maintain quality of life for the assigned crew members. While one crew takes the boat to sea on its regular cycle of refit and a two-month patrol the other is back at home port. There, the (off) crew members have a two-week "R and R" period following their two-month confinement in the submarine. They then undergo intensive refresher training in preparation for the next patrol. Public Affairs Office, Naval Submarine Base, Kings Bay, Georgia. http://ssbn640.com/640blue_gold.htm

Captain Bill McGonegal was the commanding officer of the USS George C. Marshall SSBN 654 Blue crew and Captain Mike Gray commanded the Gold crew at the same time making patrols from Charleston SC, Kings Bay GA, Rota Spain and Holy Loch Scotland.

I was born in the west central Pennsylvania town of Carrolltown, northeast of Johnstown, on the 1st of December of 1936. I grew up mostly in Norfolk, Virginia. At the time I was in high school you had obligated service to perform, usually in the military. I chose to serve my time in the Naval Air Reserves. You could spend eight years in the Reserves, no active duty other than drill weekends and summer training to fulfill your military obligation. So I joined the Reserves at the end of my junior year in high school. When I got to college I joined the Naval Reserve Officers Training Corps (NROTC) and transferred to the Surface Navy Reserves. Since I was a contract ROTC student I was able to stay in the Reserves as an enlisted man all through college. Before graduation I made rate as Signalman Third Class. By the time I graduated with a degree in Aeronautical Engineering in February 1960 I had six years Reserve time and was commissioned an Ensign in the Naval Reserves.

My first ship, USS Rockville (EPCER 851), was a research vessel home ported at the Naval Research Laboratory in Anacostia, Maryland. A notable commanding officer under whom I served was Vernon C. Smith, a mustang who eventually retired as a Vice Admiral. When he took command he had just been promoted to Lieutenant. He came aboard Rockville as a Lieutenant, Junior Grade (LTJG). His Lieutenant bars had not caught up with him yet. He was a very positive, dynamic leader. He didn't stand for poor performance or excuses. However, if you were headed in the wrong direction on a job, he allowed you to go just far enough to recognize your dilemma before providing "guidance." You would then learn the correct way to proceed. He would, of course, counsel you concerning what you did wrong and how to avoid the pitfall in the future. He was encouraging. He was no nonsense. He knew when you knew you had screwed up, and he knew when you didn't have a clue what you did wrong. He could separate those two and he approached them differently. It was a great lesson on leadership.

Running the Potomac River going to and from home port was a great training ground for ship handling. I got to be a very good ship driver. Matter of fact, I think I'm an excellent ship driver. One time on Rockville we were riding out Hurricane Donna in a dangerous semicircle. The Captain had been on the bridge all day long because of the weather. There were 35 foot seas and wind about 80 knots and gusting. I went up to the open bridge to relieve as the Officer of the Deck (OOD) for the mid-watch, 0000 to 0400 as we were standing four on eight off. I had the mid-watch for the 28 months I was aboard. After reporting my relief to the CO, he says, "OK, use your engines if you have to. If you have any problems give me a call. I'm going to bed." That to me was a big vote of confidence. The height of eye on the bridge was 35 feet. Watching the foaming wave crests coming at you was "exciting." We managed to ride it out just fine. Many of the crew wearing their life jackets were sitting in the mess deck. But that's okay. We made it through.

One observation of the commanding officers with whom I have served that I thought was exemplary, they never lost control. No matter what was going on they always had that aura of command. They didn't yell. They didn't scream. They didn't throw things. They didn't jump up and down. They just spoke forcefully and directly to the people who needed it. I tried to do that same thing. Of course, all of my commanding officers that I thought were really good knew when to relax and how to have some fun instead of wringing their hands and worrying all the time; I tried to do the same.

While serving on Rockville I received my orders to be mustered out of the Navy, having served my required two years of active duty. As I looked at Aeronautical Engineering and what had transpired in those two years I knew I had to go back to school for a fifth and possibly a sixth year to catch up. That option was not appealing. I was having fun driving this little ship, 180 foot long, 33 foot beam, 15 foot navigational draft with twin rudder, twin screw. It just drove like a sports car and was a lot of fun. So I asked for the orders to be canceled and applied for augmentation to regular Navy, which I got.

I also got a destroyer, which I dearly wanted. It was the USS Damato (DD 871) home ported in Norfolk, Virginia. So much for seeing the world. Once I got the destroyer we operated for a short time and then went into the Norfolk Naval Shipyard (NNSY) for FRAM 1 conversion. While we were operating we practiced recovery of the "Mercury" capsule as part of Task Group Bravo. My ship handling ability came in handy. Formation steaming and underway replenishment (Unrep) were also exciting for me. My previous ship usually steamed independently and met up with another research ship at a location selected by the scientists prior to sailing. Destroyers usually steam in formation. In formation closing the distance between you and the ship ahead at night while at darken ship was quite exciting. The same could be said maintaining station during Unrep. My ship handling ability was tested and improved.

Later, our Destroyer Division (DesDiv) was assigned to provide ready gunfire support at Gitmo (Guantanamo Bay), Cuba. Our DesDiv was on station when President Kennedy made his speech about the quarantine of Cuber (Cuba) because of the Soviet missile installations having been found there. It was quite exciting. There are three gunfire support stations at Guantanamo Bay. Gunfire support station three is in the inner harbor. When assigned to that station you must anchor at short stay at night. That was the safest option and also a requirement. After President Kennedy made his speech that day our site assignment was gunfire support station three. You don't think the hair stood up on my arms? I was Gunfire Liaison Officer so that meant that if the marine spotters on a prominent hill are wiped out, my band of happy guys and I would go up to the hill and take their place, whereupon we would continue directing gunfire from our ship to the shore. Fortunately that never happened.

We returned to Norfolk and entered the NNSY for FRAM 1 conversion as previously planned. Everything seemed just fine. About two thirds of the way through the conversion work I was asked if I wanted to volunteer for the Nuclear Power Program. I said, "No thank you." The Bureau of Naval Personnel (BUPERS) responded, "Wouldn't you really like to volunteer?" Recognizing the correct answer when told I went for the interview and got selected. However, I was sort of anxious. I didn't know what was going to happen next. I really wanted an assignment to the West Coast. California would be just fine and Hawaii even better. I finally made it. I was assigned to Vallejo, California for the school session, then to Idaho Falls for prototype training.

Fortunately, through all of this I had to drive my little '63 Corvette Stingray all the way across country. It was sort of fun. I remember driving through Yellowstone National Park. I spent the night at one of the cabins at Old Faithful. The next morning I got up and headed south around the ring road. I noticed there was fresh snow on the ground and that was okay. I had my top down as I drove south. I had my movie camera and was taking movies as I drove. When I got down to the bottom end of the road near a park exit there was a sawhorse across my lane of the road. I drove around the sawhorse and on the other side there was a sign that read, "Road Closed." Well, it wasn't closed for me. That little Corvette drove right through the snow. I had a lot of fun doing that.

Got back to Naval Submarine School, Groton, CT and that was fun. There were a lot of students who were draftees of the nuclear power program. Additionally, there were lots of experienced ship drivers in the class. Even so, you had to be qualified Officer of the Deck (OOD) to volunteer for submarine duty. At

162 - JEFF FLESHER

that time the Navy was just starting to put some of the new inductees direct from commissioning through the course. Upon completion of Submarine School, I was assigned to the Guardfish pre-commissioning crew at New York Shipbuilding Corporation, Camden, New Jersey.

We were the third crew that was ordered to the ship. We were the one that finally got the ship built, out of there and on its way to Hawaii, our new home port. My commanding officer on Guardfish (SSN 612) was Gulmer Augustus Hines Jr., called Bud Hines. He was a great CO. He was the consummate submarine commander. I was the MPA and as time went on I became Navigator. We had an interesting Pearl-to-Pearl Operation. Returning home from that operation we ran aground on Ahua Reef on Christmas Eve. I was in the CONN when that happened but did not have the CONN. My roommate was the Navigator. That was a tragic mess. When we finally got pulled off the rocks we proceeded to port. Later we did all those things one does before entering the shipyard for inspection and repair. Through it all Captain Hines maintained his composure and provided me an excellent example of how to handle yourself in a very difficult situation. He had his Change of Command on time and as planned. The Navigator got orders to the Pentagon and I got married. It was an interesting time. From there I was ordered to Dam Neck, Virginia to go to Fleet Ballistic Missile Navigation (FBM NAV) school.

Following completion of the school I was assigned to USS George Washington Carver (SSBN 656) Gold Crew as Navigator and senior watch officer making 5 patrols in her. My CO was Don Ray Briggs, another mustang and a very smart guy. He was an excellent CO. He had been an Aviation Electronics Technician. He was smart as a whip and I really looked up to him. He also taught me a lot about leadership and how to be a good CO. He was about the most technically-competent (electronically speaking) CO I've ever seen. On one patrol there were some problems with sonar and he went into the Sonar Shack and started working around some of the gear. About three or four hours later one of the sonarmen walked out of there and said, "The Captain just set up a rig to give us a sonar hearing test." He said, "It's the best one I ever had." Captain Briggs knew a lot about electronics and he also knew how to deal with people. He had a way of helping people solve a problem by asking well-framed questions. He was good at determining who could do what and how to trust them with their job. He also knew when to give them some guidance. He knew when to step in and get personally involved.

Following my tour on Carver, I was assigned as Weapons Division Director of the Officer Training Department at Naval Submarine School. My immediate supervisor was Dwayne Griffith. He was very smart and quite a gentleman. I learned a lot from him about dealing with people, especially civilians, in an office environment. He was very good at anything he did.

After Submarine School I was assigned as a student to the Command and Staff Course at Naval War College in Newport, Rhode Island. It was a very interesting and challenging course of instruction. At War College the students were assigned to smaller groups of five or six people. We were then given the opportunity to give a talk to the group about what our experiences were before we got to the War College. After I completed my talk our sponsor who was in charge said, "Would you like to give a lecture to the class about FBM's?" I said, "Sure." So, I prepared the slides, prepared my talk and practiced it for him. The guy said, "That was great." Presenting the "lesson" to the class of about one hundred or more was exciting. When I finished the lecture several people came to me and mentioned how good it was compared to all the other stuff, which was usually done by PhD's who couldn't hold a pointer steady.

Following Naval War College I went to USS Skate (SSN 578) in overhaul at NNSY as the Executive Officer (XO). It is probably the worst job I ever had mainly because I demanded the Skate due to its home port after overhaul. I wanted to be in New London. Additionally, overhauls are far worse than re-fits. I got to Skate as it was completing a 14-month overhaul that would drag on to 28 months. The Commanding Officer, Ronald Eytchison, was very good at holding the command together during the protracted and sometimes exciting overhaul. He was quite well spoken and very good at dealing with contentious situations. I learned a lot. Skate was nowhere near on schedule. We had to struggle to get the boat out of the yard. Between the time I arrived to the time the ship departed the yard the failings of the shipyard had gotten the Shipyard Commander fired and replaced by Joe Williams, Jr. That was a real blow for the Engineering Duty Officer Community.

Finally, after completing overhaul, we went to Roosevelt Roads in the Caribbean for weapons system tests and certification. While we were in Roosevelt Roads, Lebanon "blew up." Skate was ordered back to Charleston, South Carolina as fast as we could go. Upon arrival at Charleston we offloaded excess personnel and loaded provisions for an "indefinite" deployment. All the other weapon certified operational SSN's deployed to parts unknown. Those units that had failed their Operational Reactor Safeguards Examination (ORSE) were given a re-exam in a day and given the "OK" to continue operating. Weapons were topped off and all the boats were sent to sea. Their destinations were unknown to me, but probably the Mediterranean just in case. Since we didn't have a weapons certification yet we assumed the job of being target ship for the surface forces exercising out of Charleston. I found the performance of the surface units opposing us to be less than satisfactory. I was glad to be in Skate.

From Skate I went to PCO school and the USS George C. Marshall (SSBN 654) Blue Crew. I served four years and two months as Commanding Officer and made eight patrols in

Marshall. My assumption of command of Marshall is sort of prophetic. I took command on April Fool's Day in 1977 and relinquished command on Memorial Day in 1981. I wonder if there was a message in that?

About the hardest thing that we had to do was a refit. Refits are designed to aggravate you so badly that you just want to go back to sea no matter what. There are also times during refit that changes must be made because of personnel conflicts between the ship's personnel and the Tender Shop personnel. At one point during my first refit in command I ordered one of my officers to stay on the ship and not deal directly with the Tender personnel. I made sure the chief petty officers or other officers carried out the face-to-face exchanges with Tender personnel.

The ship did other things that were sort of fun. In the Holy Loch, Marshall had to move from one side of the tender to the other. Boats were being moved around to facilitate refit work. As a tugboat was not available for us we went around from one side to the other on the diesel and the secondary propulsion motor (SPM). That was interesting. When we finally got tied up alongside, being the third boat outboard, we had no phone and no brow. I had to shinny across the mooring lines to go to the squadron office. They asked me, "What in the hell was going on?" I asked "How do we communicate?" Shortly thereafter a brow was provided for us and we got a telephone so we could talk.

I tried to maintain my cool at all times because I knew that if you lose your cool and start behaving excitedly the whole crew puckers and their effectiveness diminishes greatly. You can't act like an idiot and expect your people to be professional if you're not. I can think of one example that occurred in the Marshall. We were conducting a dependents cruise out of New London, Connecticut. Because of a number of circumstances, we were about 50,000 pounds heavy. As we were diving to periscope depth in the "bathtub" just past Race Rock the ship sank like a rock. The Chief of the Watch (COW) got flustered and couldn't deballast the ship by blowing depth control tanks and couldn't pump out the water. I ordered a 20 up, ahead full and normal main ballast tank blow. It took the COW a while to get his head back together and deballast the ship. We got back to periscope depth with no further problems.

The father of the chief who had the dive quietly asked his son, "Do you always do this?" The chief shakily responded, "No." There was another chief in the Control Room standing with his father by the dead reckoning tracer. The chief's father had also been in the Navy. He thought the diving sequence was a drill just to show how competent and how smoothly the diving party could handle a casualty. In hindsight it did look like a drill. Everything went smoothly. Nobody yelled. Nobody screamed. Nobody said, "We're all going to die." The event was handled professionally and demonstrated to our guests the competence of my crew. It was a lesson to all of us on what to do before leaving port: recheck your compensation and the water conditions at the dive point. I learned a number of lessons that day and others previously learned were reinforced. But one attribute that was front and center is: if you don't keep your cool, no one will. I don't know if you've ever seen a captain "lose it." Fortunately, I have not.

After each refit I liked to do angles and dangles. It let us know how well we were stowed for sea and provided us with confidence in the operational capability of our ship. The navigation fathometer in the navigation center would be set up to record the ship's depth during these excursions. We would go through 10 up [ten degree rise], 10 down, 20 up, 20 down, 30 up, 30 down. We would then go to a full bell and put both planes at the full dive. When the ship got to 20 down the planes would be returned to zero and then hands off the controls. Without doing anything else we would watch the boat recover. Following the evolution the fathometer record showing the ship's depth excursions would be annotated and posted in the crew's mess. In so doing, the entire crew could see how the ship reacted even when you don't do anything but take your hands off the controls. The ship will recover itself. I used this to build confidence in the ship's capability.

I remember my leading Radioman (RM) telling about a junior RM who came into the Radio Room at about 10 minutes after midnight. The junior RM looked at the routing board, and said, "Hey, the Captain hasn't seen the message board yet." My leading RM says, "Well, go find him and get him to sign it." The junior RM responded, "The Captain's been up for 10 minutes. Don't know where he is." I hated staying in bed or staying in my state room. I walked the ship, all through the compartments; up, down, back, sideways, every way. I looked for things that might need fixing and to see what work was in progress. I could also see if any help was needed on any work in progress.

I let the wardroom and the chief's quarters run the boat. I told them I'd already done that stuff and I'm not going to do their jobs. I'll support them when they have problems so let me know. The chiefs got a big bang out of that. As a matter of fact, I had two chiefs that claimed I drove them out of the Navy, a storekeeper and a radioman. They said they got to know what they could do on a submarine with me, then went to an SSN and tried the same thing. They were shut down hard by the CO. They said, "I don't need this. Screw you. I quit." So, they got out of the Navy after that (which is a sad thing). That sort of behavior on the part of the CO is inexcusable. As a CO I think if you don't let the people do their jobs for which they are trained then you're going to have a hard time. Those guys know what they're doing. They've been doing it their entire career. All they need is a chance to do it and it'll work just fine.

The most unique thing about submarines is that you must solve your problems yourself. If you can't do that you shouldn't be in submarines. In a service-ready surface group, as was Damato, you could highline someone from the carrier to come aboard and fix your problem. Carriers usually had civilian representatives for just about everything, especially electronics. You are a self-contained world on a submarine. If you can't fix it yourself it can't be fixed. I was more inclined to make sure that we could fix everything. If there was someone who thought a piece of gear could not be fixed, I would have to be convinced why not. Otherwise we would give it a try.

Fortunately, I had good engineers. One was a graduate of the Maritime Academy graduating in engineering. He was quite knowledgeable and capable of performing nearly any engineering repair. There were several times after he came aboard he would tell the leading chief to perform a unique job or repair. The chief would usually respond: "Oh Eng, you can't do that." He would say, "Oh yeah, let me show you." He would show the chief how to do the job or repair. After two or three of these occasions when he told his men to do something they didn't know how to do, they would say, "Would you show us how to do it?" Word went around very quickly that this guy is an accomplished engineer and could do "anything." Welder, pipe fitter, whatever you want to call him. He could do it all. That's a case of making sure you allow the people who have the training and ability do their job.

I tried not to put myself in the position of being the "expert" when I wasn't. You've got to know your limits. To be a good leader you've got to be technically competent. Whether it's driving a submarine, running a reactor, or getting your weapons ready, you've got to be a technical expert on technical things. You then need to plug the holes in which you discovered you are not an expert. You must realize the people working for you are also experts in their field and many times they're more qualified than you. The trained sailors have to do the job. All you have to do is point them in the right direction and give them the tools they need to do the job. Hovering over those doing the job and frequently asking: "How are you doing?" is unproductive. Let them do their stuff. The Engineer will tell you how many hours he thinks it's going to take to do the job assigned. When the hour approaches ask how the job is progressing. Upon receiving the report, the leader now has actionable information. You don't have to be the guy driving the bus all the time to be a good leader. You know what is supposed to be done and you have to supervise from a distance to make sure that the end result is what you anticipate.

On one occasion during a refit we had a group of contractor personnel working for the Bureau of Naval Personnel (BUPERS) come aboard to talk to the weaponeers. Questions were asked such as: "Who stands watch? Who does the maintenance? Who is the guard?" The degree of cross training blew the contractors' minds. Knowing that the same sailor who stands the watch on the panel can also be a missile maintainer, stand the watch in the torpedo room or be the guard in the missile house appeared to be a complete surprise to them. It seemed like they had never been on a submarine before and never knew the amount of cross training required to make a submarine operational. Submariners are fast learners.

Following my command tour I went to Submarine School as the Navigation Department head and then fleeted up to Executive Officer. I was there from 1981 to 1986, and I retired in October after 32 years of service. From there I had various jobs including certified licensing examiner for the Nuclear Regulatory Commission (NRC) for commercial pressurized water reactors and publications preparation for the Navy and NRC. My final job was a Manufacturing Engineer at Yardney Technical Products. We were making lithium ion batteries that are literally out of this world. Do you remember the Mars Rover that was operating on Mars for 13 years? Those batteries were guaranteed for 90 days. We built them.

On the subs we worked hard and we played hard. No half-way measures were tolerated. Do the job right the first time or not at all. You have to respect your men and appreciate their efforts. You must also tell your men that you appreciate their hard work. Do not talk down to them. They need to know you respect them and their ability. You also have to have fun while doing your job. If you are not having fun you're not doing it right. I always had a good time going to sea. I enjoyed the hell out of it. I don't see what could be better. It was so much fun. Of course, you had good, well trained people and you did enough training while underway to make sure they maintained that level of confidence and expertise.

I think the thing that turns Submariners into Outstanding Leaders is the isolation of their vessel. When you are underway, you are a world alone. You listen all the time. You listen to your own ship and the rest of the ocean via sonar. When you can, you listen to the broadcast, be it normal submarine type of a specialized broadcast just for your mission. Calling for help is not in your lexicon. If you can't fix a problem yourself, you find a work around and continue your mission. If you have to abort your mission it is a major humiliation, unless of course there was absolutely no other course of action available to you.

Preventing mission abort demands the involvement of the entire crew. You never know who will come up with a solution to whatever problem is facing the ship. Leadership demands getting the best out of your crew. That means the entire crew. No one on my ship was too junior to offer a suggestion. You would be surprised what can be learned from the crew's life experiences. Ignore them at your own peril.

Finally, I must give my parents great credit for how they raised me. My firm foundation was established in my home. I am thankful for what they have given me and I did my best to emulate the core values learned there. I hope I succeeded.

Myron P. (Mike) Gray
Captain, USN (Ret.)

I talked about it at our reunion a couple of years ago, with Captain Gray and it amazes me how much responsibility a 38-year-old man can have. I can't fathom, even in the military, any other career path that can give a 38-year-old man a submarine with that many weapons on it and that many young crewmen, that much responsibility, that much authority to change the world. It amazes me that the military, that the Navy prepared him and he did it. In my mind, he did it flawlessly and it seemed like it was just an easy thing for him and it came easy. But in talking to him it obviously wasn't.

Doug Ackley (Chapter Five) interview excerpt

I came from the Midwest. I was born and raised in Lawrenceville, Illinois, which is a little town and it varied in population from like 4,000 to 6,000 people in southern Illinois. It was a rural community although it did have oil wells and oil fields around where I lived. My grandfather and my father both worked in the oil fields and there was a Texaco refinery in my home town. I was born out on an old oil lease so I wasn't even born in a hospital.

While I was in high school I was active in a lot of things. I played three sports; baseball, football, and basketball. I graduated from Lawrenceville High School and I went to the University of Illinois on a Navy ROTC scholarship. I graduated in 1957 and that's how I got my commission in the Navy. I was an engineer, got a degree in petroleum engineering, actually mining engineering with a petroleum option because they didn't have a petroleum engineering degree like maybe Texas or Oklahoma.

Kind of an interesting story, how I got into the nuclear submarine business. Because I had a pretty good academic record in college, wasn't a superstar, but enough that I qualified for the nuclear program. Oh, by the way, I did play baseball when I was at Illinois. When you're in college and you're a scholarship guy every summer you go on a cruise. And the way I got interested in submarines is between my junior and senior year I went on a submarine cruise and it was on a diesel boat out in San Diego. When I went back to school and got to selection for what we were going to do I signed up for diesel submarines.

One time the commanding officer called me, he says, "We've got this new program in nuclear submarines, they're going to take direct inputs from the Navy ROTC and the Naval Academy. You're qualified to go interview for this." I think you should go take a shot at it." I said, "Well, Captain, with all due respect, I really want to go into the diesel submarine business because I liked the people and the camaraderie." He waited about two or three weeks and he calls me back in, he says, "You know, you don't have to accept it, but I think you should go interview." So being a good sailor, I knew the right answer when told.

I went to Washington D.C. and not knowing a lot about what the whole thing was. I had heard of Admiral Rickover but I didn't really know what to expect. We sent four guys up from the University of Illinois. Two of the guys were ahead of me, they had like a 4 point, 3.95 or 3.90. I had a good average but it wasn't up there but the strange thing is that I was the only one out of the four selected for the program.

Everybody always asks about the interviews with Rickover. Actually mine was kind of nondescript except I had a D on my transcript on a junior theoretical applied mechanics course. It was an advanced engineering course but the reason that I got the D was because the professor didn't like jocks and in the spring semester I was on the traveling team at Illinois. I was only in class about half the time and I did B, B plus work in the course but I got a D. I went to the guy and I said, "What's with this?" He said, "Well, I don't think you can learn if you don't participate in class." I said, "Come on, I did all the work." Anyway, he left the D on my transcript and Rickover gave me a ration of crap about, "Where'd you get that D? You must not have been studying that." I told him just what I told you about baseball, and he thought about it for a minute, he said, "Yeah, if you hadn't been chasing that little white ball you could have studied." So he chewed be out. I thought, well, maybe that's probably it. I'm not going to get selected. But I did. So that was the start of my Navy career.

When I graduated I went to nuclear power school. For the officer's it's six months academic work. Then I went to proto-type in Idaho at the enterprise prototype A1W, and finished that up in 1963. And then on my way from there to submarine school, I got married. My wife Alice was from Billings, Montana and then our honeymoon was driving across country to go sub-marine school.

Back to what I said about baseball, about sports. Since, I've kind of looked at why I would have been chosen by Rickover and some of the other guys weren't. I think it all had to do with Rickover wanting people that had, one term that was used, fear of failure. He wanted people with spunk, that were going to stick with it. I think because I was an engineer, I had good grades, and I still was able to do well in the Navy ROTC unit and play baseball, I think he probably thought that was a posi-tive.

I finished submarine school and went to the USS John Adams, my first ship, SSBN-620 as a JO. They were being built up in Portsmouth Naval shipyard. Just before I reported in there, it was the spring of '64, Thresher had gone down the year before and it was built there. I ended up being supply of-ficer for about nine months, two patrols and became qualified in submarines. Then I was RC division officer and I had chief, his name was Chief Wolf. He wasn't a real old guy. He was an

E7 but he was an experienced guy, nuke ET. I remember him telling me years later when I ran across him someplace, he said, "Yeah, you know the day I met you, I went back to the chief's quarters and I said, I didn't know whether to salute him or burp him."

They sent me to strategic weapons school after the John Adams, which was kind of unusual because back then the nukes weren't doing that but they were going to try an experiment for some guys to go ahead and be strategic weapons officers. I was one of about eight guys back then. Now they're all nukes, there are no general service officers or whatever but back then that was kind of unusual. I ended up as a weapons officer on the Lewis and Clark SSBN 644. When I was on the Lewis and Clark, I had a bad CO, good in some ways, but bad enough that I said, "If this is the way it's going to be, I don't think I want to do this." I actually turned in my resignation because he was a drunk when he was in port, not at sea, he was a great ship driver. He liked me. I ended up on the bridge doing a lot of ship driving in and out of Charleston, South Carolina, we were home ported in Charleston. I learned a lot of my ship driving from that guy.

When I was on the Lewis and Clark, I thought I was going to stay in the Navy so I kept a little black notebook and in there I had sections on weapons, on general stuff that later you might need to know to make you a better officer. One of the sections was on leadership and I wrote at the top of it "If I ever become a commanding officer, here are the things that I want to remember." I wrote a lot of things in that section. Well fast forward, my XO was working on me hard to stay in the Navy and I went on an inspection trip out of Charleston, down to Pascagoula for Puffer, which was in new construction. I was a weapons inspector and the guy heading up the inspection team was the CO of the Sam Rayburn. His name was Carlisle A. H. Trost and he later became CNO [Chief of Naval Operations].

Well, Trost was a great guy and just the antithesis of this idiot that I had as a commanding officer. He and my XO worked on me the whole time. He says, "Okay, what's it take to keep you in the Navy?" I went back and I talked to my wife, and I thought she wanted me out of the Navy but she really didn't and I went back to them and I said, "How about if you send me as an ROTC instructor at the University of Washington in Seattle," because we'd always wanted to go to Seattle. I'll be damned if the detailer didn't have a slot for that. I pulled my resignation and the rest is history. I had a great career. I went to graduate school when I was at the University of Washington in my spare time almost got a master's degree in political science but I couldn't quite finish it. I needed another quarter or two at the University of Washington full time to finish but that was Vietnam. Things were tight and the Navy wouldn't let me stay and finish my master's degree.

I went from there to Operations Officer and Navigator on the Sunfish, SSN-649 in Charleston. Made a couple of deployments including a Med deployment out of there. That was my only SSN but it was a great job because I was the third officer. We spent a year in Norfolk Naval shipyard in a non-refueling overhaul and because they had sent me to weapons school, I had not passed my engineers exam. The CO was a good nuke; he had been CO of a prototype. I guess he thought I was smarter than I was. I was standing one and three in the shipyard; it's tough, and trying to study for the engineer's exam. I went up and took the engineer's exam and I failed it the first time and if an officer fails an exam twice, then you're done. By that time, I had a wife and two kids. So it was a pretty stressful. When I flunked it that got the CO's attention and he gave me two or three weeks up in New London where they had a preparatory school for the engineer's exam. So the next time I went, I passed it of course.

Went from the Sunfish directly, no shore duty, as XO of the Andrew Jackson 619. I reported in the shipyard and after about six months relieved the XO who was there. We finished the shipyard and I was an XO almost four years. I had three COs, which is kind of unusual. One of them was great, the other two were not so great but it's all in the deal. Once we got out of the shipyard we made our patrols out of Holy Loch. Well, being XO, it's a tough job, but it makes you ready if you will to be a CO, although there are some things you get surprised at in command even though you've been through it all as an XO. I went directly without shore duty again to Prospective Commanding Officer school in Norfolk. Then you have to go through a refresher course, up in PCO schooling in D.C. It's about three months long where you're actually at Naval Reactors studying.

I went in command of Marshall 654 and I was there three and a half years, made six patrols, from 1978 to 1981. We did an ERP, extended refit period at Holy Loch. It turns out that patrol and that particular event were really what shaped the rest of my career because when we did that ERP we put together a briefing and it was a very good briefing. When I got back, I briefed the Admiral in New London and he said, "Well, you need to go down and talk to Admiral White" who was Sub-Lant at the time. Steve White. I went down and briefed him. He loved it. When I got ready to be transferred off of Marshall, back then, the upcoming jobs were deputies at the squadrons. I was slated to go to Charleston as a deputy. All of a sudden I get a call from the detailer who's my friend that had been the CO of the Will Rogers, our sister ship. He said "How would you like to go to Italy?" "Italy?" I said, "Larry, I'm supposed to go to this good job in Charleston." "Well," he said, "I think this job in Italy is going to be a good job." When I was in New London that last evaluation cycle, I was the number one CO in New London. I went to the Admiral and I said, "Who did I piss off?" He said, "Well, I don't know. Let me call Admiral White." So, he calls Admiral White and he hung up the phone and he said one word. He said, "Go." Again, I knew the right answer when told.

I was on the staff of the Commander of the Sixth Fleet. I was the ASW [Anti-Submarine Warfare] officer. Interesting tour because we were home ported to Gaeta, Italy. We lived in Italy for two years. My boys were in high school at the time. It was really a good job and we got to see a lot and I was the only submarine guy on the sixth fleet staff at the time. I was the second senior in the Ops Department so I got to see a lot besides submarines. When the OPS officer was gone, I got to sit in his chair and worry about burn rate on fossil fuel ships and stuff like that. My wife and kids went over there kicking and screaming and two years later when we were going to come back, they didn't want to come back. We had a great group of people on the staff; we later had reunions. It was really a good tour.

When I finished that tour I got orders to go on the pre-commissioning unit on USS Georgia, a Trident, which at that time was a major command. I mean my eyes just bugged out. Basically, what happened with that whole time period was Admiral White, Admiral Rodin, who's the sixth fleet commander, wanted a post command nuke on his staff. The submarine billet had always been manned by a diesel guy. I was the first post command nuke that went into that ASW job. As my reward for doing that Admiral White assigned me to be the CO of the Georgia. That's how that happened.

I went to Georgia pre-commission. I was on there a little over two years. I was the Gold Crew guy, the Blue Crew CO was already there and I helped him get the ship out of the shipyard. We did the shakedown and after we did the shakedown, post shipyard, drove it down without any missiles on it of course through the Panama Canal. Dipped down under the Equator so all the guys could get their shell back and then drove it up to

Bangor in late 1984. I made two patrols out of Bangor. We did an FOT [Missile test] on the Georgia that was kind of interesting because we shot north to south rather than east to west. The reason they do that is the missile system, the strategic weapon system, has biases in the system. So periodically they shoot north to south to get a different set of data to insert into the algorithms for the weapon's system. When we did the OT, a four missile OT and it was shoot two, wait, then you shoot two more. When we shot we were positioned off San Francisco and we got the message right at dusk. We set up and shot the missiles and I guess it generated UFO reports all the way down the California coast to Mexico because when the missiles went up in the dusk, because these things had big fire balls, everybody saw it. I didn't know about it until we got back but I guess we caused a big stir.

I went back to the Pentagon and again, kind of an unusual path, but I became the program manager for the SSBN security program. This was a program that really looks at all the physics that has to do with submarine detection, trying to quantify it so that we know what the vulnerability is. We looked at everything from sonar, radar, LIDAR, trace contaminants, hydrodynamics, I mean all kinds of things. It was headed up by a three-star admiral at the time, Vice Admiral Bruce Demars, who later became NavSea. He became Admiral Rickover basically.

Admiral Demars had an EA, his administrative assistant officer, a Navy Captain, a submarine guy. There was a gap and so Demars pulled me and made me his EA and again, timing is everything and opportunity. He asked for me to come over and work with him, which I did for six months and then after the new guy came in I went back to my other job. Then lo and behold, I get orders to be the Squadron Commander out here in Bangor, which had all eight of the Tridents. The only eight driving submarines there were. I was flabbergasted. I said, "Holy mackerel, how did I get that job?" But again, it was opportunity. And it was Admiral Demars that put me in that job.

That was a great job. We had eight submarines, so you had 16 post command submarine new captains. They were major command guys. All of them thought they were going to make Admiral. A bunch of prima donna's. They were all good. I mean, don't get me wrong they were all good guys. It was kind of like herding cats but it was a great job. And it was interesting. It was interesting riding the ships, the different ships in different ward rooms and different crews. And again, in the leadership thing you see different ways of people doing business. I was squadron commander for about two and a half years.

I didn't make flag the first time around when I was eligible. I got offered, well kind-of offered, to go be Chief of Staff at Sub-Pac by Admiral Colley who had been my XO on the Sunfish. At that point I kind of saw the writing on the wall and I told him, I said, "No how about sending me to be the Chief of Staff for the Navy region here in Pacific Northwest?" We were going to stay in the Pacific Northwest, ultimately we decided, and so I wanted to start establishing myself here. So that's what he did. He sent me to the Navy region. I was the Chief of Staff for a little over a year and then I retired.

That ended my Navy career but it didn't end my association with the Navy because one of my PhD friends, we ultimately became best friends, lifetime friends because we hit it off so well, had since gone to the Applied Physics Laboratory at Johns Hopkins University back east. And APL Johns Hopkins was the biggest contractor we had in that program that I ran in the Pentagon. He called me up and he says, "Hey, I need help." I basically didn't have to look for a job. I went directly out of the Navy to the Applied Physics Laboratory at Johns Hopkins. Worked there for seven years, got promoted, I think I was working 65, 70 hours a week.

At one point I finally said, "That's enough. I want to retire." I told him I was going to leave. And he said, "Ah, you can't leave." Because I'd been around the program for a long time, I knew a guy that was working as a consultant for through an SAIC program. Science Applications International Corporation. It's a big defense contractor and they had a very flexible consulting arrangement and where you didn't have to work as set days or set hours or whatever. You made an arrangement with the contractor, or with the government and you became a contractor for them, and you got paid for whatever hours. I investigated that, said that's a good deal. The SSBN security program at the Pentagon basically hired me on as a contractor and put me out here in Bangor on the Admiral's staff as a civilian. I worked the issues at the fleet for the SSBN security program. There were a couple big issues and a couple of really good things that we did. I was going to do that for, two or three years, maybe four. Sixteen years later I finally quit at age 74.

Because I had time off, they were flexible, my wife and I could do a lot of travel but we still had other things we wanted to do and I retired in 2014. We did a lot more travel, and it's a good thing that I did that because my wife passed away in 2017. We had an opportunity to do things that we wouldn't have done if I had still been working. I've been here in Silverdale since. I've got a lady I've been with now, she's a retired Navy Captain as a matter of fact, I've been traveling with. We kind of take turns at her house and my house. She lives here locally. I'm doing well. My health is reasonable. So that brings us up to current.

When I was a kid, even on into high school, I was a shy guy. I wasn't the life of the party necessarily. But because I was a good student, I was valedictorian in my high school class, and because I played sports and because I was good at it, I constantly got shoved up front. Not necessarily wanting to be there but just because I kind of got shoved there by my peers I guess. I ended up having to be out in front of people or having positions of responsibility and so you have to learn then what works for you, and what doesn't work for you.

Over the years I generated my package of things where I said, these are the things that work for you. And not all things, not all the ways of doing business work for every person because it has to match your personality. For example, when I was XO on the Andrew Jackson, my second CO was a PhD nuclear engineer from the Naval Academy. Really, really smart guy. When he came in to be CO he called me in the state room and he said, "Okay, now I want you to be the bad guy, and I'm going to be the good guy." He wrote his leadership paper and all that and it was really good. I liked it. Loved it. But when it came down to running the show he could not execute that leadership package because he didn't have the personality for it. He didn't have the patience. I kept him from firing three or four officers because he just didn't, he couldn't, he could not be the good guy. He wanted to be, but he just couldn't. We were a good match because I could kind of offset him in that way.

As a matter of fact, a lot of the stuff that he had with his command philosophy, I took some of it and used it. I could make it work because of my personality, he couldn't. I think you always have to learn what works for you. The other thing that shaped my command philosophy, I'll go back to the little black book. I lost it for a while after I had command. One day I was rummaging through things and I found the little black book. Well, there was the leadership section in the thing. I went through it; I must have had 25 items there. Some of it was normal things, praise in public and reprimand in private. But there were things such as don't tell people they're stupid. I mean on a nuclear submarine the people are not stupid. They may not be informed. They may not be trained properly. Maybe you haven't trained them properly. A lot of the items that were in that book were the antithesis of the negativity that I got from that CO on the Lewis and Clark. When I wrote my leadership or my command philosophy and got the two out later and I looked at them side by side, almost everything I had in the little black book I had in the command philosophy on a positive note. I really did learn leadership from that bad guy because you throw away the things that don't work and then you pull in the things that do work.

Getting back to growing up, ultimately in high school I got shoved out in the middle and got President of the junior class and all this other stuff but I had to learn to get out in front of people and it continued in college. I was mostly in the Navy ROTC unit. I took to the Navy stuff like a duck to water because it was just easy for me. Discipline was not a problem. I continued to develop. I continued to have to be in leadership positions. Then of course as a junior officer you still have to be a leader because you're a division officer but you're young. You don't know everything so you really have to depend mostly on the Chiefs and the more senior enlisted guys because you don't know crap about things. That means you have to develop trust.

When I was a division officer and a department head, like on the Lewis and Clark, I wasn't particularly vocal within the command with regard to certain things. I was still learning my way on how to work with people, with how to deal with the enlisted guys and what's best and how you do it. It wasn't until I was a Lieutenant Commander on the Sunfish that I finally woke up and said, particularly about having opinions, I said, "You've been at this long enough that your opinion might be just as good as the next guy's." I think that helped me develop the confidence. You have to be confident because you have to feel like you understand so that you can execute the next principle and I think it's what made it work on the George C. Marshall. You need to push the responsibility down the chain of command, as far as you can get it and as completely as you can get it.

I guess it's trust but verify. But you have to let people do things and you have to let them learn and sometimes you have to let them make mistakes because they won't learn otherwise. But you have to be confident enough to know when you have to step in and not let it get out of control. If you allow the responsibility, if you shove it down as far as you can, the command, or any organization will be stronger because then you've got back up. I always told the officers don't you dare let me make a mistake, I said, "You speak up because we're all in this together."

Now as a commanding officer, ultimately, I had to make the decision. You may not agree with it, but it may be okay because I've got more experience. Well, on the George C. Marshall the guy I relieved, the CO I relieved, they had good exams and stuff but he ran the ship much differently. When I first came on the ship back in engineering spaces people were coming and asking me permission to do things and my response was, "Why are you asking me that?" I said, "Why don't you go ask the Chief?" I mean it was just people would not do things without him saying, "Jump." It took me almost a year to undo that on the Marshall. People were afraid to do anything unless the Captain said so. And luckily, I had two XOs that were good too and that made it easier.

Another example of why that's important is, remember the submarine the Greeneville? It ran into that Japanese ship out in Hawaii. Basically, what happened is that every year you have to do an emergency blow. You have to test the emergency blow system and the way you do that is you go up, periscope depth, you search all around, make sure you're ready and then you go back down to a deep depth and then you blow to the surface using the emergency blow. That's basically an uncontrolled blow. You have to go up, search, make sure that you're not going to run into anybody when you blow out of there and you have to do it in a timely manner because somebody can then get into your zone of safety. If you have delays, then you should stop. I've done it. I've stopped the evolution and said, "No, we have to go back to periscope depth" because we weren't ready to do it.

When they did it the weather was rough and they were trying to get back in port, they were pushing. The CO ran a ship where nobody brought him bad news because if you brought him bad news you got your butt chewed. They went up. It was rough. It was a sea state three or four. They couldn't see very well. Went back down and somebody should have said, "Captain, we better go check," and they didn't. Well, the ship got into that zone of safety. He went ahead and blew because he was in a hurry and he had VIPs on board that wanted to get in port and he hit that ship and killed 20 some people I think it was. The ironic thing is if you told me there was a ship on horizon and said, "I want you to go down and submerge and then I want you to blow and I want you to hit the ship," you probably couldn't do it. But that accident happened because of the command atmosphere that said, "I'm afraid to say anything because I'll get my butt chewed."

The other one that I hope I came across with was it doesn't need to be dreary. I always said, "If we're not having fun, we're not doing it right." In addition to all the work we have to do, or all the work you have to do and when things get tense, you got to do what you got to do, but you really ought to generate an atmosphere where the crew enjoys what they're doing. They feel they're rewarded. They feel they're recognized for what they're doing and if you don't have that atmosphere on the ship it's not very pleasant. And that's the atmosphere that we had on the Lewis and Clark. People were just not very happy.

There are some other axioms. You've got to treat people like they're people. I always wanted you guys to do what you were supposed to do because you wanted to do it, not because I told you to as the Commanding Officer. In the Navy you can give people orders but as you well know people will do that be-grudgingly and only put the minimum of effort or detail. You have to be consistent in the way that you handle things be-cause if you're not consistent, then people don't know what you think.

Having two commands is interesting because on the Mar-shall, I'd been an XO, I had a lot of sea duty but you never know whether your method is going to work. You always have that anticipation of is this the right way to do it? By the time I got to my second command, I knew what worked and I knew how to treat people. It was just easier. It was easier because you learn what works for you. You got to do the things that work and where you see the results, where you see the feed-back, where you see the way people respond. It's interesting, when you talk about leadership, you never know as the Cap-tain and Commander or just being in charge of anything, you never know what impact that you're having on people. I guess the current chief saying is lead by example. That's another ax-iom. You can't do one thing and say another, or say one thing and then do another.

When I took over as a CO I'd been XO for almost four years. I'd had every job on the ship essentially and I thought, "Well, I got a pretty good handle on this stuff." You know what? The one thing that was the hardest for me, it was Captain's Mast. Because it's one thing to sit there around the table and watch it happen but it's another thing to be the guy at the end of the table. Because what goes through your mind is, you got some young guy that's standing there in front of you and he screwed up. There's no doubt he screwed up. You get to thinking, "Well, why did he make that mistake? Or why weren't we paying at-

186 - JEFF FLESHER

tention? Or why didn't we see it?" Then you get to questioning whether there was something systemic within the command that didn't prevent that. Now you're standing there and you say, "I know I got to do something with him." But you're saying, "Who do I talk to as soon as I get over Captain's Mast, because we've got to fix this?" You have to evaluate things as you get inputs based on do you have a systemic problem that's causing this issue.

The keynote of my command philosophy was individual responsibility because in the light of day you are responsible for your actions and nobody else is responsible for that. Nobody else makes you do it. You have to make a decision to get yourself in the situation and that's your responsibility. You can't blame it on everybody else. You've learned on submarines to take responsibility and you've learned to complete things. You've learned to show up on time. You just learn so many things. You may not realize it and I said, when you get back out in civilian life if you don't stay in the Navy, I said those will be good tools for you. But it's funny though it changes you and I think, in the most part, I think for the better.

You have to listen. If you're always projecting, you're not listening. On the submarine you learn to focus, you learn to be calm because you can't be yelling and screaming. Although I admit some people do. When I was in PCO school we used to all get together at the end of the day and we would talk and by the time you get to PCO school, then you think well everybody does things the same way and, of course, there are procedures as far as the operations detail. But I was surprised at the diversity of the ways that people ran ships. But again, it goes back to the personality thing. You got to do what works for you. It's that simple. I would say that's what happened to me; I learned what worked for me and continued to do that.

Chapter 11

First Strike

Frank Stewart
Captain, USN (Ret.)

In January and February 1991, as Operation Desert Storm began, Louisville carried out the first war patrol conducted by an American submarine since World War II. The patrol began with a 14,000-mile submerged, high-speed transit across the Pacific Ocean and Indian Ocean to the Red Sea. Shortly after noon on 19 January, she launched Tomahawk cruise missiles against targets in Iraq, becoming the first submarine to launch Tomahawks in combat. For this war patrol, Louisville was awarded the Navy Unit Commendation.

I graduated from ROTC at Cornell University in 1971 and obviously it was a Navy program. You get through the nuclear power pipeline and you go to your first ship. There was a guy from Idaho. He wanted to go east. I wanted to go west. I was going to Norfolk. He was going to Pearl. We managed to get the bureau to switch that. I ended up on the USS Barb, a 594 class submarine as a JO out of Pearl. I was on there for three and a half years under the same commanding officer. It wasn't sup-

187

posed to exactly be that way, we had a relief onboard when I had about seven, eight months to go, then a CO on another ship in the squadron got fired and you know how that works.

The reason I mentioned that is because I learned a lot from this guy. It was really difficult as a LTjg at the bottom of the food chain so to speak because what was really important and what wasn't seemed to have the same priority to him. I said, "Man, there's got to be more to life than this." I mean, I'd written my letter of resignation. I was ready to go. I said, "This is really fun." Now, I'm a single guy at the time and I said, "This is really fun but..." I made a brief op with it before we went into overhaul. Went to a refueling overhaul with it; the pain and agony of the shipyard, well and truly branded.

Then I had an opportunity to go on a small squadron staff out of La Maddalena, Sardinia. That was an eye opener for me because they were all the attack submarines that were coming into the Mediterranean on a routine basis. This is mid 70s in the Cold War. I probably saw 15 or 16 different submarines and submarine COs pass through there. You realize that there is room for individual application and ways to make things work and do it much better than what you were exposed to in your previous life. So I've got to make a decision at that point because by now I've got six, seven years in the Navy. I said, "You're either going to get out of here now or you're going to go for the brass ring." By that I mean, you determine to do what is needed to become a commanding officer of a ship. If you don't want to do that, then you might as well just leave. So obviously I did that.

I went from Italy to a department head tour on another SSN, it was the USS Parche (SSN-683) out of Mare Island, California. I rolled straight from that, I mean literally, it was about a week off, to become the XO of another 594 SSN, the USS Haddo (SSN-604). So that's six and a half years at sea. Following that I went to Washington DC for a couple years and then started the PCO pipeline, tactical PCO and the Naval Reactors component.

Upon completion of the PCO pipeline I went back to the USS Barb and had struck a deal with the detailer and it actually came through. He said, "If you go to the USS Barb and you get some op time and then you take it through decommissioning, I will give you the fast attack of your choice in San Diego, California." So I said, "Okay, you've got a deal." I decommissioned the Barb and then I went to the USS Louisville. That's how I ended up in Louisville, Kentucky, but there's a story beyond that. After that, I drove a desk at the fleet headquarters following a tour on squadron staff in San Diego.

I got to spend an arduous year in Australia at their initial Australian College of Defense and Strategic Studies course. By the way, I got married, let's see, between the department head and the XO tour back in 1982. I still am but that's a whole other story. So then I come out of Australia and after 25 plus years of SSN experience the only way I can keep going to sea is to go to a Trident. It was the Henry M. Jackson out of Bangor, Washington. The one not named for a state. I said, "Yeah, this is going to be tough," but I did it. At the end of that tour I was twenty-seven plus years in the Navy. I wasn't going to be promoted to admiral so I said, "If you can't hang the going to sea carrot in front of me anymore, it's time for me to leave." So that's when I retired. When I left, I was the senior submarine officer, qualified in submarines, still serving on a submarine.

The reason I'm in Louisville, Kentucky in two words is Saddam Hussein. I was the Commanding Officer of the USS Louisville when Desert Shield/Storm kicked off. We left right after Christmas in 1990 to head across the Pacific, Indian Ocean up into the Red Sea and participate in Desert Shield, which was going to be Desert Storm. We ended up firing the first war shots from the submarine, Tomahawks, since the close of World War II. Now I mean we knew what we were doing and evidently the Navy, well the Submarine Force, wanted to publicize this and normally they never say anything about submarine operations as you are well aware.

So we're sitting up there in the Red Sea about four or five days after the first few shots and we've got a few more to shoot. In starts coming these family grams that say, "Hey, we heard about you on CNN. We heard about you guys on the news." I said, "I know it wasn't us." So I fired off a message to the Group Seven squadron commander and said, "You've got a security leak somewhere because here's what's happened." Within the hour I get a, "Oh, we forgot to tell you. We let the world know that submarines are playing in this war."

I recall we had pulled into the Philippines for upkeep and I had gotten a call. I talked to my wife and she said, "Well, I just got this invitation from Jack Hillerich from Hillerich and Bradsby Louisville Slugger inviting us back to the derby." That is in early May obviously, first Saturday of May, and this was the middle of April. I said, "Well, we've got about 5000 miles of ocean and 2000 miles of land. I don't think it's going to happen." Lo and behold it did. We basically got detached out of there about four months in and rolled into San Diego on the Monday before the derby. Jack Hillerich of Hillerich and Bradsby comes out and meets the ship with a special edition Louisville Slugger baseball bat that we give to everybody in the crew. The media's there and all the rest of that stuff. We come back for the derby and do all the millionaire's row. It was all a hell of a time.

He and I just became, I guess what you might say, good guy friends. We communicated once or twice a year and I'd see him maybe every couple years or so. Finally, as I was winding up the tour on the old Henry M, he says, "Well, what are you going to do?" I said, "Well, I know what I'm not going to do." I said "I'm not doing anything high tech. I'm not doing anything nuclear power." He said, "Well, why don't you keep me in mind?" One thing leads to another, change of command, and retirement, seventeen days later, I'm in Louisville, Kentucky making baseball bats. So that's how I ended up here and I've set a record. I mean my wife and I moved nine times in sixteen years in the Navy and I've been in this place for twenty-two years.

After thirteen years with them and having three of the Hillerich family working for me, I always knew blood was thicker than water. One day they say, "Hey, you've done a great job at teaching these guys all this stuff. It's time for one of them to step up and it's time for you to go elsewhere." I ended up working in the defense side of business development for a small tech company in southern Indiana. Then at the end of 2015, at the ripe old age of 66 and change, I said, "I'm done." So every day is Saturday since then although I do a bunch of volunteer work.

Obviously you learn as you go. Like I said, way back on square one, I learned how not to do it. That is to make everything the same priority. The other thing I learned early on in this game is that it's almost like the mini bully pulpit. When you're the Captain of a ship and you say something you may be saying it in a fairly lighthearted way but if you ask somebody a question about why is this that way? All of the sudden it becomes an action item; whether you wanted it to be that or not. So you have to be very careful about how you have conversations.

Probably one of the biggest things is you've got to know your people. I hate to use the word empower because everybody does it, but you've got to push stuff as far down the chain of command as you safely can. As I used to tell everybody, "Do your job. Hopefully I won't jump in too early, but before it's too late," and "Make sure you got clear guidance and direction. If you don't understand what we're about to try to do or what you've been asked to do, then before you start doing something get it straightened out."

Other pearls of wisdom. Keep me honest. I couldn't stand yes men. The teachable moments are always when you ask the hard questions. Somebody would bring something up and I would ask them, "Okay, what do you recommend?" They knew that was coming and I told them, I said, "It's perfectly fine to tell me you've got an issue and it's also perfectly fine to let me know that you don't have any recommendation but you're working on it. So don't try to bullshit me because I'll see right through it."

One of my big things, and my kids hated it, now two adult sons, I said, "What's the reference say? What's the governing document demand that we adhere to?" Whether it is technical on the ship or operational on the ship or in terms of my kids, what's your homework guidance? What are the wickets that you're trying to satisfy here? Another great thing I learned early on is if you think you should tell your boss, then you should tell your boss. Don't have an internal debate about should I or shouldn't I? Even if it's zero-dark-thirty in the morning if you're thinking right now you need to do that, then you should do that.

Also, one of the keys is to get buy-in from your sailors, to somehow be able to articulate to them what's in it for me? In other words, how do I fit in the picture? When you're talking with a guy who's checking onboard and you go over their records and talk to him, and say, "Look, I realize that I'm as old or older than your father. Odds are, you didn't exactly listen to him and you're probably not going to listen to me, but let me try to help you understand where you're going to fit in this scheme because you're brand new here and you're the guy who's going to be at the bottom of the food chain for a while." For the mechanics, they'd always end up in lower level or the engine room. I said, "All right, lower-level Louie, here's how it works." I would say, "You've got the evaporator down there. Guess what happens in this ship if we don't have pure water?"

Then the upper level, you got the main engines and turbines. You're just trying to personalize where they fit and how it contributed to the mission.

I did have a reward program. I told the crew this, "Let me be right up front with everybody, life is not fair and neither is it here. Here's how it works. Good behavior and good performance, good deals. Average behavior, average performance, average deals. Poor behavior, poor performance, no deals at all." I mean that's the way and everybody understood that.

There are four guiding principles that I think are important. Act with integrity, tell the truth, keep commitments, and treat people with dignity and respect. I think I swiped part of that from Steel Case Manufacturing many, many years ago. Obviously, you can get sidetracked quite easily. One of my mantras was keep the main thing the main thing. Some days the main thing is different than others so you had to make sure that we're all pulling in the same direction. To the subordinates as you try to push everything down to the lowest level where it could effectively be managed, I said, "Remember this, when in charge, be in charge. Don't abdicate." I guess one last pearl of wisdom is, I said, "Always remember, it is easier to relax the restrictions than it is to tighten them up."

Okay, so what did I do when I'm sitting there in that state room or I'm wandering around the ship? Management by walking around and talking to people find out what's going on. I would tell the XO and the department heads and myself early on, my job was to effectively figure out how to eliminate self-generated crisis. We, and me especially, should be looking far enough down the road that we can be working on the day-to-day stuff. Obviously, the further down the chain of command you got, the more the day-to-day stuff was really, really important. But you always had to make sure you understood where you were going, say next week or next month. I wasn't so exotic as the five-year planner or the three-year planner, none of that. I'd take it maybe a month, two months, or the next major event on the deployment schedule or upkeep schedule or whatever it was. I went at it because I said, "If we can effectively eliminate the self-generated crisis, then when the external crisis gets dropped on us, we have room to work on that and not really impact what we're trying to do on a daily basis. Because if all you're ever doing is putting out your own fires and somebody drops a bigger fire on top of you, guess what? The fires just keep getting bigger."

On the submarine you have a captive audience, nobody's going anywhere except where the ship goes. People are quick to understand that it is a teamwork environment. You can't just leave. If a casualty happens, you're in a bad space to start with, being several hundred feet underwater. Odds are being on the surface is a much better place than where you are right now. But there is an inherent risk to just making that call. Again, if you're in the middle of the ocean, it's much different than if you're operating local op areas.

The teamwork concept of everybody has a job to do and when you go to battle stations or you're combating a fire or hydraulic oil leak or any of that kind of stuff, they get it for the most part. With a crew of say 140 or 150, you find that five or six are really upset with where they are. They're recognizing they volunteered to be upset with where they are. But it's important to explain again where they fit in the puzzle. Explain why it's important. If everybody does their job we're going to come out of this okay. If we don't and somebody starts screwing it up, then regardless of the casualty it might become something even worse.

I really do think a lot of it is you just have to understand where you are and how you fit. Not only how you fit right now today but what can you do to prepare yourselves to take on more roles and responsibilities and advance? What can we, by the "we" I mean the rest of the ship, do to help you achieve that? Its growth and professional development because when you're finished, when you walk across the brow for the last time, t's what training did you do? Did you train your relief? Whoever your relief may be such that somewhere down the road they can roll in and do what you've done, only better? Because your only real legacy is how did you improve the system when you were in it? How did you develop the people to take your place when you're gone? Because once you're gone, they pat you on the back on Friday and they'll talk about you on Monday, but they'll forget about you on Tuesday.

It's like when you first walk on a ship as the brand new CO. Obviously having done it three times you learn quickly that you have a window of opportunity measured in, the numbers I always used were probably two to three months. Where if you really want to change anything, you do it then and they'll buy in just because, "Oh, it's the new guy. He wants to try something else." You can get it implemented but if you start waiting much longer than that you lose the inertia that comes with being the new guy.

You do the best you can with what you got. Like I said you always try to make it better. If your objective in life is not to make it better for your relief then you've got the wrong mindset. I hate to again use one of those continuous process improvement things. But let's face it, that's really what you're all about. In any organization, it's okay. The thing I used to always cringe about is, "Well, we've always done it that way." Okay, well, we're not going to do it that way anymore. Let's try something different.

You start getting people that are interested in pushing the envelope and asking their questions. "Why are we doing this? It doesn't make any sense." When they start asking that and then they start coming up with some better ideas and then you implement the ideas, and a few of them start to work, then it becomes almost self-fulfilling because then more people will

196 ~ JEFF FLESHER

try it. "I don't like this. What are we doing about this?" You start feeding the culture where you're getting the ideas from the people who are actually doing it right there, right then, right now, and it's coming up in my direction, which makes it a whole lot easier to implement than something that's getting pushed down from the top. As you well know, buy-in is critical.

It's not exactly a story but it's related to a lot of things that happen on a submarine. You know how it goes, here's the officer on the deck and here's the team and we're getting ready to do some exercise and we're in the position we're supposed to be in. Everybody's getting ready to go to battle stations or whatever it is. I recall going up there and talking to the officer of the deck and I said, "If you're not nervous right now, you don't understand what's about to happen." Those were big exercises but sometimes it would be a bit too cavalier. Obviously if it was too cavalier then I failed to make sure that they understood the significance of what was about to happen. But I always enjoyed that. So, if you're not nervous right now, you don't understand what's about to happen. Because I am a bit nervous right now and I've been down this road a couple of times. Of course, you've got to have a sense of humor in this business. We also tend to take it too seriously sometimes.

A good example was where the watch section finds the aircraft carrier many, many miles ahead. This was an exercise out in the western Pacific. I said, "Okay." They're trying to run the gauntlet and we're the bad submarine and they've got their escorts. They're trying to get through, this is north of the Philippines. The exercise ends at 8:00 o'clock in the morning. We picked them up, I don't know, 10:00, 11:00 o'clock at night. So, I tell the officer of the deck, "All right, you got this." I said, "You go down there and you just run flank for about three, four hours because we know which way they're going. Then you slow down long enough to make sure he's roughly where you think he is." It's 7:30 in the morning, it's going to quit at 8:00 o'clock." I said, "All right, you just run for about 10 minutes, we'll clear baffles and come up. As you well know he should be where you got him plotted." Sure enough, bang he comes up. I said, "Okay, shoot your green flare." Boy, the battle group was pissed. Louisville had beaten the aircraft carrier. You just empowered them. They were so happy. They just did what they needed to do and they got it done with fifteen minutes to spare.

Even as that young division officer it was my job was to make this better for the next guy. That may not always be on paper; evaluations, inspections, all of the rest of that stuff. It just may be the way the whole organization is run. If you're lucky, you have developed a lot of people who have moved up through the officer corp or through the enlisted corp. They become leading petty officers, chiefs, chiefs of the boat. You have instilled in them the fact that, as I said, it's time to go after the brass ring because if you don't want to go after the brass ring, then you're just wasting your time.

The ring is different depending on people and where you are and what it is that motivates you. It may motivate you to say, "I don't want to do this. I want to go do something else. I've learned a lot here." I really appreciated whatever it was I took with me and I can see having more fun and more professional challenges elsewhere. You pat them on the back and you thank them for what they've done. The key is recognizing what people have done for you and don't be upset when they decide to leave. You make the decision based on the facts you have; it's the best one you've got. Now my baseball analogy. You follow the guidance of Leroy Satchel Paige. "Don't look back, something might be gaining on you." Once you've made that decision - Go. Don't play would've, could've, and should've, and I wonder what.

Chapter 12

Perisher

Christopher (Chris) Groves
Captain, RN (Ret.)

Among his many assignments and duties, Chris Groves was responsible for all sea and shore based submarine training including the world famous and possibly most difficult command course in any service, the Perisher course. Failure in the program means not only the end of a chance at command but also the end of assignment to submarines. Formal training for submarine Commanding Officers was introduced in September 1917 and since then there has been a steady flow of students ready to undertake this most intensive of courses. Since its inception the course has qualified 1,164 UK officers and 408 foreign and Commonwealth officers to command submarines and hence it remains an elite club to which only a few ever achieve access.
Excerpt from: 26 June 2017, The Royal Navy Forum,
Submariners Gather to Celebrate Perisher Centenary

I joined the Royal Navy Submarine Service largely because of my father. He joined the Royal Navy in 1960 and I came along in '67. After 10 years in General Service, he joined the submarine service in 70. I can remember as a four or five year old, sitting on his knee on a diesel submarine. The Navy was part of my life all the way through, and everywhere we lived was linked to dad's job. We lived in Portsmouth and Plymouth, and then we ended up for a couple of years in Australia while he did an exchange with the Australian Navy. When I got to that stage of, do I go to university or not, I had a conversation with my father which went around, "I've got a place to go to Swansea University to do Geography, dad." And he said, "Okay. What are you going to do with that?" I said, "Well, I'm going to join the Navy, dad." He suggested that maybe I could join the Navy without going to university and still get a degree through the Navy. So, I did. When I first joined the Navy I was pretty convinced I was not going to join submarines. I thought I was going to go into surface warfare and be a fighter controller, controlling aircraft from ships. That all changed when in my first job in the Navy I was a midshipman in HMS Ark Royal.

We were on a big long deployment out to Australia. On our way out to Australia as we were coming into the Mediterranean we were doing a NATO submarine exercise. I can remember being on the bridge for the middle watch - that's midnight to four o'clock in the morning - and submarines would mark their attack by firing a green flare into the sky. By the time I'd witnessed five of these in my four hour watch, while I sat on what was supposed to be one of the premier antisubmarine warfare capabilities in NATO, I thought to myself, "I'm in the wrong branch here." So I transferred to submarines and never really looked back.

When I eventually left the Navy, I left early; I retired at 47 as a Captain having been responsible for all submarines sea and shore training. I knew what the journey was going to be to my retirement from the navy. Fifty-five is your retirement age. I knew what the journey to 55 looked like but felt I had to be able to prove myself in some other field so I decided I was going to leave early and do something completely different, completely separate to defense.

I joined the oil and gas industry. They took me on to do a leadership and development coaching role offshore on oil rigs. It was going to be part of a big change management program. I took that role on up in Aberdeen, Scotland and really enjoyed it. It was really exciting to see a new industry and to see a different way of treating a team effectively to deliver something operational. The teams are largely financially driven obviously but also in a similarly high risk and safety critical environment but with a completely different set of individual motivators. They were all mostly motivated by money and time off, whereas I had always been used to people who were motivated by the role, challenge, kudos and job satisfaction.

After some months I was asked to write the strategy for decommissioning fourteen oilfields and two oil installations for the oil company. At the end of that, after a year delivering that strategy, I became the field manager for the first oilfield in that Company that was going to be decommissioned in the North Sea called Beatrice. I did that for about a year. I'd been out of the Navy for about three years by the time I got to that stage. Then QinetiQ, the company I work for now who do an awful lot of work for the UK MOD [Ministry of Defense] and particularly the Royal Navy Submarine Service, just completely out of the blue dropped me an email and asked if I would like to come and have a conversation around running a submarine growth campaign to do with developments in the submarine area. I've been doing that for about three and a half years, so that's where I am now.

After I'd spent the first two and a half years in the Royal Navy in a few surface ships as a trainee, I transferred across to the Submarine Service. Did my basic warfare training in HMS Dolphin in Gosport in the Submarine School there. I did all of my escape training in the submarine escape training tank in

Gosport as well and then I was very lucky to get sent to a diesel submarine for my first job. I went to HMS Opportune as the torpedo officer and I spent about eighteen months on Opportune cutting my teeth.

That was a really, really good way to learn submarining because everything was pretty much manual. Nothing was really automated, so if you needed to make water move around the submarine then you'd have to open all of the necessary valves to get the right lineups and run all the pumps. There was no automation of it at that stage. You were directly involved in operations like snorting and making sure that you could keep good trim in a small submarine in rough weather. That's raw submarining really. It was a fairly small team compared to the nuclear submarine. We had 60 odd people in the ships company commanded by a Lieutenant Commander. So quite junior in many ways in a command perspective. The wardroom was quite small there were only five warfare officers and two engineers, one marine engineer and one weapons engineer.

Everybody had to muck in and everybody was busy. We all were multi-roled, effectively. I think that's the reason we got more responsibility at an earlier age on a diesel submarine than you did on a nuclear submarine. I was very lucky that I had a command team that were extraordinarily effective driven largely by the Captain, who was an excellent coach and mentor.

I think the great thing about the submarine service is that you change roles about every eighteen months to two years. On each occasion you will have experienced at least one commanding officer but maybe a couple. So throughout a career of lots of jobs in submarines you get to see lots of different command and leadership styles. I would say certainly from my perspective that you probably learn more from a bad Captain than you do a good. But my first Captain was a great Captain. A really inclusive guy who was prepared to muck in. Was not a shouter. In fact, I think some of my worst telling offs came from him. Never raising his voice they were usually one line comments such as, "That could have gone better." Because you respected him so much you really felt you'd let him down. It was worse to have felt that you'd let him down than it would have been to have got a good hair-drying or pineapple-ing in the shouty kind of sense, a bollocking kind of sense. I guess from a leadership perspective he taught me an awful lot.

He wasn't perfect. He made mistakes but he would learn from them. He was very self-aware. He knew what his short-comings were and he was quite happy and not too proud to fill those shortcomings with his team. He wasn't always a great ship handler. He wasn't great at driving the submarine on the surface and berthing it but he would often delegate it. I've come across a lot of Captains who would never delegate that sort of thing. They would say that was the Captains job. I think I learned quite a bit from him.

One fond memory I have, we were about to deploy to the Sea Training organization to put us through our paces. We went out, just the ships company, for a day beforehand called Cobwebs designed to blow the cobwebs away. We went out to sea and we needed to test both of the watches in how to put a snort on; how to run the diesel at periscope depth. We really weren't very good at it and we kept on making mistakes and getting the routine wrong and really, we should all have known it. We got back alongside and the Captain turned round and he said, "That was just not good enough" Instead of turning round to the heads of departments and saying, "Sort it out" he turned round to the XO and said, "Right XO, tomorrow at lunchtime we're going to give the whole of the ship's company the after-noon off." And he said, "Then we, the wardroom, are going to make sure that we can put a snort on."

I can remember being sat alongside at lunchtime. We'd kicked the whole ships company off with the exception of those that we absolutely required and he said, "Right! I'll go first!" And he sat on the ships control spot as though he were a junior officer and he grabbed hold of the microphone and he kicked off the snorting routine. After about three commands he made a mistake. And after a number of expletives he stood up, and he gave the microphone to the XO, and he said, "Right XO, your turn." The XO got up there and we all went through it. We all made mistakes but by the end of the afternoon, we were absolutely brilliant at it. He turned round to us all and he just said, "Right, I think we can do that now, let's go to the bar." And we went for a beer and that was the way he set the tone for training and for continuing improvement and working as a team from that day forward. Great guy.

I then went inboard and did a shore job up in the headquarters in Northwood where I was what's called a submarine controller. I was responsible for water space management and that sort of element. The great thing about that job was it was all about overt and covert operations. I ended up with very regular contact with the Admiral who ran the Submarine Service and the Staff Officer Operations; very capable submariners and very capable operationally but both really cared about their people, which is so important. I left there and I went to be the navigator of a nuclear submarine, HMS Splendid.

She was coming out of a refit period where she'd been in refit for nearly five years. I'd never been on a nuclear submarine before. It was new to me. I was taking on the role of Navigator, which is pretty intensive when it comes to work and a fair amount of responsibility. I had an interesting Command Team with a Captain and Executive Officer who had very different personalities. I learned an awful lot from a demanding Executive Officer but he made my life unnecessarily miserable and was one of those guys who was just always on your back. Emotional intelligence is important here as I was not the kind of individual who needed somebody to be on their back so I didn't really appreciate that very much.

At this time in my career, I started to question my direction and nearly left the Navy at one stage. I was pretty down and my wife said, "Right. We've got to do something about this." I ended up phoning my old boss in Northwood and I said to him, "I'm considering leaving the Navy." He said, "No. You cannot do that." He lived close to Plymouth which is where I was. It's about a three and half hour drive to Northwood. It was about half past ten in the morning. He said, "Meet me at my house at four o'clock this afternoon." He got in his car and drove all the way from Northwood where he was doing a really, really busy job. He and his wife gave my wife and I tea in his conservatory that afternoon. We had a great conversation and there's no doubt about it if it hadn't been for his intervention I would perhaps not have carried on in the Navy. Emotional intelligence is a really, really important attribute that you need to have as a leader. Not everybody's got it. He had great emotional intelligence. He could read an individual and treat everybody as such. You need emotional intelligence to be able to do that, definitely.

Splendid, taught me that a leader doesn't necessarily have to be good at everything. My Captain not the greatest of war fighter but he was a brilliant navigator and he was a great ship handler. He also had emotional intelligence. He left much of the war fighting things to the XO who had less emotional intelligence and was a hard taskmaster. As a team we adapted and overcame. It wasn't a textbook leadership situation, but we were a pretty tight and effective team in the wardroom despite the strange leadership structure. Myself personally and professionally, I had a great relationship with the Captain because he was passionate about navigation and ship handling and I was pretty reasonable at it. He taught me quite a lot and was an excellent guy from that perspective. I learnt lots from that team and how to do it and not to do it and interestingly how to do it in a different way. I think one of the other elements that makes you successful in command is you can be a good leader and you can have good emotional intelligence and you can be good with people but you do need to have a considerable amount of the professional expertise and experience behind you as well to make the whole package.

I guess if I look back at my career, it was my diesel submarine introduction which really gave me the building blocks of how to be a submariner and what it was all about. Why it was important and what you needed to concentrate on. My time as Navigator in Splendid gave me the building blocks when it came to navigation and ship handling and that's absolutely critical in my view; that professional bedrock. I embraced navigation and did well enough that they then sent me to be the navigation instructor at the submarine school afterwards. I taught a whole generation of submariners navigation for two and a half years. I was then very lucky and went to a surface ship to command a patrol boat at the age of twenty-eight. I got my first taste of leadership in command and that loneliness of command, and what it's like to make a decision when the buck really does stop with you. Particularly safety and decisions involving people's lives and livelihoods if you like.

I think it was a great opportunity to be able to make some mistakes and generally get away with them and learn for later on. I think about the mistakes I made in ship handling and driving the ship. Mistakes where things were taken to the limit, enabling me to find my personal limits, including overstretching my limits in a couple areas. Particularly I learned a lot about sea states and wind because it was a pretty small ship. It was only twenty odd meters and I had a whole bunch of inexperienced university students that would be with me for most of the time so the ship's company weren't always particularly effective, experienced or efficient. So the buck really did stop with you. You'd have to have the courage, the moral courage to step in when required. So, moral courage I guess is another area I think which is an absolute requirement of a good leader. Emotional intelligence, moral courage, and absolute standards are important. You need to set the bar and make sure that everybody understands where that bar is and everybody understands they need to meet it.

I then went to be third in command of a nuclear submarine, an SSBN, HMS Victorious. I had been on diesel submarines, SSNs and now a bomber. I'd seen them all and I'd done the shore appointment by teaching navigation and more importantly, the job as the submarine controller that looked at the other end of operations, the higher management of operations. I don't think I could have been more blessed in terms of the building blocks for professional expertise. In my bomber I came across another Command team. The Captain was quite remote and the XO was highly professional and extremely hard working.

Predictability is a key element of leadership. You can be particularly hard or unreasonable but as long as people know you're going to be unreasonable then they can adapt and deal with it. Being unreadable is extraordinarily difficult. An unpredictable and inconsistent leader doesn't allow people to adapt to a style. On one day expecting one thing and another day expecting something else creates great uncertainty and discomfort for the team. Be consistent.

As a commanding officer you write a set of what are called Captains Instructions to Officers and they're kind of your values, beliefs, and how you want your submarine to be run. It can include whatever you want. There's no real specified format for Captain's instructions, although you do tend to get them handed down and amend and personalize them. I've got my old instructions and re-read them recently. I wouldn't write them like that now as you continue to change quite a lot post command and it is seventeen years since I was in command of the submarine. I guess I've changed since then as well through the whole experience. I remember writing my Captains Instructions to Officers and when you first join the boat you do this thing called clear lower deck so you get all of your officers and ratings together and you give them a quick five minute transmission about how proud you are to be commanding them and set your stall out for your time as Captain.

One of my points which was picked up on many occasions afterward was that I would consider that anybody who shouted on my submarine for anything other than a point of immediate safety or immediate danger would have lost it. I wouldn't accept it and I lived by that mantra. I never shouted other than if somebody needed immediate safety attention. I never shouted. I just wasn't that kind of person and I didn't think there was an excuse for being like that. During my early career I learned an awful lot about how not do things which I think completely shapes how you should do things. You definitely learnt more from a sub-optimal commanding officer than you do a good.

I was lucky and got very quickly promoted and selected to command HMS Torbay which I did for 28 months and had a great time. I commanded both in maintenance alongside and on operations. Commanding a boat that's coming out of deep maintenance, going through its workup and full generation stage and then into operations is a challenge and requires a flexible leadership style. I was very lucky to do a number of operations including some minor intelligence gathering operations. I was also very lucky to be in HMS Torbay as it was the trials platform for the brand new submarine command system and the brand new submarine sonar system that was going to go on the new Astute class of the submarines that were taking over from the Trafalgar class. I ended up doing an extended deployment across to the United States and going down to the AUTEC range doing quite a lot of work with the Americans, both in their PCO course and reference firings and trials and a lot of testing and evaluating this brand new kit. Taking that to sea was interesting and getting a ships company trained in the use of this new kit, developing new tactics at sea which was great. I enjoyed that.

I guess every commanding officer thinks that their ship's company's is the best ship's company that ever existed and I was blessed with a very capable ship's company. We grew as a team from deep maintenance; taking her to sea for the first time with a new bunch of equipment, doing a whole load of trials, and then taking her through the sea training phase. I think that there are different approaches to when you're being inspected or looked at from externally. I think as a leader that can be quite an uncomfortable place to be but it depends on how you approach that whole phase as to how it goes. I'm convinced that I did it in a reasonable fashion and I think what you have to do is embrace that organization that's coming to look at you. You really have to treat them as a tool that's going to make you better rather than as an organization that's just going to come in and is looking to dig holes in you and tell you how bad you are. If you do that and you get your ship's company thinking the same way then you gain so much more out of the experience and out of training.

I think another point I would raise in submarine command certainly is about training. Everything you do is a training evolution whether you're fully trained or whether you're on operations or whether you're in that basic stage of bringing a submarine ship's company together. Everything should be treated like a training evolution and you should always inculcate that in your people. I think that if you do that then all of your ship's company starts to treat things as a training opportunity.

I turned round to my heads of department and I explained my sort of philosophy about training. Never should there be a time where we weren't training and expecting to get something out of what we were doing. We were not going to be a submarine that ended up on a passage going from A to B. We would always be looking for opportunities to make ourselves better and once we thought we were on top of our own games, the one thing I said to my head of departments was, "Look at your deputies, and can they do your job? And if you can't say, 'Yes, they could do my job,' then you've got some more training to do." From a resilience point of view, from a succession planning point of view, from a job satisfaction point of view, it was essential. I was convinced that if everybody on the boat looked at their one down and ensured that they could do their job then you couldn't go wrong.

And that was always my mantra. So for my XO I would take not significant risk, but would take calculated risk and I would give him long periods of time where he was effectively in everything but name doing the role of the Commanding Officer. I would encourage him to then take all of the watch leaders to do his job as the Executive Officer and then the watch leader would encourage the watch navigator to do the watch leaders job. So you're always training your one down for the next role up and I think that was a good mantra. Good way of dealing with things.

I'll go back to that never shouting piece and give a sort of example for effect. It's a fond memory I have. A sort of story I guess. We were doing an underwater look which is where you take your submarine to a depth that's very shallow where you can raise your periscope and remain safe, but be able to visually see the underside of a ship. We would practice it not routinely but fairly often. We'd got ourselves to be pretty good at it and on one occasion we were setting ourselves up as a training scenario to do an underwater look on a frigate that was working with us. It didn't go particularly well. The Coxswain, who I really rated, was a fantastic ship controller. One of the

Coxswain's jobs was to sit on ship control at diving stations or action stations when it was important. He would make sure the submarine was the right weight, making sure it was on depth, and making sure that the submarine was in control. In the run up to this underwater look we were all over the place. I kept my cool. We managed to get in, we did the job and we came away. After three hours at action stations doing this underwater look we got to the end of it and fell out. I got up out of my chair in the control room and I just turned round to the Coxswain. So I said, "Hmm. That could have gone better, Coxswain," and I walked out of the control room. Nearly ten years later, I was the Captain responsible for submarine sea and shore training. I'd just joined the job and he was a Warrant Officer Coxswain working in the organization and I ran into him for the first time. Without even batting his eyelid he just came straight up to me and bear hugged me in the middle of the base. He stepped back from me. He said, "Boss, it's really, really good to see you." I was chatting to him for a long time and he said, "What you said to me, do you remember that underwater look, boss?" I went, "No, Coxswain not really." And he told me that whole story and he just said to me, "You said, 'Coxswain, that could have gone better.'" And he said, "Boss, that was the worst bollocking I ever had in my Navy career," is what he said. I'll never forget that.

So after I'd commanded Torbay I went off and did some staff training. I ended up working in the Ministry of Defense for Chief Defense Staff in what's called the Chiefs of Staff Committee a team of three that did all of their staff work basically. That was quite intense. That was right in the middle of the Afghanistan, Iraq, Bosnia, end of the Bosnia defeat, and the start of maritime piracy in the gulf so that was quite busy. Then I went off to be the commander of HMS Illustrious, the aircraft carrier which was a different type of command. One of the easiest jobs I ever did in the Navy I think because I had nine heads of department who were all Commanders with all of the deputy heads as experienced Lieutenant Commanders and ratings. You had a great orchestra that just needed the right conducting.

I went across to the United States and was the Submarine Liaison Officer in the US. I was responsible for submarine liaison between the US Navy and the UK, the Royal Navy. That was quite fun. I had to go to the Pentagon about three times a week and engage with N87, the Navy Yard, and Groton, Norfolk, SubPac, the entire US submarine Force. I had about ten other Royal Navy officers who were on exchange in various places in the states. From that I got promoted and went and wrote the Royal Navy people strategy in 2012 and then I went off to be a Captain in charge of submarine sea and shore training. With that I was responsible for the submarine command course, for all of the submarines working up and I was responsible for all shore training as well.

I guess there are a lot of people who would think that the Perisher course is a hugely expensive, asset-rich, requirement just to provide half a dozen submarine commanding officers each year to go and be captains of submarines. There's been a constant push to try and create a course which is less asset intensive. There's been a move to try and move it to a more a synthetic environment which has happened but you cannot get away from the requirement to train and test, more importantly test, individuals under pressure and you cannot recreate that pressure in a synthetic environment.

It's a course that is designed to provide some training, although you should have the skills before you go on the course and it's really about honing those skills. It's a six-month course, the first four months are the piece where you get assessed both ashore and then at sea. You spend a month at sea in a submarine and the course goes through the full gamut of submarine operations and puts you through the hoops really.

It's a test of stamina, mental fortitude, and mental agility. It's a test of your people skills and leadership skills both in peacetime and in war. What I mean by that is both under pressure and not under pressure and then it's a test of your war fighting capabilities in submarines. Your ability to command a submarine from a practical perspective.

I guess most people in the Navy would say it's the most demanding and most difficult course in the Navy. I wouldn't argue with that too much! When I look back on it, it was a bit of an endurance test and the most stressing piece of it was never really being a hundred percent certain that you were going to pass the course. It's such a seminal moment in your career if you don't. You don't go back to sea on a submarine again; you'd have a complete rethink in your career if you don't pass it. So the advice I was given, which was good advice, was "Before you go on the course, think about failing. Think about what you're going to do when you're told you've failed. Write that plan down somewhere, and then never think about failure again." That was pretty good advice, I think. Clare, my wife, and I had decided exactly what we were going to do if I didn't pass the course. We knew what that was going to be, and from that moment on we didn't think about it again.

I guess I look back on it quite fondly. I probably was quite lucky. I came top of the course as it happens but I look back on it quite fondly in that probably I didn't really feel the pressure that some others felt. Maybe because I wasn't put under that pressure because I think teacher had confidence in me, the teacher being the Commanding Officer of the Submarine Command Course. So I probably was not given the external pressure from him that others got. I think at the end of it I certainly was a better person for it, professionally and as an individual as well. I was certainly more confident and when I left that course I was pretty happy that I could go and drive a submarine.

It was a real test of stamina in every respect; physical, mental, just tiredness. The whole course is designed to put you under all of that pressure and one of the ways they really put you under pressure is to make you tired. Seeing how you'll react. Interestingly people change massively when they're under pressure. There is absolutely no doubt about that. People's leadership styles change completely and one thing that I thought was really powerful about Perisher is people when they're under pressure and they're against it, they revert to type. You can put on a face in lots of scenarios but when you're under pressure your true self comes out. Your true personality comes to the fore and you can't hide it. It really is a test of an individual's character. You see people change completely when all of a sudden things start to fall around them and they revert to their true selves. That's why it's such a great test of a future submarine Commanding Officer. You see how they think, you see how they act, you see how their decision making changes and you see their true drivers in life when they're working under pressure.

The other thing I found really interesting was the ship's company, they spot it straight away. They know the good guys straight away. They can read people really well in those scenarios. I guess what I'm saying is there is a natural ability in leadership which you can't get away from. I guess it goes back to that nature/nurture question in leadership. There's no doubt about it that you can learn, and train, and adapt your leadership styles for different scenarios and different situations and you can be taught some basics around how to lead and manage.

I get back to this emotional intelligence thing. It's so important. If you don't have good emotional intelligence, if you can't read your team and your people and you can't motivate them in the way that you know is going to be effective for certain respects you're in and you can't teach that. That's just natural. I think you can learn it through experience perhaps but I don't think you can teach it. If you don't have that natural ability or you haven't developed that natural ability through experience you'll get caught out. Your team will see it straight away. They'll know you for the person you are.

I go back to that sort of Perisher piece and the importance of leading in an operationally realistic environment or being tested in an operationally realistic environment. I had an individual on my course with me who mentally, mental arithmetic and agility, was brilliant. No other word to describe him. Brilliant. He was better than Teacher himself at it. He could keep himself safe on the periscope. His mental maths was unbelievable. His ability to do sines and cosines and tangents in his head and work out look intervals and ranges and all these things was phenomenal. We had gone through the various phases of the shore training side of Perisher and I can remember we had finished the tactical phase in the simulator - so about nine weeks of working up for war fighting situations. He and I went on an industrial visit to Barrow where they build the submarines. We were staying in a hotel and one night we were about a week away from going to sea for the final phase at sea and he and I ordered a brandy. We sat there and we had both agreed that we were both sat comfortably at the top of the course from all the feedback we'd had to date. I said to him that I would bet my house on him passing the course and we then went off to sea.

The first three or four days on the submarine you end up working with two to three frigates who are all charging the submarine and you're trying to stay at periscope depth. It's a driving test effectively on how you keep the submarine safe visually without recall for any other sensors. And the minute he got to sea the real world started to interact; the sea state was suddenly not calm, waves were splashing over the periscope, and he couldn't see through the periscope as well as he could do in the simulator, he was finding it difficult to get the information he needed. I go back to this, "Your true self comes out." All of a sudden he completely lost his confidence. So then he started to make mistakes. Things that he'd never made mistakes on before. Then he started to interact differently with the ship's company and then to shout at the ship's company, and lose his temper. He'd never done that before and Teacher noticed it immediately. From that moment on Teacher decided he was just going to raise the pressure and just start to try and make life a bit more difficult for this individual and he went downhill. Never managed to recover from it and he failed the course in week three at sea. Leadership under pressure and you're ability to operate under pressure is a key element. I think that in a submarine you need to be able to do that and not everybody can.

I guess I learnt something about myself from that but it absolutely emphasized the importance of training and exposure to realistic environments in that kind of a space where you're expected to in the future, be the one person in that submarine who's responsible for the whole thing. It is an immense responsibility but you can't allow it to cloud your judgment or get to you in any way. You just have to take it on the chin and get on with it really.

Chapter 13

Brothers of the Phin

Timothy W. (Tim) Oliver
Captain, USN (Ret.)

Brothers and Sisters of the Phin is a phrase used to describe the family-like connections shared by submariners everywhere. All submariners belong to this family and it is not unusual to find generations or actual siblings serving on boats. Tim and his brother Dave were both submariners and Commanding Officers.

Tim is also the Executive Director of the Naval Submarine League. The Naval Submarine League was founded in 1982 to educate the public about the importance of a strong undersea arm of the U.S. Navy. Several events are scheduled each year which enable government, industry and academia to identify, study and develop potential solutions to undersea warfare challenges. A quarterly journal, The Submarine Review, and ten chapters (some at submarine ports) enable submariners and submarine enthusiasts to be informed.

NSL History, https://www.navalsubleague.org

I have a six-year-older brother and a younger sister. My brother ended up as a two-star admiral in submarines. He was always wonderful to me, which isn't always the case when the younger brother wants to tag along. We've always been close. To both be in submarines is a tremendous thing to share. He's quite a writer, so when I read his books and talk to him, it's great to be able to understand the situations he's discussing.

I didn't think he'd make Captain. He can be in-your-face confrontational; if somebody was doing something that he didn't think was right he was going to be in the middle of it. I think he was so successful because he thought things through in advance; he looked for the ways that something might go wrong. As a result, he was able to recognize possible problems and take action. I think he became an admiral because people wanted him around; they knew he was a smart guy who would keep them out of trouble.

I saw my father as a really strong influence on my development. He demonstrated honesty, respect for others, and leading by example. He taught me that if you want to be a leader you must set an example. Lots of people like to be popular, but I learned early on if you're going to be a leader, don't expect that you're necessarily going to be popular. The other thing I took away from my dad was to work hard. He stressed that to whom much is given, much is expected. Dad also believed that you learn through teamwork, but you know yourself through individual sports. I ran cross country because Dad wouldn't let us play football. We grew up in Indiana. When I didn't turn out to be the hotshot basketball player that I thought I was, I ended up wrestling. I also played tennis. With individual sports you develop the ability to stand on your own.

I went on to the Naval Academy. My brother had gone there and, of course, that was the only place I wanted to go. I excelled. I had a pretty good idea about what the coursework would be before I ever got there. At the Naval Academy you receive peer evaluations from the very beginning. I've always been a humble person and although I had a lot of ambition, I was never a braggart. Throughout high school I had served in multiple leadership positions, so I wasn't shy about stepping forward. But I think people recognized that I truly cared about them and so those peer evaluations were very positive and pushed me to the top. At the end of the last year at the academy, I was selected to be the brigade commander for the Fall of senior year, the leader of the 4,000 midshipmen. Working to be the best was just something that drove me.

One of the things that I saw at Annapolis was that not everybody who takes a leadership role is willing to live up to those standards. At that time, there was a lot of Mickey Mouse at the Academy. Some people made a game of breaking the rules without being caught to be "one of the guys." I remembered what my dad had taught me – if you're going to be a leader, you have to set the example.

In my senior year I had an independent study program, called a Trident scholar. There were sixteen in our class. I was also selected by the Academy to compete for a Rhodes Scholarship. I didn't win the scholarship, but it was a fascinating process. My advice to others would be to read books that cover a wide variety of topics beyond your regular curriculum. People want to know what you've done outside the classroom to gain perspectives and draw your own conclusions.

My first tour as an officer was on a nuclear-powered ballistic missile submarine, an SSBN. I transitioned from being on top of the world at Annapolis to being unqualified and inexperienced. It was demanding, which I didn't mind. But there was a totally new lingo that you had to learn, which was demoralizing. I had a boss who chewed me out because I had reported a problem in an equipment status log. He said, "You don't put things in that log. The Captain looks at the log every day, and then he's on my ass." How did I react? I hated confrontation, and I didn't like anyone to think I didn't know or understand things. In retrospect, I shortchanged myself. No one expects you to know everything about your new job in such a demanding environment. Embrace it! I should have asked more questions. As long as you show that you work hard and take your business seriously, people will respect you and help you. Try to bluff your way through, and you're bound to have a more difficult path. When you tell people you don't know something and then you learn it, that process reinforces your understanding of yourself and what you're doing.

I almost got out of the Navy because the SSBN was such a demoralizing tour. But I said, "I've invested so much; I'll try one more boat." That boat was the USS Skate. It was seventeen years old at the time, and I had more fun on that tour than all the others. I was in charge of all the boat's auxiliary equipment. The boat had been in overhaul for 29 months, and I reported as a lieutenant wearing gold dolphins. I had a wonderful reception, and I was put in charge of making all the underways and landings. When we made our first deployment, all the department heads were lieutenants. I think the fact that the Commanding Officer (CO) and the Executive Officer (XO) let all the young department heads run the boat is what made it really fun. From a leadership point of view, the more you can let people take ownership for what they're doing, the better they will respond. They get the satisfaction of doing a hard job, and people appreciate it when the boss recognizes them for their good work.

On one underway, we hosted the head of the Atlantic Submarine Force. Vice Admiral R. L. J. Long was a future 4-star admiral. To this day I remember his comment to the wardroom that the Skate was his jewel box. He inspired others to be proud of what they were doing and to know that what they were doing was important even though, heaven only knows, the boat had been run hard and was difficult to maintain. It was an inspiration to have that kind of leadership tell you that you were doing an important job and doing it well.

I went from Skate to the USS Silversides where I was the Engineer. My advice about being a department head is to teach your people how to do their job and then let them do it. After you teach them what is expected, hold them accountable. When your people know you're working hard and have the same high expectations of them, they will rise to the challenge. On Silversides we were homeported in Charleston. We got to do a special operation, which is a very rewarding submarine mission. After that deployment, we took the boat to a non-refueling overhaul in Norfolk. The majority of the families chose to remain in Charleston. This combination of a challenging deployment immediately followed by demanding preparations for a relocation away from families could have been difficult to handle. Through extensive planning and communication with the crew, they knew that their leaders were doing all they could to take care of the crew and their families.

Despite the complexity of the overhaul, we completed it in eleven months. What were the keys to this success? First, our people knew the importance of what they were doing. Only volunteers are accepted into submarine duty, and they do it to prove that they can be part of an elite group. They also knew that the boat's leadership was taking actions to support them and their families. Finally, the crew wanted to make sure the work was done right the first time so they could get back to their families in Charleston. Sometimes, even if you do the planning and do the hard work, you aren't able to control the shipyard environment. In this instance, the people in the shipyard saw that the submarine crew wanted to support the shipyard to get the ship overhauled successfully. As a result, shipyard workers showed that they would rather work on Silversides than others. We weren't calling them sand crabs, and it wasn't "us" versus "them." The boat's attitude was, "Hey, we're here to get this job done together."

The demands on the crew in overhaul are enormous. The crew is responsible for the boat, and the shipyard can't move forward without the support of the crew. To maximize the ability of the crew to support the shipyard and to not exhaust the crew, I designed a watch bill to bring in a whole fresh group of watch standers in the engineering spaces about 11:00 every weeknight. They'd take over from the duty section, the day section, and send them home. Then the new group would stand the watches through the night and into the next morning. This team made sure all the paperwork from the previous day's work was in order. They were alert and able to get done what was needed to be prepped for the next morning. Then, when the shipyard arrived, the boat was ready to start the workday at top speed.

From Silversides, I went to Admiral Rickover's staff. The Admiral had thirty-four direct reports – just try to imagine that. The Admiral had an unbelievable work ethic and grasp of so many technologies. He had a unique way to supervise the work of the 300 to 400 people that worked at Naval Reactors. Any time a letter or a document was going to be sent from Naval Reactors, the author produced multiple carbon copies. This was back in the days of carbon paper to produce pink, and yellow, and green copies. The pink copies would be delivered to the Admiral's office every day. After twenty-four hours, if you didn't have the pink come back with questions from the Admiral, you could send the letter. As one of my initiatives, I proposed that submarines didn't need to carry classified manuals that were only used when the submarine was in a major overhaul. If you didn't carry them, you didn't have to enter periodic changes that were issued, and you didn't have to inventory them and send off a computer sheet to Naval Reactors to say that, yes, in the last year you hadn't lost any manuals.

But none of the Naval Reactors engineers who were responsible would agree that their manual wasn't needed on board all the time.

I wrote a letter that proposed a change that nuclear submarines did not need to send an inventory of all classified manuals to Naval Reactors every year. This letter earned me an invitation to go downstairs and explain it to the Admiral. He asked, "Do you really think that's needed?" I wasn't ready to defend my position, and I backed down. The lesson I learned was, if you're going to be a leader, first think through all the possible situations that you might encounter and decide what your various responses will be and why. Then, when the time comes, whether it's a fire on the submarine or a crotchety old Admiral that's questioning your ideas, act upon your beliefs. My shortcoming was that I had always been blessed with good instincts and intelligence. But the sooner you learn to quiz yourself and walk through all the "what if" drills, the better you'll be prepared to take action under stress. Another great way to practice thinking through situations is to write for publications or journals. The process forces you to think through positions and get used to taking a position. If you're going to be a leader, you need to train yourself to be unafraid to get in that arena and talk and defend your positions.

Enthusiasm is another key leadership quality. For some people it seems to come naturally. People will follow somebody who's enthusiastic because they inspire confidence and they're fun to be around. Enthusiasm is infectious. When my son wondered if he was making the right decision to study opera in college, I told him, "Okay, you're going to study to be an opera singer. If that doesn't work out, don't worry. You're enthusiastic. Whatever you're doing, you're always enthusiastic about it, so you'll be successful." He's still an opera singer, and he attracts people to him not only because he has a great voice but also because he's enthusiastic about whatever he's doing.

On USS Parche I was the XO. It was a great experience and very rewarding. One of my leadership role models was the skipper, Pete Graef. He said, "I've got to go to Washington and brief our deployment, so you're in charge. We need to be out of dry dock by the time I get back. So, get it done." It was his way of giving me the responsibility to do something important. Sure, he had watched me and trained me, but he gave me the chance to demonstrate I could do the job. It was a reinforcement of the principle to teach people, give them the opportunity, and then hold them accountable for what they do.

For my command tour, I was selected to be CO of the Glenard P. Lipscomb, an electric-drive, nuclear-powered submarine. She was a one-of-a-kind boat and had been operating for over twelve years. During my predecessor's tour the boat had a major electrical problem with the propulsion motor generator, and the boat had been tied up at the pier for twenty-seven months for repairs. It was a miserable experience for the crew. After repairs were completed, the CO took the boat to the Mediterranean where the propulsion problem happened again. So, the boat returned from the deployment for me to relieve as CO. I can remember Admiral Kauderer saying, "Well, we can either let you run it at reduced capacity or we know how to fix it. What do you want to do?" I said, "I'll run at reduced capacity." After I had been in command for a short period, I realized that the number of people assigned to care for the propulsion motor generators was the same number as were assigned for all the other nuclear submarines but none of those submarines had propulsion motor generators! For twelve years, this submarine had operated without the extra people needed to properly maintain those generators. We submitted a request for additional electricians, and the request was approved. People want to do a great job, but leaders have to recognize when their people need more assets and make sure that they get them.

I didn't understand why people were opening doors for me, literally, opening doors for me. I wasn't used to the deferential treatment you receive because you're the commanding officer. It became obvious that the example that I set, or any CO sets, is what others are going to emulate. The example that really got my attention was when we had contractors on board during an underway. They were working in an isolated space. They came in to tell me what a wonderful crew I had. They said they had been able to perform their demanding work under difficult conditions and the crew had made the difference. Crew members would bring them food and ask what they could do to help. That's when I realized how the example you set as a leader is reflected throughout your organization.

One of the fun events I created as CO was to surface the boat and have a swim call in the middle of the Atlantic. We were transiting from Puerto Rico to Norfolk. As a leader, you need to think of things that you can do that will be memorable for your people and that they can tell others. There is so much about submarines that you can't talk about that you have to provide these young, red-blooded, Americans some things they can discuss. That's just another part of positive leadership; you look for ways to bring fun into your organization to build morale.

Being a submariner means that you understand and embrace high standards. The sea is an unforgiving environment and operating such a complex boat demands high standards. We've all seen situations where high standards were not enforced. Living with low standards doesn't motivate people. People want to be proud of their organization. A leader sets the high standard and doesn't accept anything less. When people who won't meet the standards are tolerated, good performers notice and become demoralized. Everyone wants to be part of a winning team. The leader sets the standard needed to achieve that winning status. The really good leader figures out how to have fun in the process!

Take care of your people. As a negative example, when I retired from the Navy as a Captain after 26 years, the organization I had been leading was disbanded, and I spent my last year working at CinCLANT Fleet [Commander-In-Chief, US Atlantic Fleet]. There was no retirement ceremony for me. There was no recognition. I just finished the month and walked out the door. Eight years after I retired, I married Ginger. She had never been involved with the Navy. I took her to a retirement ceremony for a friend. All of this was new to her. She said, "Where was your retirement ceremony?" I said, "Well, I didn't have one." She understood the significance of that, and said, "I'll fix that." And, she did. For my 60th birthday, she sent off e-mails to every boat that I had been on and asked people to write their experiences about me or to be there at the event to tell their stories. She posted the stories on the walls around the room, and she arranged for others to speak. It was a wonderful experience because so many people remembered me and wished me well. I still, to this day, think that the keys to being successful are to be prepared by studying the "what ifs" and to take care of the people around you.

David R. (Dave) Oliver Jr.
Rear Admiral, USN (Ret.)

Dave's diverse career has included extensive experience in government and industry as well as the military. Immediately before he retired, Dave was the CEO of the EADS North America Defense Company (Airbus). Before that Dave was in Iraq where Paul (Jerry) Bremer selected him to become the Director of Management and Budget for the Coalition Forces. He served in the Clinton Administration as Principal Deputy Undersecretary of Defense for Acquisition, Technology and Logistics, a position the President appointed him to while Dave was working as an executive at Northrop Grumman Corporation following a thirty-six-year career in the Navy.

Dave has written extensively on leadership. His books include; Lead On, a practical guide to leadership, Against the Tide, Rickover's Leadership Principles and the Rise of the Nuclear Navy, and A Navy Admiral's Bronze Rules: Managing Risk and Leadership. He has also written a guide to working effectively in Washington, intrigue based novels, and a biography of his wife Linda Bithell Oliver entitled Wide Blue Ribbon.

https://daveoliverbooks.com/

I went into the Naval Academy because I was looking for something that was difficult and the Naval Academy, going into the military during the Vietnam War, was the hardest thing I could imagine. My grades were good and I was admitted to every place I applied, Yale, Harvard, MIT, but our family had very limited means and the Academies were more exotic. I couldn't get an appointment to West Point, but got a fifth alternate to a selection at the Naval Academy. The Air Force Academy wouldn't start up for a few more years. I always felt they looked down the list and let me in as they had hired a new

228 ~ JEFF FLESHER

wrestling coach, were building up the program, and I had lettered in the sport.

After three and a half years at the Academy and experiencing all the different aspects of the Navy, I still had no idea what I was going to do. I was tentatively planning to go into the Marine Corps. I mean I wanted to do something exciting, right, and we were still at war in Vietnam. I liked to keep myself in shape, to run, do push-ups and physically challenge others. To make your selection you used to walk down from your room to the Battalion Office and sign this big sheet to indicate your selection.

Our Company Officer was a surface guy. We all respected him. As I'm walking, I felt him fall in beside me. He said, "What are you going to do?" I said, "I think I'm going to be a Marine." He says, "You don't want to be a Marine, you'll be doing push-ups until you're 50 years old." I thought about it for a few seconds and replied, "Good point, I'll be a surface officer, like you." I didn't care, I just wanted to go out and do something and he was cool. He says, "You don't want to be a surface officer like me. You want to go onto submarines." I said, "What's great about submarines?" He replies, "That nuclear power thing is going to work." I said, "I don't think so." This little conversation gives you a feel for how deeply I was invested in submarines. At the time the USS Nautilus, SSN 571, the first nuclear submarine, had been successfully steaming around the world for nine years, but alas, there were girls who came to the Naval Academy on weekends and, at the time, I could be easily distracted.

I said, "It's not going to work." He said, "Yeah, I think it's going to work." I repeated, "It's not going to work." He says, "You know what, it pays $100 extra a month." Well at the time, pay for an ensign was $233.33 a month, so I shut up and made a quick calculation. A hundred dollars extra a month? What could I do with a hundred dollars extra a month? I had just bought a used Mercury convertible for $500 cash. For a $100, I could go on a date every night, right?

I said to him, "Which is the sheet I sign up for submarines?" He says, "Right over here." I signed up for submarines. I mean I'm not saying I'm shallow, but I'm shallow. I was a kid. I wanted action. I signed up for submarines and then the senior Marine at the Academy put me in charge of being the drill officer for the Naval Academy for the summer. He and I and his wife, who was also a Marine, would run ten miles in the morning, then do push-up contests, then I would drill the Midshipmen. I was an acting Marine for the next six months at the Naval Academy even though I was signed up to be a nuke. I loved it. You give me a task; I'll do it, whatever it is.

After I signed up to be a nuke, I went to see Rickover. I was the first graduate at the Naval Academy who was a literature major. Everybody took the same courses to become a civil engineer but I took another six hours each semester so I could also get a major in literature. I was thus taking twenty-five hours of courses instead of nineteen so I could get my engineering degree and also obtain a literature major and a history minor. I describe my interview in *Against the Tide*, but essentially Rickover looks at me essentially says, "You are missing the purpose of a university. These professors are around to explain things to you when you get stuck. You get stuck more often in math and physics and the hard courses. You can always figure out the soft sciences on your own after you are out of the university environment. You are wasting your time on the history and literature. I said OK, and dropped them, adding a 5th year of mathematics and another semester of nuclear physics for my final semester. That was a load that kept me off the streets! Rickover had specialized in education and understood me.

At the time I was doing this, after you have been through nuclear training, you go out into the fleet and spend three of four years on a submarine and then come back to Naval Reactors in Washington, DC to take the Engineers Exam. You took an exam for two days and then if you failed, they keep you around for a third day. They kept me and another guy around for a third day. Rickover's number two guy was named Bill Wegner. He kept the two of us in his office for the third day right in front of his desk. Every time a message would come in he'd read the message and then he'd ask one of us a question about it. After about six hours he said to me, "What do you want to do, you want to go east coast or west coast?" I said, "I need to call my wife," and he said, "You'll be the engineer on Nautilus" and he turned to the other guy, Bill Owens, who would one day become Vice Chairman of the Joint Chiefs of Staff, and said, "You go to the west coast, you can be the engineer on Sea Dragon."

Before I left Washington, Rickover gave me his home phone number to call. I was a JG and he was a four-star Admiral. Anyway, Rickover says, "You call me at my home if you have any questions." When I got to Nautilus I found out that they had just fired about half of the chief petty officers. I actually did call him at his home twice, okay, just bypassed everybody else in the Navy and called him. I worked my butt off all hours of the day. I'm on that ship every day of the year over the next three years, had over 1,000 fires, several flooding's and twenty-three officers were relieved for cause. I'm the only officer who was not fired.

I left there, went to Washington and worked for Admiral Zumwalt, the Chief of Naval Operations. Zumwalt had twenty-one captains on his personal staff, and he replaced one of them with me. I was a Lieutenant Commander. I worked for him for two years. When I finished working for him, he writes a fitness report that simply says, "Finest officer in the Navy."

I get promoted three years ahead of my peers and I did all sorts of things. Smuggled arms to Israel, several other events about which I've written. Decided to do my master's about Middle East oil, Middle East relations between Israel. During that time of course we had the Six Day War and I had smuggled to Israel the air to air weapons they used to shoot down the Egyptian jets and received a set of Israeli wines in thanks.

I had introduced the President of the United States to the President of Kazakhstan (via the Secretary of Defense Bill Perry), which enabled the US to smuggle nearly a third to their nuclear weapons out of Russia. After I'd been out in industry, working for a couple different companies, the Clinton Administration brought me back in and I was the number five person in the Defense Department as a political appointee. A couple of years later, I went to Iraq with the Coalition of Provisional Authority. I was the director of management and budget for Iraq.

Then I became the Chief Operating Officer for Airbus in the United States for ten years. I helped run some political campaigns for the Governor of Virginia. My wife was Hilary Clinton's lawyer. Linda was the first woman who had a career whose husband was selected as a flag officer in any of the services. She was the first General Counsel for the Naval Investigative Service. Then she was the head of small business for the Department of Defense.

At the beginning of the nuclear power program we had too many sons of bitches around and they lasted for a long time. I was really trying to get rid of those guys and it was the reason I wrote my first book (Lead On). I was still active duty and I was doing my best to get rid of as many of those guys as possible. There were too many drunks and there were too many SOBs. I had done my best when I was a Captain to get rid of the drunk and mean guys.

The reason I wrote the book about Rickover was Rickover was really an introvert. He accomplished great things - perhaps more than any man of the twentieth century – but he wasn't an exceptional leader. He was a really great manager but he was such an introvert and he was so shy, he was not a really good leader. I believe I knew him well and I understood him, but he was so shy, he didn't do well with other people. He adopted an approach that worked for him. A whole bunch of people thought that his approach was perfect. But it definitely was not. He overcame his own flaws, just like he overcame other things, but it wasn't a good way. While he had the intellect to overcome himself, when a whole bunch of nukes started copying him, they didn't have his intellect to correct themselves. At the same time the submarine force had gotten to the point that it was improving the professionalism every cycle. In other words, they understood their own secret sauce, which was extraordinary talent and constant improvement. They had to sort of be careful or you would grind yourself into the dirt because you've got to understand talent can walk. About every third cycle you need to rewrite everything, you can't just do it all the same way again, and again, and again, and again.

I think there's a bright line between leadership and management. I used to say, and I still do, everybody should strive to be a good manager because everybody can be a good manager and you really ought to work at that. The problem is everybody wants to be a leader. Nobody wants to say, "I'm a good manager, but I'm not a good leader." The crux of it is there's a really small percentage of people who are really good leaders, but that's okay because it's an even smaller percentage of people who are ever going to be required to be good leaders because they're not going to be tasked with a problem that's going to require that leadership to come forward. They're not going to be required by this great fire or this great tragedy that requires their innate leadership to leap up. Probably, maybe 2% of the people ever in their lifetimes are going to be faced with a leadership situation, the rest are, if they can be really good managers, by God, that's it and they can just feel proud as hell of themselves.

I'm going to tell you a story. It used to be when we first had nuclear weapons aboard submarines. When we had them on SSNs, when we had nuclear torpedoes, guys were worried about the Soviets recovering them if we had a submarine go down in shallow water. What we did was we put open cases of dynamite underneath the torpedo racks and put fuses on each stick of dynamite. The idea was because everybody smoked at the time, we had those big lighters, those big Ronson lighters, the idea was if we got in trouble you just throw your Ronson lighter into one of those wooden cases. It'd catch light with the fuse, the dynamite ignites, and that solved the problem.

I was on a boomer, so we're sitting in the wardroom one night watching a movie and the word comes "fire in the torpedo room." All the officers ran back to the control room and I'm the only guy that runs into the torpedo room and shuts the hatch. I'm in the torpedo room with about three other guys, A-gangers, and I'm saying to myself, "How much longer do you think you guys in Control are going to live if I don't stop this fire. You're going to live about an eighth of a second longer. But you guys are going to control me from the control room over sound power phones?" It was a bilge fire. Somebody had thrown a cigarette in there. That's when I got to learn that nitroglycerine, you heat up dynamite and the nitroglycerine subsumes and drains out of those dynamite sticks and drips in the bilge. Anyway, it was quite exciting for a while. That's what I mean about the difference between who is a leader and who is a manager. All those officers who turned left and ran to control, those guys are managers. They self-selected right there when they stepped out of the wardroom and turned left instead of right. I don't care what you spend time telling them or how much you spend time in class, at that moment when they said fire in the torpedo room bilge, they self-selected and it didn't matter.

Everybody tries, everybody, I never met a guy that wasn't trying. The range of capabilities is extraordinary. There may be a guy that you think has a lot of capability but once you subtract the fact that he's scared, and the fact that he's worrying about his aunt and his grandmother, or the fact that he's taking drugs, you drop his ability down to this really small number, much smaller than you think it is. Once I had an officer who actually was senior to me, but he worked for me. The problem was he could only do two things. He could do that one pretty well but he could only do one. Doesn't matter how mad I got at him, he could only do one. That was it. So I finally got rid of him. It wasn't his fault; he shouldn't have been in that position. It was my fault for leaving him in that position. That's what you've got to remember.

My experience was that it's really hard to look down. Just like sunflowers. All these guys are smiling up at you; it's really hard to see down one level. It's impossible to see down two. You cannot see the assholes. I used to be in charge of all personnel for Submarine Force Pacific. When I took over our suicide level was 100,000 times higher than it was for the civilian world age-corrected. That's awful. I finally realized it was a problem and I decided to take care of it. Of course, it was because of some jerks. I had a boss who would let me do practically anything I wanted to so I dug up my jerks and he let me throw them out of the Submarine Force. I brought the suicide rate of this horrible number down to zero. I kept it at zero for two years.

Then I left and went off to do other things and ten years later I'm back in the Pacific and now I'm an Admiral. Suicide rate is back at the same extraordinarily high level, right? I said, "I'm not going to put up with this crap." I called all the guys, the senior leaders together and I said, "I've gone through this before, I'm not going to go through it again, I'm telling you guys, if you have somebody that commits suicide, I'm going to come after your ass, and your ass is grass." The problem immediately stops. Had no suicides for another two years, except one; some kid killed himself, an ensign. I had somebody do the investigation, they finally come and talk to me and they said essentially you didn't realize this guy was working down three levels, he was a complete jerk and he forced this guy to kill himself. I go look at it and I just missed all sorts of things I should've picked up on. This guy was a jerk. My fault.

I used to go down, when I was in Newport News, new construction, I'd go down every morning there was a jail down by the waterfront. I had RC division and ETs, and I'd go down and sign for half my division who were in jail because they'd be in jail every morning. I'd go down, pick them up, feed them breakfast and they'd work all day and all night. Then about ten o'clock at night we'd get through and they'd go out and drink. They were brilliant sons of bitches who apparently came from bad backgrounds but if they made it through to live to be about twenty-two they were going to set the world on fire. They were going to be terrific guys, and you knew it. You could see it but when they were nineteen, God they were terrible. God, it was great fun.

Rickover always had an expression that said, "If you can't do it all, you can't do it." That was what he thought about it. If you can't do it all, you can't do it, which means there are no excuses. He didn't want any excuses; he just wanted you to do it. On Nautilus, I kept trying to get started up and the reactor kept scramming and this went on for four or five days. Finally, late at night one night I call Rickover. I call him at his apartment. Here I am, I'm a JG and he's a four star Admiral and this is before there was a squadron engineer. I didn't call the CO either because I didn't think the CO would know. So I called Rickover. There's this pause, and he says, "Put the phone down and go back," to a place above the reactor, "Count ten plates back, ten grids back after you walk in the door and then reach down and there should be a switch underneath the deck plate. If it's in the front position, move it aft." I walk in there and I unscrew the deck plate and there's a switch with no nameplate on it, and I moved it aft, and walked back, and Rickover had already hung up the phone. I make the startup and it works. As it turns out they'd installed it that way in 1953 to add a sensitivity plus 100 in the event that there had been any problems in the startup so it would crash on startup. They'd never taken it out and somebody had moved that. At this time, this was 1970, so it's 17 years later, smart guy.

You've got to keep the bad guys out. You have to understand, a leader is responsible. A leader has to shoulder responsibility for everybody else. You have to practice it. When I was in high school, I noticed that the people who did well were able to speak in front of other people. They did things like debate, what was called interpretive speaking, things like that, and I was not very good. I was okay, but I wasn't really good. I decided that I would practice that and I would enter those contests. I took every opportunity that I got to do that and I accepted every invitation to speak that I was offered, not because I was good at it, because I wasn't, but I wanted the chance to practice and to improve. If I learned the ability to express myself when I reached a point that I had an idea to sell, I knew I needed to have the tools to sell it, so I needed to practice those tools. If I wanted to be a leader, then I needed to practice the characteristics of being a leader. If you aspire to be a leader, you need to practice those things that make it up. It's just like anything else, just like practicing a sport. You need to shoot a lot of baskets if you ever had the hope to get one in a game. If you aspire to be a leader, you need to do that every time, every chance you get, so it becomes second nature. You do it, you try to do it all the time, and when you don't do it, you know it's a failure of yours.

I was teaching leadership at the University of Maryland, there was a great book about the guy who redid the prison industry in Massachusetts. It was titled, "Over the Wall," I think. He did it by talking the Governor's wife into changing, they were incarcerating 12-year old's as if they were adults, and this gentleman talked her into basically changing to a juvenile system. It's a really good book. One of the reasons I really enjoyed teaching this was the first day I went to class to teach this, I had 30, 35 MBA students, about five or six of them were spaced out on marijuana and about, I don't know, another equal number weren't paying no attention at all. By the end I had nobody who had smoked marijuana before they came, and I had them actively broken up in groups where they were giving each other lectures and practicing what they had learned out of class. They were all into it.

I'm over in Iraq, I didn't believe there were any weapons of mass destruction, but I went over there because they asked me to go and they knew I didn't believe there were weapons of mass destruction, but they asked me to go because they knew I was a good manager. I told Jerry Bremer that he needed to fire the head of the Oil Ministry because he was an incompetent manager, and Jerry says, "Unfortunately, President Bush likes this guy," and I said, "I don't care, the Iraqi Minister is stealing from us and you've got to get rid of our Senior Advisor because he's making everybody look bad." Jerry and I actually got along, but Jerry says, "I can't do this because I have some limitations."

I went back to my office and go back to working on the budgets. About two days later, Jerry calls me and I go up there and here's the Oil Minister Senior Advisor looking at me. Jerry says, "They are rioting in the oil fields, you know I've got 100,000 people out there rioting in the oil fields," and I said, "Here's a chance for this Advisor that you love to go out there and fix this problem." Jerry says, "He doesn't want to go out there, David." I said, "Okay, give me your megaphone, let me borrow your car." I go out but I don't take any soldiers with me, right? I just go out there because we don't have enough military to do a show of force. I go out into this oil field, everybody's shooting, there are guns everywhere, holy crap. I climb up the oil derrick because that's what you do. You climb up the oil derrick so that you can turn around and speak. All these guys are gathered around you with their guns and all sorts of stuff, and everybody speaks English over there, by the way, so I don't need an interpreter. Then I said, "Okay, let's talk about what we need to do to resolve this," and then I resolve it. I was thinking about it as I was climbing because when you have your back to all these guys with the guns, that's actually the problem. Once you get up to the platform and turn around, your problem is over with. It's actually that climb, it's that 35-feet when you have your back to them that is the leadership part. Once you turn around, the problem is over with, once you're up there. A lot of guys can't make that 35-feet climb. Those 25-28 steps are leadership steps.

I truly believe what I said. I think every one of us owes it to each one in our team to become a great manager, to do the very best, and if circumstances arise that some of us great managers will become a great leader, then we'll have the necessary background. If that happens, you don't need to worry, because you'll reach down and grab that part of yourself that you need.

Chapter 14

Big Al the Sailors Pal

Albert H. (Al) Konetzni, Jr.
Vice Admiral, USN (Ret.)

There's a reason they call him "Big Al." He's big, musta been built when meat was cheap, cause there sure is a lot of him. As a submariner, the first thing you say to yourself is "Man, I'll bet he banged his head on a lot of overhead gear in rough seas." The man is slightly smaller than Oklahoma. But, there is something special about the man. Wherever Big Al goes, he leaves a wake of total and absolute respect.

Dex Armstrong on Admiral Konetzni's retirement,
Submarine Sailor.com

I'm very fortunate in my case. I was born and raised in New York and when I was in high school the folks moved basically out of New York up to Westchester County, went to a parochial school. Didn't have a lot of money and the Naval Academy came about as an option. This is in the very early 60s and I wasn't even sure where the Naval Academy was. It could have been Indianapolis as well as Annapolis. To make a long story short due to a special set of circumstances, one was being able to play football in high school, number two having pretty decent grades. I was able to get an appointment to the Naval Academy of all places from I think North Dakota as a qualified alternate. Went there sight unseen.

I went down there in June of '62 and very quickly picked up a nickname of Zero for being dumber than a box of rocks because I filled out, of all things, a DD-396 form wrong with pencil and corrected it. I learned a lot because that whole year taught me an awful lot. When your nickname is Zero and you have magic markers, I know that they were first sold in 1962, dressed up like Peter Rabbit for the whole year wearing a dunce cap you learn what prejudice and hazing can really do. I fit pretty well at the Naval Academy and played some sports and that kind of stuff and thought I'd be a pilot because that's what everybody did. I thought I'd get all the good looking girls that way. I remember I talked to Lieutenant John McCain down in Pensacola before he was a prisoner thinking, "This is what I got to do. He's got all these girls on his arm."

But as we got close to graduation, it became clear to me that high speed relative motion was not my forte and because they needed submariners, and this is 1966, I was able to go down for the interview with the old man, with Rickover. Got through that and got into the program. I wasn't sure I really wanted to be in the program lots of times because things like the proto-type and all that stuff were just not to my liking but I made it through and got to my first ship, which was the Mariano G. Vallejo out in Guam. Spent a couple of months on top of that on the Razorback just trying to get some surface quals and that kind of stuff on a diesel boat. Long story short, I fell in love with it.

I really enjoyed the camaraderie. The fact that I was in an organization where every individual counted; even the newest guy on board was as important as the old man. I sensed that people knew that. So that's really the history of it. After that first tour, I had a great skipper in Arnie Johnson. He's still alive. Went to the Naval Academy as a company officer. At the time I had about 135 young midshipmen who were under my tutelage and was able to use some of the leadership skills that I'd picked up on my first ship. When that was over, I think like all of us, you wind up saying, "Okay, what do I do next?" I thought I might get out but I figured I'd give it one more shot and became the Engineer on the William H. Bates down in Pascagoula and then things just rolled from there. But as I said camaraderie, that closeness, that family, that has been the biggest turn-on for me all my life.

I went to Pascagoula to new construction on what was supposed to be the USS Redfish. That's when Rickover used those words that, "Fish don't vote," and they named that ship the William H. Bates after the very popular Congressman from Massachusetts. When that tour was over they needed XO's so I went straight to my Executive Officer tour on the Kamehameha. That was in 1976. That's actually where I met Bud Atkins. He was a COB on that boat and we had a great time together just trying to make it through and became friends forever. When that tour was over at the end of '78, I went down to the Bureau of Personnel as the Submarine Placement Officer, the XO Detailer.

That was a great tour of duty because I worked for Frank Kelso, he was a Captain then. He was the boss. Then after that in '80 I went to my command tour on the USS Grayling, SSN-646 down in Charleston and great, great tour. Couple of spec ops, a couple of bad trips, still very close friends with those guys. In fact, I go to most of the ship reunions. After that tour was over I went back to the Naval Academy of all places as the Deputy Commandant with Admiral Chuck Larson who had been my boss and roommate in the Mediterranean when I was in command. Spent three years there; wonderful tour of duty. I was kind of like the dean of discipline. Then came down

242 ~ JEFF FLESHER

to Squadron 16 in '87 down in King's Bay, Georgia, which was a great, great opportunity. The old boomers, the old 41 for Freedom. I know you were talking about you worked for Mike Gray. A wonderful friend of mine and we had commanded at about the same time and I still think just lots of things, good things, about Mike.

After the squadron tour, I was in the CNOs Strategic Studies Group, from '89 to '90 and I basically went to be Chief of Staff for SubLant and I was selected for flag in '93. It has been a good run, I must admit, and I think it has been successful primarily because of all the guys that I've worked with. I heard a story once. Colin Powell, I'll never forget him, when I made flag at the Capstone Program. I guess that was '93. He gave about a 10 minute speech when he was Chair, but it was the best speech I've ever heard. There were three things that I remember. First, he said, "Hey, don't forget those guys whose backs you climbed over to get where you are," and clearly he was talking about the sailors and the soldiers. Second, "Don't forget that you're a general officer or flag officer. Nobody cares whether it's one, two or five stars." And the final thing he said was, "Use your authority while you have it. Do something good for the nation." Those things really stuck with me.

After I made flag, my first job basically was back at the Bureau. I was a policy guy doing women in combat, HIV, tattoos, you name it. That was in the 90s and then my wife and I went over to Japan and I was Submarine Group Seven commander over there in Yokosuka. That was from '95 to '98, then I went to SubPac from '98 to 2001, and wrapped up my career as the Deputy Chief of Staff as a three star at Fleet Forces Command, the Atlantic Fleet in Norfolk. So, after thirty-eight years I thought it was time to hang it up but it was certainly a lot of fun and my wife and I will never, ever forget it.

I already told you the name at the Academy, the nickname Zero. If people want to turn a person into a sub human they can do that. I came away with a feeling after that, particularly getting in the Submarine Force that you've got to realize that every person has a mom, that every person has a dream. Every person wants to go and be something. And it hit me that in the Submarine Force, most of the close camaraderie that we had I really wanted to be part of because I took care of my folks that worked for me, but boy, they took care of me.

Those Chief Petty Officers wanted to teach me everything they could. They wanted to mentor me. They wanted to make sure their imperatum was on me and that's what has really kept me going through my whole life; that these guys are all equal. They see each other as dear friends and I keep thinking about the Submarine Force right now. It's the only organization in the country that has privately run memorials in every state. It's the most active. The submarine veterans, it used to be the Submarine Veterans of World War Two and now is Submarine Veterans Incorporated. That camaraderie does not leave those guys. To me that's pretty phenomenal.

What I generally have done over my life is to say, "Hey look, first of all, you need to have, in my mind, self-discipline." I looked at the ten areas the Naval Institute had printed out. I said that these areas are great leadership terms or techniques, not only for individuals, but for corporations and groups as well. The one that hit me the most is you have to have self-discipline. We certainly had that in the Submarine Force. We don't care if you stayed out all night, but you're going to be up at five working.

I also think that you have to have self-esteem. I would much rather be on a ship that thinks they're better than they are than one that thinks they are worse than they are. But we also have to look ourselves in the mirror and say, "Hey, I'm okay. I screwed that up, but I'll get past it." So, I think self-esteem is very, very important. I think that self-confidence is also important because, quite frankly, when you have self-confidence it's easier to do things. The task becomes simpler. You don't get fearful and I have always believed that on a ship. Lots of investigations at the end of the day for collisions and groundings but most of the time what's missing is that the Officer of the Deck, Quartermaster of the Watch, whoever it might be was afraid to talk to the skipper. They delayed too long. That's because somebody had taken that self-confidence away. I think self-projection, the ability to communicate very clearly, is also very important. I talk about that all the time. These are some of the things I feel very strongly about when you look at leadership and all of those things I've certainly learned in the Submarine Force.

I can tell you my best leadership story that really goes together. It's April of 1983. I've taken the Grayling to the Mediterranean. We've already been successful up North and we think we're going to kick some butt. When I go to the Med, most of the time, I didn't load up with stores as much as other people because I wanted some room to move around and go to La Maddalena and load up. Long story short, after a very successful run chasing the Russians around the Mediterranean, I got a note from the Group Eight commander. He says, "Hey, as your reward, we're going to send you into Tangier and Morocco." I said, "Oh, that's good." So we go to Tangier, Morocco, and you got to anchor out. We had a pretty well-trained crew and we had an escort ship, which was an ARS, a rescue ship.

Of course, the first night, I always call it, was like crazy night. It's amateur night. Everybody goes out. They've been out at sea for 70 days tracking the Russians and I remember after probably drinking too many beers that I needed to get home. I needed to get back to the ship. Being the senior officer present I was able to go ahead and use this LCVP, a landing craft that the recovery had, the ARS-40. It was pouring rain and I had to make, I call it the leap of faith, from the landing craft to my ship with the round hole. And I had a kid there who later retired as a senior chief, a wonderful kid, African American. He probably weighed half of what I weighed even then. He grabbed my hand. He was the topside watch in the pouring rain and he grabbed my hand and made sure I didn't fall between that LCVP and my ship.

Clearly, I would have either been crushed or certainly broken a couple of bones. I get down to the ship. I'm happy as hell, and wouldn't you know, I had planned for everything except for what occurred and it was disappointing to me. Some pretty bad weather came in and what occurred is I knew that anchor chains were made for 70 knots of wind over the ship and seven knots of current. Long story short, I had to give up a nice luncheon with Chuck Connors of Rifleman fame who was filming a movie about the Russians in Afghanistan. Again, this is '83. About six o'clock at night, it's close to sunset, playing cribbage down in the wardroom and the quartermaster comes back and says we're fixing the ship's position every three minutes. And he says, "This fucking ship's moving, Captain."

I act like a macho man. I go to the bridge and my fat rear end knocks the bridge suitcase out. So the only communications I have is a headphone and I said, "Holy shit, we are moving fast." I kept thinking I was dragging the anchor. I've always said you go through about three levels of despair. The first level is you just get a little louder and say, "I can do this." In the second level, you calm down and you start thinking, "Dear Lord, I got to pray to you, but I need a little help on this baby right now." And in the third level you quite frankly throw it in the Lord's hands. Long story short, in this case, I yelled and screamed. I got the word back to engage the clutch. Thank God the kids were smart and the guy who actually engaged it was a young second class electrician who wasn't even qualified as the auxiliary electrician aft, but he engaged it.

I could hear it up on the bridge. I remember saying, "All back Full," and we pulled away. First time I've ever seen a submarine basically not veer. We would have been a black whale on the beach there at Tangier Bay. We got out of there and two days later picked up the rest of the crew. No damage at all. To me, two leadership things about individuals are phenomenal. Number one was the young kid who's topside watch and who would not let my hand go so I wouldn't fall between the LCVP and the ship. Second was everybody on board were heroes, but this one kid heard it. He wasn't even qualified but he knew what I wanted and that clutch got engaged and we got out of there. For me those are the best leadership lessons I could ever think of. Great examples of submariners.

Chapter 15

Flag Officer Submarines

Niall Stuart Roderick Kilgour, CB
Rear Admiral, RN (Ret.)
(Chuckles)

Admiral Kilgour served as the commander of the Royal Navy Submarine Force as Flag Officer Submarines/Rear Admiral Submarines. He was universally called by his nickname Chuckles. Even in the short period of an interview it is obvious why. His enthusiasm and positive attitude are palpable. When asked about his nickname he replied, "Chuckles came from my first submarine, HMS Orpheus, I was forever grinning at life, and the First Lieutenant on board called me Chuckles, and of course that was picked up because for some reason people thought it was appropriate. Throughout my Naval career, whether I was Admiral Chuckles or Commodore Chuckles, or Captain Chuckles, and it's not a bad nickname to have. Young commanders, Captains, they would say, 'Admiral Chuckles, can you come and help us out here.' But mostly, it was a very friendly nickname to have and it stemmed from my very first days in submarines."

I was born in 1950 and I went away to boarding school at the age of eight until thirteen. I had for some obscure reason always wanted to join the Navy from about the age six. So, my parents sent me to the Nautical College Pangbourne which was a private boarding school but with a Naval and Maritime focus and I survived that. It was an enjoyable time. It wasn't very academic, but I loved rugby, boxing, sport and that sort of side and made friends for life. While I was there at the age of fifteen, I went for a Naval scholarship to Dartmouth and managed to get that and so, at the age of eighteen, I entered the Britannia Royal Naval College at Dartmouth and that was for a three-year time span. The first year was basically professional exams, discipline, leadership, and sport as well. We spent three months at sea in the Dartmouth Training Squadron so it was one term professional, one term at sea and then you came back and finished off your professional exams. After that you had a year at sea as a Midshipman.

I went to, initially, a carrier HMS Hermes; she was a small carrier only 25, 26,000 tons I think, but with big aircraft; Buccaneer and Sea Vixens on board. That was an exhilarating six months. It's quite the most staggering thing watching the Fleet Air Arm land and take off from a small carrier. After that six months, I then went to a fishery protection minesweeper based in Scotland. And that was chalk and cheese from a big ship to a small vessel facing force nine gales in winter all around the Northern UK coast and the UK coast in general.

I had a fantastic time in that midshipman's year and then we went back to Dartmouth for a final year of academics. There were obviously exams, there was the discipline, sports, the leadership, activities on Dartmoor and that sort of side. I managed to pass out from that. In academic terms I was always able to pass exams throughout my time from the age of eight onwards but I had one difficulty and that was engineering science, or applied maths. That was the first time that I learned I had to get up early in the morning and do some work! Fortunately, I came pretty close to the top having realised that if I didn't, I wouldn't really have a good career in the Navy.

And so that was my early time and then I went to, what we call, Fourth Year Courses. They go through the various disciplines in the Navy, Surface, Fleet Air Arm and so on. I decided I wanted to join submarines. And so that happened. I went to basic training in HMS Dolphin, Gosport, opposite Portsmouth along the South coast. Went to my first submarine, which was a diesel submarine, HMS Orpheus, where I qualified on what they call Part 3. You have to learn all the systems and then have an exam. I was the torpedo officer, casing officer and the correspondence officer, and the gash hand, really.

After about seven months I then went to the nuclear course at Greenwich, to give me a basic nuclear education before going as the ship's communications officer, correspondence officer, and torpedo officer, in the SSBN HMS Repulse (Port Crew). I completed five or six patrols on there. So that was two and bit years. I then came off that and the Navy said, "Right, we'll send you to the advanced navigation course." Now, having never navigated anything in my life that was quite a steep learning curve. It was four weeks of exams, which again I had no problem with and then a really good, demanding three weeks at sea in a frigate throwing this ship around at 28, 30 knots in some of the most dangerous waters around the UK. That was a steep learning curve but I managed to pass. What that did was give me huge confidence at sea. After the advanced navigation course I went to navigate a frigate, HMS Ambuscade, for a year out of submarines, which was enormous fun.

Following that, I went back to an SSBN as the Navigator again to Repulse Port coming out of refit. Work up and a DASO in the States, enormous fun. I had about two years in Repulse. As you'll probably realize, on an SSBN, you don't really look through the periscope much so I had hardly looked through a periscope by the time I came out at thirty, thinking, "It's time I went to go and command one of these things." Fortunately, I was selected for the commanding officer's course, The Perisher, and that was an entertaining five, six months.

Lots of attack teaching ashore and then three weeks attacking at sea up to four to five frigates and then open ocean followed by inshore warfare conducting submarine business. I managed to pass that. Then I went to sea for my first command of HMS Porpoise, the oldest diesel submarine in the Royal Navy. Had a fantastic two years doing that then had a bit of time in the South Atlantic in the Falklands just after the war. Came back went to staff course and then was appointed to the Britannia Royal Naval College on the Staff.

I was head of leadership, head of one of the big divisions in the college and had a fabulous two, two and a half years there. I got promoted to Commander. Did three or four months on the AUTEC range in the Andros Island Bahamas with trials work and then got selected to command HMS Courageous, a nuclear attack submarine, which I did for two years. Had a very enjoyable time doing that. Then went to be Commander SM of the third submarine squadron for a year, then was appointed to be the Submarine Operations Officer (SOO) for the Flotilla, which was a great surprise because all previous SOOs had been, what I would call Northern runners, but they stuck me in the deep end and I ended up having a fantastic two years. It was after the Berlin wall had come down but before the USSR had broken up and the USSR were in their last final flings of throwing submarines out into the Atlantic for us to play with and so that was indeed an exhilarating two years.

It would have been, just coming up to December 1991 and it all went quiet. I got selected for Captain, went to Naples as the DACOS Ops in Naples. This again was an exciting time, because it was right at the start of the Bosnia crisis. Admiral Boorda (USN) was the Commander in Chief in Naples, and that was a busy and exhilarating time. I introduced the first ever wartime water space management for submarines since the war. Because the good Admiral Boorda was a fiery Commander in Chief, and the Serbs had two submarines that were running, he had commented that if he saw a periscope he was going to bomb it! We had various NATO submarines going in and out of the Adriatic and so I thought we ought to introduce wartime water space management and so that worked. From that, I was really fortunate, I don't think there's been many UK NATO Officers who have been given sea command in the Royal Navy after being in a NATO job. But very nicely, the First Sea Lord appointed me as Captain of the Sixth Frigate Squadron, and in command of Norfolk, a type 23 Frigate, and then Montrose, another Frigate. I had an excellent two years then with a Work Up across to the States twice, down to the South Atlantic and all over the place, so I enjoyed that.

The system then said, "Come into Fleet Headquarters and go and be Assistant Chief of Staff of Operations" in the rank of Commodore. I was also ACOS J3 in the newly formed Permanent Joint Headquarters, which had just been set up as a new organization, so I was doubled hatted. Again, a hugely exciting busy period of ops. I then went to command the Amphibious Task Group as a Commodore and I had three years commanding the Amphibious Task Group, anything from eight to twenty ships at times and several deployments including to Sierra Leone. At the time it was the biggest Naval task group since the Falklands so that's all fun. After three years, I was promoted to Two Star Flag Rank, to be Flag Officer Submarines and Commander of Operations of the Fleet. So that really is my Naval career.

I came out of the Navy in September 2004 looking for a job. I had two or three 'coming seconds' in applications for jobs, that's because I was useless at interviews. But after that,

I bucked up and there is a place called the Hurlingham Club, which is 42 acres, by Putney Bridge on the Thames in London. It is a Sports and Social club, I like people, and it was always a busy environment with committees and people issues. It was a big staff, around 300 at times, and thirteen and a half thousand members. I had ten years there, which I enjoyed enormously, and retired at the age of 65.

I always say, a submarine is in a dangerous environment really and you require every single member on board to be doing his job 100% of time. It's the most fantastic team work and you always realize that actually, these are intelligent guys as well. So you have a great mutual respect. And as the Commanding Officer, having gone through the Perisher course and passed, you have professional competence. That gives you enormous self-confidence anyway. I think the younger you can command, the better, because when you're young you take risk, you enjoy yourself, you're not really fussed about the future career prospects. What you are doing is enjoying yourself.

I had a fantastic time as the commanding officer of HMS Porpoise, as I said; she was the oldest submarine in the Navy. I only had two occasions trying to get to deep diving depth on her, and she was reduced to 500 feet, which was the maximum. I never made it down there because we had floods each time I tried. My first alongside in command was Bermuda after a difficult passage in winter in awful January gales with terrible weather and bits flying off the submarine casing; our steaming light was sheared off. It really was foul weather but it was a wonderful learning curve. And to have your first alongside in command in Bermuda is a good laugh, I can assure you.

After that I went to play with an American 688 SSN. I think the US Navy wanted to see what a diesel submarine versus a nuke was going to be like and how easy it was for the nuke. I was required to snort every four hours over a ten-day period. For the first two days, we got banged every time by the US

SSN, so I decided, against the rules, I wasn't going to snort every four hours for the next cycle. I would snort once after eight hours. And we lost the US SSN for six days. And I was then getting a little bit concerned that maybe they'd deserted and were pissed off because I'd broken the rules. But the US went active and of course as soon as you go active, you know where it is, so you can go in and try and have an attack, which we had attempted to do. I got a shot off, it wouldn't have hit, but it was an indication, which I gave to the US to say, against a diesel submarine if you go active he knows where you are and therefore you need to be very selective and careful if you're going to transmit actively.

My second alongside in command was Palm Beach, so this was high powered fun stuff. On the transit back to the UK, a thousand miles out from Palm Beach, that's when I went deep to complete a deep dive. That's when we had a flood, wrote off one of the engines, the water had by-passed three non-return valves because we were a bit rotten and so went into Port Canaveral to get fixed there and then back across the Atlantic. We were a target boat as well so I did a lot of running to introduce the Stingray Torpedo. I was the target for the Stingray Torpedo to be dropped on me. Either by frigates or by maritime patrol aircraft. That was an exciting business because they had turn away heads which didn't always work so they hit you at 50, 60 knots, which was interesting.

We were often in shallow water, doing all that sort of thing and also a bit of SBS, Special Boat Service, running with canoe work and so on. And that was ideal timing, obviously, to get, first of all the Stingray down to the Falklands and secondly to train some Royal Marines SBS in working from submarine. Then towards the end of the Falklands war, the submarine was due to pay off and went into London for a final visit. I was due to have a big party with all the former COs of the Porpoise, but they were mostly down in the South Atlantic so we had a lovely party with all their wives. Much better looking! And then took her to pay her off in HMS Dolphin. So that was my first boat. Courageous was also a nuclear submarine target boat and it was also a trials boat for the Spearfish Torpedo so I had lots of runs over to the AUTEC Range to do firings of the Spearfish and to act as the target boat for the Stingray Torpedo.

I think the job that I really had to pay attention to was SOO, SOO CTF 311, and that, of course is where I came really in close contact with the Americans and was often over to Norfolk, Virginia, to SUBLANT Headquarters. I got to know the group over there really well. Had a very close rapport and friendships with Captain Jim Durham USN who I still very much keep in contact with. Being successful in the SOO job was absolutely key. I worked for two Commander-in-Chiefs and Flag Officer Submarines there. Overall in my career, I've worked at close range with six Commander-in-Chiefs. I understand why they all went on to be First Sea Lords. They all had presence and very good brains.

I'd always been rather understated but I was also quietly confident and of course the fundamental bit about submarine leadership is competence is absolutely number one and the ship's company will find you out straight away. I always think professional competence is really important. There are some people who aren't necessarily decisive. I always was reasonably decisive, whether it was the wrong decision or a right decision. The ship's company always knew what I wanted them to do. Of course, the ship's company always wants you to succeed and once you realize that you know they're all on your side.

I learnt, and it came naturally, never to show emotion when you're on the periscope or in the Control Room. Never display hesitation or emotion. Never shout. All the things that the ship's company hate and of course it shows indecision. I always had a quiet confidence in what I was doing anyway. I had a very easy rapport with the ship's company. I respected them. I liked them, but I think it's absolutely key that you never try and become one of the boys. As much as I liked them, I always maintained a distance to a degree but it was a friendly distance. And the other factor of course was that the lads get up to mischief and they make mistakes and you have to discipline them and the right application of discipline is absolutely fundamental to the atmosphere on board a ship or submarine. They know when you've made a good judgment and if you go off-beat you can tell. The atmosphere changes in a heartbeat. I'd say to the youngsters I'm with always pay attention to discipline and the fairness of it and if you get that right then the ship's company will be with you every time.

You have to be a reasonable character, and of course, youthful command, I was always up to mischief with the submarine. Parking in the wrong place or stopping off hiring boats to take the lads ashore for a quick beer and things like that. I got into trouble one or two times but nothing really serious really. So, they like character, they like confidence, they like decisions, they like good administration of discipline, and they also don't want you to be one of the lads. They want to see a distance from them to the Captain and I think that's how I commanded. Of course, I enjoyed it and when you're enjoying something you're normally doing it quite well. I go back to what I said earlier on that the younger you command the better because you take risk and you have fun and you're not thinking of your next promotion. You're enjoying it and if you're enjoying it the whole ship's company is enjoying it as well.

I went on to command surface ships and I always remember thinking that when you surface in a submarine it's like going on holiday. So when I commanded various ships on the surface it was almost like being on holiday all the time. And again, that made it very easy to command. I always say that in command you have lots of responsibility but you have the authority as well, which makes it much, much easier. When you're working for someone else, you have responsibility, but not the authority and to have both together is a fantastic relaxer.

I am Chairman of Trustees for the Navy Club, which dates back to the 1790s, and I'm a Chairman of a local trust in our parish. I live in Somerset in a small, very rural village on the through road to nowhere but with good communication links close by either to London, Bristol, Exeter, motorways and so on. So I have had an enjoyable life I would call it.

I am also President of the Submariners' Association. Basically, the Association is a mixture of both serving, but mainly retired submariners and there are branches all over the UK. So, you've a Nottingham Branch, a Plymouth Branch, a Derby Branch and so on. It enables the old boys to maybe once a week get together in a pub have a drink, talk about the old days, and enjoy a rapport. It is mostly retired submariners, mainly lower deck, who have loved their submarine time, very proud of it, and enjoy the various branch gatherings.

There are a couple of main events. The focus for UK Remembrance is the Cenotaph, which is the main one for the British Legion, as close to the 11th of November. The Submariners Association always have a submarine remembrance parade the week before the Cenotaph. There is a lovely submarine memorial, the submariners equivalent to the Cenotaph on the Embankment on the Thames just opposite the Middle Temple and the Inns of Court. It was created around 1922 I think. It's a brass memorial with plaques and names on and so on. Not huge, but we have a really brilliant Sunday with a remembrance service. Our Patron is Admiral of the Fleet, the Lord Boyce, who was a very distinguished submariner. He is always there, as is Admiral Sir James Perowne, again another great submariner and Vice Patron. It is always a good turnout, and continues to show respect for those who lost their lives in submarines.

Chapter 16

Commander, Submarine Forces

Chapter Sixteen
Joseph E. (Joe) Tofalo
Vice Admiral, USN (Ret.)

NORFOLK - Vice Adm. Joseph E. Tofalo relieved as Commander, Submarine Forces in a change of command ceremony aboard the Los Angeles-class submarine USS Newport News (SSN 750) in Norfolk, Virginia, Sept. 11, 2015. Vice Adm. Joe Tofalo will continue not only the legacy of the submarine force, but also that of his parents. His father was a 35-year career naval officer and his mother a Navy WAVE, one of the first enlisted women in the Navy. In his introductory remarks, Tofalo shared his happiness for taking on his new role through a lighthearted story.

"I was sitting having a cup of coffee with Suzanne this morning and I said to her, 'Honey, did you ever think in your wildest dreams, that you and I would return as Commander, Submarine Forces?' And of course, Suzanne, always one to keep my feet firmly planted on the ground, not skipping a beat, says to me,

'Joe, what makes you think for a minute that you are in any of my wildest dreams?!' Like I said, Suzanne is always one to keep my feet firmly planted on the ground and we are thrilled that those feet are planted right here in Norfolk, Virginia." Vice Adm. Tofalo also expressed his gratitude to his shipmates, friends, family and wife. "Suzanne, we've come a long way since USS Flasher and that little apartment at the end of the Ocean Beach fishing pier," said Tofalo in closing. "I can tell you that my wildest dreams would not have been possible without you."

Excerpt from: Commander, Submarine Force Atlantic Public Affairs Sep 17, 2015

You might say I'm pretty hardcore Navy, the son of a career Naval Officer and WWII First Class Petty Officer. My parents were part of the greatest generation, World War II obviously shaped them significantly. My father, a Naval Academy graduate Class of 1942, graduated on December 19, 1941, so 12 days after the attack on Pearl Harbor. Imagine being a Midshipman then, the rest of the school year canceled, no first semester exams, no Christmas vacation, no second semester, just go to war. Dad spent the entire war on USS Portland, went aboard as an Ensign, and came off a Lieutenant Commander just four years later, earning 16 battle stars. They were torpedoed at Iron Bottom Bay in the Battle of Guadalcanal, participated in the last battleship-on-battleship fight in history with the last "crossing of the T" at Surigao Strait, and he was in the battles of Midway, Coral Sea, Leyte Gulf, and Okinawa. Pretty much every major WWII Pacific naval engagement—he was there. He was even Officer of the Deck on USS Portland when the Japanese came aboard to surrender at Truk island, one of a few smaller surrender ceremonies that took place simultaneous with the main surrender ceremony on USS Missouri in Tokyo Bay. For me, he was a naval hero.

My mother was a First Class Petty Officer, one of the first enlisted women in the Navy, in a unit called the WAVES, Women Accepted for Volunteer Emergency Service. She was a First-Class Yeoman. My childhood was probably more driven by the Navy Yeoman than the Captain, she ran a tight ship! She was an amazing woman, dedicated to her family and the Navy, and a hero of mine too. Her father was a strip miner on the Mesabi Range in Minnesota. My father's father was a poor Italian immigrant, a farmer and shepherd, from central Italy, a no-stoplight town called Sasso di Castalda. He came to this country in 1907 with only $14 in his pocket, and rose to be a Section Foreman for a central New York railroad.

My father went to a one-room schoolhouse, the teacher would beat his left hand to force him to write right-handed. He enlisted in the Navy at seventeen, had a hammock on a battleship and somehow got into the Naval Academy through an enlisted commissioning program. Somebody saw something in him and damn if he didn't graduate number two in his class at the Naval Academy, and ultimately got a Master's Degree in Electrical Engineering from the Massachusetts Institute of Technology (MIT). He was a really smart guy that, again, came from pretty humble Italian roots. My mom and dad moved twenty-six times in dad's career, and I did a half-dozen of those moves, plus about twenty-five more of my own in my career. I was born in San Juan, Puerto Rico when my father was stationed there. His career had an ordnance and guided missile focus, Gunnery Officer on USS Portland, and then with his MIT Electrical Engineering Degree, he got into the guided missile business as that was becoming of age. He ultimately was the program manager for one of the Navy's first guided missile programs; the Talos missile. I'm told he had the nickname of "Father of Talos."

My father commanded two ships after his World War II service, the destroyer USS Stockholm, and a deep-draft major command auxiliary, USS Yancey. With both of his parents "off the boat" from Italy he spoke fluent Italian, so as a senior Captain he got orders to the U.S. embassy in Rome, meaning I got to live in Italy as a kid. It was great. Funny story, my grandfather, Rocco, the one who came from central Italy in 1907 and became a railroad man, he was old when my father told him of the exciting Rome assignment. Dad was really proud that he was going to Italy to work in the embassy and represent our nation back to the country from which we came. But when dad told Rocco, his father started crying. Rocco said, "Son, I worked so hard to get us out of there, I'm so sorry you have to go back!" There's a Godfather III reference in there somewhere..."just when I thought I was out, they pulled me back in." It's all perspective, right?! But a great experience in Rome, we actually had a private audience with the Pope as part of dad's embassy duties.

It was just a tremendous Naval career for my father and my mother, who met on a Friday night soon after the war, and dad asked her to marry him the following Saturday. The war was over, it was time to move on. They were married for 50 years, with four children. My brother was also a Naval Officer, a submariner too. I graduated from the Naval Academy in 1983, and as a midshipman I thought about being an aviator for a little bit, even worked on my private pilot's license and parachute wings. It just wasn't my thing. I was very excited about submarining and it really appealed to me. It's got a heavy engineering underpinning, it's a small and elite force conducting highly classified missions, and it's the foundation of our nation's strategic deterrent. So, I became a submariner, and it was the best professional decision of my life.

I loved it all, and would do it all again in a heartbeat. My first tour was USS Flasher, conducting classic Cold War missions in WESTPAC. I was engineer on USS Michigan, my first boomer, with a front row seat for watching the fall of the Soviet Union through the lens of an Emergency Action Message team member. XO of USS Montpelier, this time a fast boat going to Europe, the Mediterranean, and the Persian Gulf. Back to an SSBN as CO of USS Maine. Then Squadron Commodore in Pearl Harbor, an SSN squadron, then Group Command as a Flag officer in Kings Bay, mostly SSBNs. So, I literally went, SSN, SSBN, SSN, SSBN, SSN Commodore, SSBN one-star, and then Force Commander. Truly blessed—a lucky guy. I also had the good fortune of being the Director, Undersea Warfare, OPNAV N97, as a two-star. That's the submarine force's Requirements Officer, and kinda like the submarine force's CFO.

When I retired from the Navy as the Submarine Force Commander, I got my current job working for Huntington Ingalls Industries (HII), the nation's largest military ship builder. HII has built 70% of the United States Navy, and has two shipyards. Newport News Shipyard in Newport News, Virginia, and Ingalls Shipbuilding in Pascagoula, Mississippi. Newport News is the only builder of our nation's aircraft carriers, and one of only two builders of our nation's submarines. Ingalls is the only builder of LHA big decks and LPDs, one of only two builders of Arleigh Burke destroyers, and the only builder of the Coast Guard's National Security Cutter. So, I'm proud to say I'm a shipbuilder. I work in the Washington, DC office, government and customer relations. It's a great job with a great company, and I get to be involved in building the Navy that I love and the submarines I was passionate about, just a great way to continue to contribute.

What is leadership? Wow, where do I begin? You manage things, but you lead people. But before jumping into leadership, you have to have some context. For me, that always started with standards. Standards are the things you set for yourself, others, your team, and your command, but it starts with yourself. Then leadership is how you achieve different goals in everything beyond yourself. The goals in submarining as I saw them were 1) combat readiness, 2) mission accomplishment, and 3) taking care of your people.

In the Navy and submarine force I found that you have to think about standards early and all the time, because you typically don't have a lot of time, relatively speaking, to affect change. A nominal two-and-half-year CO tour is not a lot of time compared to the guy in the private sector who does the same job for 25 years. In the Navy, with pre-established and finite tour lengths, you quickly have to lead and get results. You can't survive on, "well that's how we always used to do it"—after day #1 in command, you own it. You've got to quickly establish what your standards are whether that's the amount of time from "Prepare to surface" until the OOD shifts his watch to the bridge, how fast the crew achieves Battle Stations after the General Alarm is sounded, what's the standard time for a leave chit to be routed, or what is the standard for crew attendance at the varying professional schools. I'm a nuke so I'm probably a little bit more metric-based than some. But if you can measure it, you can change it, and then you can use that to quickly get to the desired outcomes for combat readiness, mission accomplishment, and taking care of your people.

The danger of the stereotypical nuke and the desire to understand and measure the underlying data, is that can easily be confused with the perception that you also want to personally control the applicable issue, to micromanage it, and it took me awhile in my own leadership journey to sort that out. On the contrary, I do not want to own it at all, I want you to own it, but I do need confidence in what you are doing and how you are doing it, so that I can comfortably, and more efficiently, let you run with it. I think this is where we start to get into one of the leadership paradoxes that you think about. That tension between being 100% responsible and accountable, but figuring out how to give others the leash needed so they can safely, effectively and efficiently do hundreds of things for you simultaneously.

So how do we do that? We have standards that are well understood and consistently applied. Those standards are set forth in things like CO Standing Orders, Night Orders, trip wires (e.g., if this happens, call me or sound off). Leadership needs to create the space for the team to maneuver on their own, like a submarine navigation moving haven, with standards in that example like the minimum distance allowed to other surface ships or land, Yellow/Red soundings, when to transition to the Modified then full Piloting Party, when to set the Maneuvering Watch, etc. Leaders get these standards operationalized via plans, and the quality of the team's backup to their leaders improves with the quality and understanding by the team of that plan. The lower down the chain-of-command you can safely move that process of operationalizing standards into plans (this takes time and training), the higher functioning your team will be, particularly when this activity just becomes routine, cultural.

So much of this is cultural, it's a mindset. For example, as CO I would not have the OOD request permission for things, rather I'd have him state his intentions to me for everything that required my permission. This meant he had to own the development of the plan, to the standards, but he would get to execute it, it was his. It's subtle, but the onus was more on him and his team, rather than on the CO. The CO needs to be the ultimate in backup, not the primary in execution, and this is just one example of how to do that. The other cultural piece the leader has to develop in the team is that of a questioning attitude and the empowerment to speak up when your questioning attitude requires it. Malicious compliance to standards is also not good, and can be dangerous.

The biggest skill that your team has to have is the ability to self-assess. This also starts with having and knowing the applicable standard, and then having the ability and institutional process whereby your team can honestly evaluate themselves to that standard. Standards are set, promulgated and understood, but the ability to self-assess is a skill that requires development. If there is any skill for a CO/XO/COB to teach their Officers/CPOs, it is the ability to self-assess, to find problems before they find you. Being Below Average on ORSE is not the real problem, the real problem is not knowing you are Below Average and having to have someone else come in and point it out to you. If you don't know where you are (self-assessment), or what it takes to get to where you're going (standards), you'll never get there (combat readiness, mission accomplishment, taking care of your people). I had the privilege of being the Senior Member of the Tactical Readiness Evaluation Team and the Prospective CO Instructor, so I got to ride a lot of subs. The highly functioning teams I observed worked this way, with very good self-assessment skills, and clear understanding of high standards that were operationalized by solution development at the deck plates.

I had a command philosophy in command, every CO does. Mine, like most, had an emphasis on integrity, accountability and trust. Integrity, say what you mean, mean what you say, demand complete honesty of yourself and your team. People typically don't wake up in the morning with the goal of cheating on a test, gun-decking a log, or initialing off something that they didn't do, but in the moment of choice, they may marginalize what their signature or initials are worth. Accountability, it's not just part of being in the military, it's part of life, and it must be consistently and fairly applied. Trust, submarining is built on this, it is foundational to mission-command. Trust that you did the Rig for Dive checklist to the standard, trust that you'll stand an alert watch while others sleep, trust in the CO and crew to go to sea often with no shore communications and silently execute the mission, trust in the CO by the crew to be bold but not reckless. I mention these three things, integrity, accountability and trust, in the context of leadership because they are so interwoven in the fabric of good leaders, and highly functioning teams.

Another thing that I used to tell my people is that the truest measure of a person is how they respond in the face of adversity. By virtue of saying that statement, you admit that it ain't always going to go perfect! You get duty on Christmas, some major valve/pump brakes, you BA'ed a major ship's inspection, you get extended on deployment, whatever. Life is not all sweetness and light—stuff happens. But how you respond in the face of adversity is the true measure of an individual, particularly in leadership positions. The troops have got to see that you're calm under fire, and then they will be too. A good sense of humor goes a long way here, and in general you need to be having fun; if you aren't having fun, you aren't doing it right.

One final thought on everything we've talked about so far. Whatever you come up with given the culture you created and the leadership you apply, to go do whatever mission, event or task, is not a one-size fits all solution. The standards and trip-wires set, the plan developed, the way you put together teams, the level of procedural detail needed, the level of supervision you use, the timeline and milestones you establish, all of that is going to be different depending on the people that are involved, with their respective strengths, weaknesses and personalities, the scenario that you're given, and the hand you've been dealt. Leadership is very dynamic, there is no one single answer.

Sea story? Here's my favorite leadership sea story that will hopefully tie together a lot of what we've talked about. One day, in command, with a Tactical Readiness Evaluation (TRE) being conducted on the ship, in the middle of the simulated war, the Communications Buoy jumped off its capstan and got stuck in a deployed position, meaning there was a bunch of heavy cable and a buoy the size of a riding lawn mower coming out of the sub that couldn't be pulled back in. Like I said, "stuff happens!" The slightest wrong move and the buoy and its cable would be stuck in the screw and rudder. I'm like, oh, I'm screwed, at best I'm going to BA this TRE, and who knows what else if I damage the shaft, screw, rudder, buoy, etc. The good news is the team had a culture of solution development at the deck plates, because in a crisis, you need that to happen in real-time at the lowest level possible. So we gathered the COB, Department Heads/LCPOs, divers, Deck Division, some Machinist Mates, and a couple of the strongest men on board, gave them the problem set and some command guidance, and let them work it. They had to start by quickly developing the procedure for getting to periscope depth and surfacing without entangling the screw/rudder, then the procedure for getting the buoy back alongside and stowed, with all contingencies and applicable standards and trip wires for safety articulated. All of this with the inspection team monitoring every word and action, and writing lots of notes and comments—no hiding any warts here. The crew executed the plan, surfaced the ship, retrieved the buoy and strapped it back in place, resubmerged the ship, and continued the simulated TRE war. The crew got an Above Average on that exam, and I'd like to think that it's because of much of what we just talked about.

But there's more to the story. After we got to the surface, I'm on the bridge of course, watching the XO and COB, two rock stars, tighten down the last strap holding the buoy in its cradle. On the bridge is just me, the OOD and the lookout, and we're cheering for the guys on deck and how the team had done it. And the lookout, a young Seaman, turns to me and says, "Captain, it's like you always say, it's all about how you respond in the face of adversity." Wow, you could have relieved me for cause that day and I still would have been a happy man.

I mean, it was a total victory, the command philosophy had made it to the deck plates. It just doesn't get any better than that!

Another sea story that comes to mind, is in the category of "train like you fight." We had just gotten the new Navy Fire-fighting Thermal Imagers, or NFTI, that allows you to "see" into a cloud of smoke and direct your fire-fighting actions where you could not normally see with just your naked eye due to smoke. When those first came out they were a big break-through, everyone's training with them, we know it's going to be on the ORSE, how to use it, etc., but they're expensive so we developed a makeshift "Training NFTI," which was nothing more than a sideways coffee can on a short stick! And you know where this is going. Middle of the night, General Alarm goes off, and on the 1MC, "fire in the Engine Room, fire in Engine Room Lower Level!" It was not a huge fire, but even where there is only light smoke you've got to get on it right away, every submariner knows that. I'm the ship's Engineer, so I rush down there, make my 4MC announcement, "this is the Engineer in Engine Room Lower Level, I'm the man in change, there is light smoke coming from the Aft Drain Pump Controller," and I look over and there's Seaman Smith with the damn coffee can on a stick looking at this real cloud of smoke! It was electrical in nature, so the team quickly opened the breaker, and the smoke quickly dissipated. Needless to say, that's the last time we ever used the "Training NFTI", you've got to be able to use the real thing and not break it, and you don't want folks to respond differently just because it's a drill. You've got to train like you fight!

4

Strategic Paradox

.

Chapter 17

Doing the Impossible

When the Nautilus was launched in 1954 it was able to do things impossible for other submarines. It was the first submarine to reach the North Pole submerged. It could make air from seawater and it could operate for years without refueling. The development and use of nuclear power enabled this revolution in submarine design and warfare. The advent of Naval and civilian nuclear power is widely attributed to Admiral Hymen G. Rickover and his will, intelligence, and audacity. He believed that it was possible and he brought others to this conclusion by building the support needed; technically, managerially and politically. When he started there was no reactor to install, there was no proof that it would work, he didn't even have the authority to do it, and as Dave Oliver personally observed, he wasn't a naturally good leader. Still, he pursued a vison of possibility, found a way to engage and leverage others that worked for him and in the end achieved a decisive competitive advantage. Rickover and his team had again proved the paradoxical axiom "it's impossible until someone does it."

Paradoxical thinking is a tool that can help organizations and individuals do the impossible. Paradoxes might be the problem that your company or organization originally came together to solve, like the ships that sink to gain strategic advantage. It can also lead to a personal advantage that sets you apart like the person who does the jobs others won't or remains calm when others are panicking. It can change conflict to collaboration and helplessness into action.

The notion of paradox is nothing new. They are ubiquitous and once you start to look they are easily found; day and night, Yin and Yang, work and play, birth and death. Folklore, fables and sacred literature from all cultures use these elements of wisdom as fundamental truths and guiding principles. There are also paradoxical prerequisites for business success like selling the current line and designing the new one and doing the work and learning how to do it better.

From a problem solving perspective the most important realization is that paradoxes are not linear problems that get solved and can be forgotten. They are ongoing tensions between conditions that need to be understood, managed and leveraged. This is true at the strategic, operational and enabling levels. Our competitive advantage may be thinking about something that seems unrelated or untried like forming companies that make products without factories or creating infrastructure that allows customers to design their own products.

We know that as leaders we continuously work with paradoxical requirements. We provide feedback and judge, encourage and correct, and provide stability and change things to name a few. We understand that we need to manage tasks and motivate people; a fundamental aspect of the paradox of management and leadership. We may intuitively understand the opportunities for performance leverage in each of these conditions and we likely struggle with some of them.

Throughout the stories shared by the submarine leaders we heard about preparation, practice and many good principles they had adopted as thoughtful biases. Of course, they didn't call them thoughtful biases and still they are. Much of human behavior is instinctual; an efficient unquestioned automatic selection of a pattern of behavior that we believe fits the situation. It's not that we think it fits, we don't really think before we choose; we just react. In most cases this serves us well but sometimes it doesn't.

I would like to offer a few of these useful thought biases for your consideration. A useful thought bias is a habit of mind or chosen perspective to help frame our behavior for better performance. If practiced I believe they can give us a head start and greater probability for success. We can make a conscious effort to practice helpful biases to the point that they become habits. Submariners regularly do this. Drills are a constant effort to habituate the correct behaviors in an emergency. I doubt the XO who closed the hatch in Bob Hogue's story actually thought about it. He recognized the danger and performed the appropriate immediate action. Afterwards, he, the Captain, and others thought about what happened and how to avoid the situation in the future.

A thought bias I have adopted is a perspective that people usually want to do the right thing. I know that this isn't always true and I prefer to start with the benefit of the doubt instead of the doubt of the benefit. This is an initial bias and I subsequently use my judgement to validate or modify that bias. I believe this makes me more approachable and easier to trust because I mirror trusting behavior through that assumption. So, I start with an assumption that I need to adjust as I learn about the person while the bias predisposes me toward success.

The second useful bias is a paradox introduced by Bud Atkins; the classic nature or nurture question. Are leaders born or made? Like most paradoxes we have learned that the answer is usually not Either/Or but Both/And. So the answer to the question is actually "Yes" to both options, Nature AND Nurture. Situationally or personally it may be more of one than the other while both are still paths for better performance.

Mike Gray tells us that knowing your temperament is a clue to what you can successfully pull off as your leadership approach and Ron Gordon tells us that you must play the hand you are dealt. We all start with strengths and weaknesses, advantages and challenges – that is the hand we've been dealt (nature). It is up to each of us to fix it, both gaps and aspirations, if we want to be as effective as we can be (nurture). Mike Gray did this with his little black book. Ron Gordon observed that formal leadership programs may be of limited value. Bud Atkins reminded us that learning by doing with a good role model works and Frank Stewart and Chris Groves told us we can actually learn more from a bad example. Most of the great leaders in this book faced a moment of leadership and career crisis brought about by a bad leader and that motivated them to learn how to be better themselves. A core tenant of the group was self-directed learning, starting with a realistic understanding of self and a desire to be the best, to have a brass ring as Frank Stewart shared to motivate and direct improvement; leveraging nature and nurture.

A handy instinctual tool to use as we choose further development is as simple as what attracts and repels us. You can feel the visceral response our submariners had to poor leaders, it wasn't intellectual, it was emotional and we could call it by an emotional response – disdain. Our instinctual emotional system does help guide us to choose, what we like and don't like means something. What is fun and what is painful means something. Who we are attracted to and what repels us means something. We need to listen to ourselves and what our emotional responses are telling us. In effect we think AND feel and should use both.Whether through natural talent or dedicated practice, where we are today is not the only place we can ever get as leaders. We can take whatever level of talent and advantage we have and leverage it through purposive effort. That starts with a choice; our intention. Intention is powerful and it can be changed consciously to suit our needs. John Buffery told us that he changed his intention when he got married and realized this was not just a game and he then applied himself more strongly to support his goal of being a good husband. So, let's look at intention as our third useful bias for a moment. I maintain that intention is also a paradox – what do I want to accomplish AND who do I want to be? In every decision we make a dual choice; to advance toward a goal and to express ourselves individually and collectively in a manner we prefer. This is true in all cases, not just when we are successful. It is even more important when things are not going well and we are at the most risk of abandoning the standards described by Joe Tofalo, leading to a lapse in our integrity. Intention is the motive force behind navigating paradoxes, creating and maintaining a useful tension and achieving goals consistent with our personal and organizational values.

The next useful bias paradox is - performance AND constant practice. The key to becoming good at anything is practice. Dave Oliver told us he practiced public speaking even though he wasn't good at it because he knew it was required to be the leader he aspired to be. Chris Groves observed that we essentially are always practicing and it is worthwhile to be purposive in this constant stream of preparation. Bob Hogue observed that his experience in the Navy enabled him to successfully lead and innovate with the teams in his business. He was able to leverage previous practice by adopting characteristics he found valuable and also observed that, as the organization grew, so did the need for an increased leadership focus that would empower, delegate and build competence just like he experienced when he worked with his engaged leaders and peers at sea.

If we assume all action to be practice we start to look differently at incremental outcomes. In Bob Hogue's flooding story, after it was contained the most important thing was to learn from it instead of blame someone for it. This doesn't imply abandonment of standards or accountability. It does introduce a concept often foreign in business or even the Navy – forgiveness is another thought bias for consideration. Forgiveness isn't about helplessly accepting bad choices. It is about recognizing error and starting with an assumption that the situation and person can learn from it and improve. I would maintain that if we can't get over someone's mistake, then we won't trust them. If we don't trust them we will not depend on them and if we can't depend on them they have no business in our organizations. As Rob Davis advised, "Everybody's got to pull their weight and if they can't pull their weight then maybe they should go somewhere else and not pull their weight."

Paradox awareness doesn't mean we see so many dimensions to things that we are immobilized. It reminds us that there is likely at least one other side of things and as the saying goes, if you pull a string you might be surprised by what it is attached to. I suspect that as you read this chapter and consider the paradox possibilities you are already recognizing them in your experience and our lives. For example; too much of a good thing is bad, all roads lead to home, and the submarine axiom - hours of boredom punctuated by moments of sheer terror. Paradox mastery does not imply that the concepts are balanced, or have the same level of influence or managerial effort. It means that the relationship between the components is appropriate for the situation. As a practiced habit of mind, paradoxical thinking and consideration become quite fluid and more effortless. The good news is the opportunity to practice is constant.

One of my favorite paradoxes is a provocative proposition – Massively more value for less time and effort. The first time I used this it was with a team of Lean and Six Sigma Master Black Belts and I suspect they thought I was either kidding or misguided. Of course, a group of efficiency experts would be working at capacity and meeting quality standards. They may have been but they were working too hard and the need was greater than the output. In the period of just a year or so their productivity had in fact multiplied. So, paradoxes are also possibilities, great choices we haven't made yet.

The practical value derived from paradoxical thinking ranges from heightened awareness and reduced conflict to disruptive innovation and strategic competitive advantage. Like the little black book created by Mike Gray, explore these, try what fits your situation, create your own, then practice and continue. In the next chapter we will consider ten paradoxes of submarine leadership that our group of submariners use to great effect. These also apply to any organization and can help you see more broadly and focus your effort more clearly on the path toward your intention.

Chapter 18

Paradoxes of Submarine Leadership

The technologies employed in submarines have advantages and constraints. There are still depth limitations, the space is still cramped even on the largest boomer/bomber and a constant battle is waged for innovation in sensors, signals, systems and silence. Of course, technology is only one part of the complex system required for submarine operations. There are political, financial, shipbuilding, command and control, supply chain, human resources, and managerial systems to name a few that must perform to exacting standards in order to produce, support and maintain a submarine fleet. As nations compete across these dimensions the submarine as a weapons platform will continue to pivot from one strategic paradox to the next to maintain its warfighting relevance.

The extreme demands of the submarine context with its inherent danger and complexity heightens the importance of effective leadership. There is obviously less room for error and the crew of a submarine performs 24 hours a day continuously for long periods, even months at a time, with no real time off or opportunity for complete relaxation. Paradoxically, the silent service also provides us a uniquely informative microcosm for studying individual and team performance. While the outcome of these efforts is unique, much of this enabling background is familiar to all of us as precursors to most organizational endeavors. Possibly the major difference is that in the submarine high performance is a baseline requirement not an aspiration or unusual occurrence. While the context is different from common experience there are experiences we can learn from in common.

In this chapter we will explore ten underlying effectively leveraged paradoxes of submarine leadership that enable the continuous high performance required to operate and provide a strategic competitive advantage. In most leadership environments these are below the surface, often not recognized or consciously managed. The mastery of these paradoxes typically looks like individual style, magic and good luck. While that may be true to some extent, we also see that these leaders have consciously studied, reflected on their experiences and worked at continuous personal leadership improvement in order to perform and guide their crews to collective excellence.

Essentially, all of these paradoxes underlie the universal strategic paradox of Success AND Failure. It may seem odd that the tension between these two seemingly opposite poles is the ultimate leadership effort. Like all paradoxes, we tend to favor one side/aspect over the other and it seems obvious that success is our primary goal. However, it is just as important for us to understand and use failure effectively to get there. Our goal through paradoxical thinking is to, as much as possible, benefit from both. So, the difference between these successful submarine leaders and others is that they really do leverage and benefit broadly through their innate and conscious understanding and navigation of these paradoxes and learn from both good and bad examples, successes and failures.

As individuals we tend to learn more from other's successes and more from our own failures. Their successes show a path forward from a circumstance or issue while our failures highlight areas where we need to do something different. As you reflect on the stories from our twenty-two submariners you can see many examples of the successes they achieved and the times that they worked through failure using it as an effective tool for improved performance. Continue to consider their efforts and advice as we look at ten strategic paradoxes that can accelerate your success and that of your teams.

Companies and individuals who can see a strategic paradox where others see an impossible combination can leap ahead. If you are able to create more for less, sell today's product while developing tomorrow's better model, leverage assets you don't own and see clearly what is over the horizon you are already well ahead of the game. If you can also operate as the submarine leaders suggest with maximum delegation and recognition of mutual expertise, constant criticism and support, and be able to trust even when you doubt you are creating the enabling thinking infrastructure for high performance.

Daring and Caution

The goals in submarining as I saw them were 1) combat
readiness, 2) mission accomplishment and
3) taking care of your people. Joe Tofalo

It's a test of your people skills and leadership skills both in
peacetime and in war. What I mean by that is both under
pressure and not under pressure and then it's a test of your
war fighting capabilities in submarines. Chris Groves

In the early months of World War Two it became clear
that the commanders of US Submarines were too cautious and
younger, more aggressive commanders were brought in to improve performance. Submarines of course are warships and
that performance really comes down to the ability to accomplish a warfighting or related mission. There is no question that
it is risky to take pictures from beneath another warship or
conduct covert surveillance inside hostile waters or to follow
at close quarters potential enemies without being detected but
that is what submarines do. They are a first line of defense and
the terrible promise of the last line of nuclear deterrence with
more destructive power than all of human conflict combined.

Submariners, and especially those in command, must be
willing to take needed risks and be confident in their direction
while also knowing that there are outcomes more important
than the safety of the ship and crew. While it is imperative that
submarines be operated safety with due caution they must
be ready to pivot at any time to aggressive action. During the
Second World War US Submarines were responsible for sinking a majority of Japanese shipping and almost a third of the
Japanese naval loses while being only 2% of the US Navy. US
submarines had the highest casualty rate of any US service
component in the war, approximately 20% of crews were lost

and this terrible cost was still lower than any other submarine force in the war. The Royal Navy submarine casualty rate was approximately 30% and an astounding 70% of German U-Boat crews were lost in boats that were referred to as iron coffins.

In effect, submarines were highly effective and inherently dangerous to operate in combat conditions. You may be familiar with the old submarine movie scenario where the boat attacks a convoy, sinks a ship or two and then is immediately set upon with depth charges. As soon as a torpedo is launched the element of surprise is compromised. This is still true and it also applies to Tomahawk missiles and submarine launched ballistic (nuclear) weapons. The reward of battlefield performance can't be decoupled from the risk of complete loss.

Joe Tofalo's three goals describe intent; what needs to be done and who we need to be to accomplish our missions, to be always ready. The value of the submarine is its stealth, powerful weapons and the effective ability to add an additional operating dimension to the battlefield at sea. Submariners are smart professionals and technicians and also proudly the pirates of the Navy. Famously during World War One, First Sea Lord Admiral Sir Arthur Wilson of the Royal Navy said submarines were "underhanded, unfair, and damned un-English" suggesting crews should be hung as essentially criminals. Submarines didn't fight fair because they changed the paradigm (paradox) of battle at sea from agreed rules and courtesies to total war without quarter or notice and they accepted the risk that came with the advantages.

Leaders in all organizations navigate the risk and reward paradox through choices, preparation and efforts at strategy and prediction. We plan to take market share and hedge our bets, aggressively enter new spaces and protect our turf. In effect all of our choices have this underlying aspect and leaders get famous for their ability to choose well when they can choose and respond well when they can't.

Courage and Fear

If you're not nervous right now, you don't understand what's about to happen. Frank Stewart

Don't panic. Do what you're trained for. Doug Ackley

Repeatedly we are reminded that yelling and screaming is not the best way to enable our goals on a submarine. It probably isn't in our businesses either. Those moments as Chris Groves tells us that when we "lose it" we not only reduce the potential that we will be immediately successful but also reduce our credibility and the trust others have in our stability and judgement in the future. We can't expect confidence as Frank Stewart reminds us, if our team is afraid of us. We have all seen the chilling effect that can be catastrophic in the submarine environment like Mike Gray's story of the boat that sank a fishing vessel because no one spoke up when a compromised positon had been taken by the Captain and the antithesis when Bill McGonegal calmly managed through a poor choice by the Chief of the Watch while enabling him to recover. At the same time, fear is often effective and important. Again as Frank Stewart said, "If you're not nervous now you don't know what is happening," but there is a significant difference between useful nervousness and crippling fear.

The routines at sea maintain this tension such that there is coiled readiness when action is needed. Constant surprise drills that interrupt sleep and require immediate action keep the crew appropriately on edge while also providing confidence in their performance. The effective leaders have their fingers on the pulse of the crew, the level of confidence and potential weaknesses. They have also learned to manage their emotional impacts through the quiet word as Ron Gordon and Chris Groves told us and we see broad awareness of the destructive effects of unpredictable leaders and assholes although they do occasionally slip through.

This dynamic is an underlying aspect of all organizations and certainly a tension played by all managers/leaders. Some leaders revel in the ability to make people afraid, to use their positions of authority for self-aggrandizement or as a shield to hide their lack of confidence or competence. While, as Greg Kane says, the stakes may not be life or death certainly it is about important things like profitability, career possibilities and even organizational viability. Assholes are really just about as welcome in the workplace as they are on a submarine. It is well worth recognizing as Frank Stewart did that in a position of authority your intentions, and foibles, are magnified. It really is important in either case to maintain a calm and stable demeanor as the nurturing background for the performance of others.

Bud Atkins and Jack Gallimore told us how important it was to take care of their crews. That is mostly accomplished by a combination of high expectations and support coupled with high empathy and emotional intelligence even though it may sometimes be administered in a direct and no-nonsense way. Leaders need to serve as a primary performance and character role models that are on stage almost every moment. On a submarine the Captains have this very difficult task of being the constant role model and emotional weathervane for others for months at a time with very little room for error. There is no question that they are exemplary performers. In all environments it does matter how we act. Our words and actions are magnified by power and it is critical to have persons willing to step up when called upon, to tell the truth when things are headed in the wrong direction, and to have leaders who can be both supremely confident and consistently open to listening to input from others.

Trust and Doubt

If you don't trust the person in the job that they are doing, that they're doing it right, your life's in jeopardy. You start to build up trust. But that also goes two ways. If you're assigned to do something, I learned, you better damn well do it and do it well because their lives could be impacted by a mistake that you might make. Greg Kane

They stood right out and said, "This is what we're going to do," and we did it. And they didn't tell you one thing and then go behind your back and do something else. Bud Atkins

Submarine qualification is an acknowledgement of a baseline demonstration of trust. No one can hide and as Bill McGonegal noted, "On a submarine, you're a self-contained world. If you can't fix it yourself, it can't be fixed." I often say "You shouldn't trust me until you should." This might sound a bit ridiculous and it describes the nature of trust and doubt on a submarine. Trust is not bestowed based on any factor other than demonstrated proof. You can't be awarded Dolphins through any other means than rigorous qualification; no one skips ahead of that line.

Like the other paradoxes this tension highlights that neither aspect is inherently good or bad. Too much trust can lead to getting in over your head. Several of the leaders maintain that it is essential to push down, to delegate to the lowest level possible to ensure experts are doing expert work. They would also want to see proof of the readiness to do this; expertise is also never assumed. Similarly, too much doubt erodes confidence and diverts attention. Mike Gray and Joe Tofalo remind us that, as the saying goes, "trust but verify" and in the submarine service that isn't just a saying; it is an expectation.

Too often in organizations trust and doubt are assumed to be aspects of one's character or pedigree when in fact they are directly related to performance and experience. I can really only fully trust you when I see you do what is needed in the right way when it needs to be done. Until that there should be doubt in my mind that supports you in your performance. This is a very important point – doubt tells me I need to help you. While I can extend the benefit of the doubt based on intentions and even make some cursory judgement that a person might be trustworthy, I should not substitute belief for observed behavior. These are not personal judgements they are situationally dependent artifacts of performance. They are not permanent, they are built and they erode. Submariners are not offended by doubt; they expect it and are willing to demonstrate their ability to meet expectations through all levels of rank and hierarchy.

In business and other organizations this can be a difficult tension to master due to the assumption that this is an either/or space. We want to acknowledge people, to empower them and to respect them. Respect is critical and basic human respect for each person is a worthwhile approach. However, respect isn't the same as trust. Respect doesn't require performance and on the most fundamental level does not need to be earned. Trust does.

Criticism and Support

We had this sort of camaraderie where people were helping you learn. We would test each other in lots of different ways. Sometimes it would be humorous and sometimes they were just doing it to goof off, but we would always challenge each other with what we knew. Bob Hogue

The guidance you get from senior members of the crew and the way the blend is of new crew and old experienced crews is a remarkable learning experience. It's got so much structure and so much foundation to it.
The confidence building is remarkable. Harry Baker

Be truthful in the assessments. Never butter him up, just tell him as it is. Ron Gordon

This paradox is also a constant condition in the submarine service. Sometimes it is funny, sometimes aggressive and always expected. It is a method to support the development of trust and a foundation for learning and performance. On my very first day onboard the 654 when I went into the missile control center to report to my division, my supervisor pointed to the computer printer and asked, "Can you fix this?" Now after almost two years of electronics and computer schools it may have been a reasonable assumption that I could. I answered, "No." His immediate response to me (criticism) was, "What the fuck is wrong with you?" I don't recall being offended. It was an accurate assessment and motivated me to learn. I stood watches the rest of that patrol and maybe the next with the same supervisor who patiently taught me how to fix everything (support). He encouraged and helped me become an expert technician and when it was my turn to be a supervisor I did exactly the same thing for my new technicians.

The process of qualification requires the new person to learn every system onboard and be tested by many different members of the crew until they are satisfied that the examinee knows the system, the requirements and immediate actions necessary. These tests are oral with no time limit and passing is at the discretion of the examiner. Until a person is qualified they are dangerous and at best might get in the way. It is a bit of a game and a point of pride in knowing that the tiny valve in the missile compartment can do this or where the smallest tank on the ship is located. Like Dave Hulin, one of my proudest moments was when I was able to be assigned the role of Troubleshooter for strategic missile launches. Like him, I was the person who would be called to immediately fix anything that malfunctioned. It meant that I could fix that printer and everything else in the system and I could do it quickly.

In submarines there are many supports for effective criticism; boards, qualifications, inspections, certifications; it is ubiquitous. This is extremely helpful so that criticism can be seen, not as a personal affront, but as a core aspect of support and guidance. Support is also ubiquitous, almost every achievement has a ceremonial aspect. There are awards and medals for running toward the fire, fixing critical equipment, passing strenuous examinations and doing a good job. This is not monetary as Chris Groves observed. The military doesn't compensate high performance with cash. It rewards performance with recognition, praise and social status.

This is a special area for focus and opportunity in business. It can be very difficult to separate the person from the performance and make it safe to learn from mistakes. It usually isn't that fun and can be awkward and easily misunderstood. This is also directly related to trust and fear. If a leader is trusted and reduces the fear associated with feedback it becomes much more natural and welcome. Similarly, if criticism and praise are regular features in an organization, they don't lose their value but become naturalized expectations for both leaders and followers.

An effective system of criticism and support is also needed for full effectiveness. On-the-job training with accurate performance examinations, thoughtful project reviews with identified strengths and weaknesses, regular quality reviews and systems of continuous improvement all support this intention. In business we sometimes suffer from a reliance on simplistic answers and metric summation to the point of uselessness. Just like in learning about leadership, it is easy to know the right words and it takes work to know what they really mean.

It is a natural tendency to avoid conflict and too often criticism results in defensiveness instead of helpful realization. It is important to learn how to describe performance issues in a manner that others can hear and take into account instead of dismissing as an unfounded attack. This does not mean to lessen the accountability or individual responsibility. It does mean that clarity of communication is the goal not just the satisfaction of taking someone to task. The establishment of a continuous feedback and support system and effective managerial criticism and encouragement for individual continuous improvement are the foundation. The ability of leaders to be confident and still open to critical input as noted earlier applies to everyone from the bridge to the deck plates on a submarine. This is just as much true in business from the Board or C-Suite to the loading dock or new intern.

Learners and Teachers

*They weren't worried about showing how much they knew.
They were worried about you learning and they would help you.
They would sit down and talk you through the systems and
draw them out with you. Bob Hogue*

*The biggest thing you have to learn is how to manage people
and that's hard because everyone's different. You have to learn
how to manage them, lead them, and they have to follow your
example as much as possible. Stan Mathis*

As Bob Hogue discovered, submarines are amazing learning environments and you are expected to be constantly learning. You are also expected to be constantly teaching. The learning experiences are fantastic. As Bill McGonegal pointed out, everyone has more than one job; there are multiple collateral duties and situational assignments. I was an electronics and computer technician, a line handler, bridge phone talker, painter, fire watch, security guard, radiation spill team member, access coordinator, qualification petty officer, watch standing missile launch supervisor, ship's librarian, occasional barber, custodian, torpedo loading party member, and our division's entry in the Halloween costume contest (I won). I was also available for any working party that needed me or that was comprised from the weapons department or all hands.

Beyond the technical topics, procedures, and processes, I also learned about my peers and like the other submariners enjoyed stories about families and adventures. The same supervisor who taught me to be an expert technician also shared every Frank Zappa album ever made. Like Steve Thorpe I was attracted to the Navy and submarines for the adventure and while most of my submarine experience was under water I did go to other countries and experienced other cultures. Even on

292 - JEFF FLESHER

the ship there were regional foods I'd never eaten and I pretty much learned to eat anything. Once I complained about a meal to the cook on duty and his response was "Go eat somewhere else." Not all lessons were voluntary.

Submariners are fast learners and qualification proves the learning potential and achievement of each crewmember. You are expected to teach the new people and to support qualification. It is a continuous cycle of teaching and learning that creates the capacity for consistent performance in an unforgiving environment. You also teach others about yourself. Generally, everyone is an open book. I also learned a lot about myself. I was my own captive audience in a sense by learning patience, calmness, and to do the hard things first. I also learned greater empathy, how to share, and to avoid high stakes poker games and possibly the greatest accomplishment was a sense of confidence knowing I could be counted on by others and could count on myself.

All leaders (everyone really) are always teaching others about themselves. After I left the Navy I heard a retired Admiral say that "A manager never has a bad day." I immediately though that he may have a screw loose because everyone has a bad day but what he meant was that you are a constant role model that is closely monitored. As Chris Groves and Niall Kilgour described, the crew can quickly get an opinion about a leader's strengths and weaknesses. The same is true for the leaders in any organization and as Bud Atkins observed, you must be able to walk the talk in order to get people to follow your direction and believe what you are trying to teach. Just as importantly, teams that can learn to think together have a significant advantage. If hierarchy can be recognized and good ideas can still come from anyone, then everyone is encouraged to contribute.

Frivolity and Seriousness

When it was time to play, I'm ready to play. When it's time to work, I went to work, Dave Hulin

Really good CO's knew when to relax and how to have some fun instead of wringing their hands and worrying all the time and I tried to do the same. You gotta have fun and if you are not, you're not doing it right. Bill McGonegal

A submarine environment is of course deadly serious. It is also filled with practical jokes, funny stories, and some bizarre behavior. It is critical to have these elements to manage the stress and isolation. These are also tests and the person who might easily get angry will become the entertainment for the moment. Like the other paradoxes this is a critical psychological and operational need on submarines. It reduces the space between people, allows you to blow off steam, laugh at yourself and others and bond like an extended family. One great lesson I learned was I didn't have to like everyone but I did need to depend on them and they needed to be able to depend on me too. I would have come to the immediate aid of anyone no matter how close we were or if I liked them or not. They were my shipmates and all of them were a part of my individual responsibility.

It is amazing the level of resourcefulness we can have when there is a need to entertain ourselves. For some reason we had sheets of clear laminating paper on the boat and quite a few people made key chains with every imaginable thing they could put between two sheets of plastic. We also laughed at other's poor fortune and being a good sport was an important shared value. There were few limits with juvenile humor and it provided a healthy outlet. Some of the practices like drinking dolphins (having them in your teeth after a large glass of assorted spirts had been downed) or tacking on (punching) the newly qualified person in the Dolphins pinned on their chest are now discouraged/banned. As the Navy rules continue to evolve, I suspect frivolity will too. The common experience makes for lifelong friendships and as Rob Davis shared about going to the Subvets, it is easy to enjoy time with other submarine veterans even if from other timeframes or countries.

In any environment being able to have fun together strengthens the relationship bonds needed to perform together. It is important to enjoy both work and play. We learn very easily through social play and build trust through shared experiences. This is worth purposive effort to create those memorable times like Tim Oliver and Ron Gordon suggested and to meet each other as human beings first and bosses and employees second. There is no threat to authority or credibility in being able to share a story or activity consistent with organizational social norms. Even for the most senior leaders, as Niall Kilgour advised, while you may need to stay somewhat apart, you should not be socially isolated or ignore the opportunities to create the social glue and collective identity forged through both shared challenge and good natured play.

Oftentimes in business environments managers interact transactionally with reports. Work is ordered and accomplished and conversations are performance judgements. Hierarchy is somehow indicative of intellectual and emotional superiority. We trade working together for being in charge. There is no threat to authority when we acknowledge our shared human condition. Being a person first who can also be a leader who creates massive leverage through employee engagement and trust. When I challenged the Master Black Belts with the massively more value paradox I also shared that this should be the best job we ever had. We realized both. It is more likely to achieve sustained high performance when we can enjoy even the hardest work with a sense of shared comradery.

Change and Stability

We are their heritage and they are our heritage. We pass down what we learned to these younger sailors and they honor us as we honor the WWII guys that we lost. Bud Atkins

As a leader you've got to think about, when you're gone, who's going to replace you? Rob Davis

High performance is a requisite stable characteristic in operating submarines and at the same time crews regularly have about 25% turnover each year. Boomers/Bombers have two crews so their turnover is not just the newly assigned persons but the entire crew and leadership team regularly occurring every few months. Exacerbating this situation is the youth of many crew members and the constant inherent danger and the complexity of systems.

The military in general faces this condition in every branch and country. New recruits join and must quickly learn the rules, customs and culture. They also must become proficient at jobs they most likely never had or prepared for in any real sense. Ensuring the readiness and continuity of performance is a core need for the military and of course submarines. Essentially, the stability is built on constant change and approaches have evolved over time to effectively address this condition and when it works well it is a massive advantage.

Submarines run on routines; cycles of deployments, watch standing, maintenance, inspections and even the menu. The only way you feel what time of day it is, is by what meal is being served, and whether on purpose or by chance, that is extremely helpful in being able to frame time and provide psychological stability. Familiar routines of field days (cleaning), special meals (Saturday night pizza or curry) and the changes of watch standers is the underlying structure for life on board.

When interrupted they are temporarily replaced by other routines like a fire emergency, flooding casualty or battle stations. While these can be unpredictable events, they all have a defined routine that is practiced to enable naturalized responses that provide the needed familiarity to perform.

As Joe Tofalo describes, these routines are grounded in standards and clear expectations and adherence to expectations is a critical behavior. So is knowing when to improvise because, as Bill McGonegal pointed out, it won't get fixed if we don't do it with whatever and whoever is at hand. That dynamic is a clear cultural system advantage. We know the rules and abide by them until they don't work and then we improvise (that's a great paradoxical standard).

It is an unusual paradox in most organizations that we are constantly changing and occasionally manage it as if this is a special effort reserved only for the largest scope or most disruptive events. In fact, most work in change management only focuses on change and stability is something you might get back to when you are done instead of another constant to help accomplish desired performance. With focused attention it is possible to reduce the perceived amplitude of change by also increasing and reinforcing stability. The lack of a massive conflagration in your burning platform doesn't lessen the chances for successful change. It normalizes change as a constant path for greater success while limiting unnecessary disruption and that reduces the time to achieve a new status quo.

Just as we think about what can be better we can also consider how things can be more predictable. How can we embed routine into systems and keep change in perspective as a response to contextual conditions and not a knew-jerk reaction that appears to be out of control? As stated earlier, with effective continuous improvement change becomes a stable element, not because we continuously fail but because we continually aspire to a greater realization of our intentions.

Individual Responsibility and Teamwork

The keynote of my command philosophy was individual responsibility because in the light of day, you are responsible for your actions and nobody else is responsible for that. Mike Gray

You require every single member on board to be doing his job 100% of time. It's the most fantastic team work. Niall Kilgour

Your one mistake can make the submarine sink, so you're extremely important to the team. That's a big difference. I have to do my best. I can't let the team down. Ron Gordon

I think teamwork is paramount on a submarine and teamwork goes hand in hand with leadership. Steve Thorpe

I was in an organization where every individual counted. Even the newest guy on board was as important as the old man. Al Konetzni

I don't think there is anything more important than working as a team and I think teamwork was probably the key in both my time in the submarine force and as an officer. Pat Urello

The test of qualification is a personal milestone. You may get support, you might even have a qual buddy to study with or a sea daddy to watch over you but in the end, you have to know it and prove it yourself. That baseline extends to everyone onboard and provides the foundation for effective teams based on mutual respect and known achievement. You have to volunteer to get there and you have to perform to stay there.

The interdependency of individual and group performance is obvious on submarines. While each person has specific jobs and tasks, no one can perform by themselves. Even during Captain's Mast, Mike Gray considered what could be happening in the systems to enable the individual's poor behavior and choices. Every person has a stake in the success of the rest of the crew from the obvious perspective of group survival to the most mundane things; it really is like one big family that enjoys healthy competition and does their best to make sure no one loses. There is little room for marginalized or incompetent members of the crew, or leaders who ignore either case.

One of the greatest performance aspects of the submarine forces is the teamwork and the number of teams one belongs to as a normal part of crewmembers' duties. You belong to a watch section, a division, a department, forward or aft, nukes and weaponeers as well as being part of the wardroom, chief's mess, and of course qualified and not. Everyone effectively belongs to multiple layers of constantly changing and effectively stable groups. Every team has its duties and expectations and value/reward for membership. Individual performance leads to great teams that get the work done and belonging to teams keeps everyone going through a sense of belonging.

High expectations for individual performance and accountability are more typical in business environments than are regular check-ups of team performance and behavior. This does not require sophisticated measurement, simple observation will often do. While teambuilding activities can provide social glue and a bit of fun and a chance to learn together, the best context for improving team performance is in the normal activities and regular work. Focused attention on team goals, standards, function and continuous improvement are all prerequisites to effective team management and require hands-on attention. Teams also provide a critical component of success that can be leveraged to great advantage; the collective social norms and resulting positive peer pressure to conform to expectations.

Hierarchy and Social Norms

From a leadership point of view, the more you can let people that work for you take ownership for what they're doing and be able to get the satisfaction of doing a hard job, and then, being recognized, not that they need a medal but that you appreciate what they're doing is really important in leadership in my opinion. Tim Oliver

I think first and foremost was integrity. We all learned that early on in our submarine careers. We count on each other. We depend on each other for our, basically, for our own lives while underway, and knowing the systems on the submarine we are all required to know and to operate. I had a chief petty officer tell me early in my career, it's doing the right thing when nobody is watching. Pat Urello

Military leadership is often associated with the rigor of hierarchy and the chain of command. Authority is well defined in each link and at sea the ultimate authority is the Captain. The robust hierarchy includes well defined roles and responsibilities and authority from top to bottom. Delegation may be easier with a structure that supports that from the watch standing operating structure to the departments and divisions and the Chief of the Boat/Coxswain and senior enlisted/ratings team. So, in a very real sense the clear definition of hierarchy, standards and roles makes it much easier for effective social systems that will then reinforce through peer pressure the expectations for individual and group performance.

One of the unique aspects of Navy service in general, especially true on submarines, is that authority represented by rank is separate from work performed as defined by rating. Therefore, the most advanced nuclear power plant technician has the same level of general authority as an equivalent ranked traditional machinist, chef, or electronics technician with the same expectation for supervisory competence. Of course, there is a difference between officers, Chiefs and enlisted ranks although it is much less on subs than the surface Navy due to the close quarters and lack of extra space or separate facilities.

All organizations have social norms. Oftentimes these are described by the term culture. Social norms are specific, observable and malleable. Looking through this lens we can better understand what group agreements advance and inhibit our intentions and progress. In the submarine service the adherence to social norms and traditions is a supporting element that encourages positive peer pressure to perform and conform. As several of the submariners noted, one of the worst infractions a crewmember can commit is to let their shipmates down.

It is imperative that people are trusted and capable and do the right thing when no one is watching. Doing your part is not just an expectation – it is a cultural foundation reinforced by standards, command hierarchy and shared values and norms. Combined, leadership structure, individual responsibility and group norms/culture are a powerful blueprint for sustained performance and safeguard against non-compliance and any potential single point of failure.

Frank Stewart created a foundation for this with new crew members by connecting their tasks to the overall operation and effectiveness of the ship. He connected the what's in it for me to the bigger picture of what's in it for us. This is also reinforced in submarines through the distributed qualification process and deep delegation described by the leaders, pushing it down to groups and individuals so that the systems and culture can be mutually supportive and leveraged for continuous high performance.

Management and Leadership

You manage things, but you lead people. Joe Tofalo

The fact that they included me, as I got a little more senior, in decisions, particularly Commander Chabot, he would seek advice on decisions. He would talk to people. He would make you feel like you were included. You would see those attributes in the Submarine Service over and over again. Bob Hogue

First of all, to be a good leader, you've got to be technically competent. Whether it's driving a submarine, running a reactor, or getting your weapons ready; you've got to be a technical expert on technical things. Then you've got to realize, the people working for you are also experts in their field and they're more qualified than you are many times. Bill McGonegal

Management and leadership are another paradox that seem like an either/or choice and much effort has been invested in teasing out the differences and definition. There are many approaches and schools of thought from trait theory to situational leadership, servant leadership or transformational leadership to name just a few. I believe this is another case where the answer is not either/or but – Yes! Nature and nurture, technical and people, task and people, formal and informal are all paradoxes that describe a portion or aspect of the management and leadership dynamic. These different approaches capture something important from each perspective and yet they also seem incomplete in being able to comprehensively describe the efforts. In a practical sense the terms are interchangeable and I believe they can be described with paradox. The paradox they are meant to support and the paradoxical relationship between the two concepts.

A simple way to describe the similarity and differences is embedded within the purpose of the pair, which is to accomplish intention. Intention is "what" management and leadership are "how." As stated in Chapter Seventeen, intention is a paradox that includes what you want to accomplish (goal), and who you want to be (motivation). In most situations leader actions do include both even when unstated, done poorly, at small or large scale, or through formal authority or influence without position. We express our intention through management and leadership efforts. The amount and mix of related activities is not based on a theoretical difference. It is based on the context of use, what's needed for success in the situation of interest.

On submarines, especially those with effective delegation, leadership and management are parts of everyone's individual responsibility. As you read through the stories in this book you saw management and leadership at every level on a submarine. Leadership from above, leadership from below and peer leadership. In the Navy there are expectations for leadership behavior at most ranks and this is the case in both the US Navy and the Royal Navy. This is an advantage as there is a general familiarity and expectation that grows with advancement and as stated earlier, that is independent of a specific job. Senior leaders are seen as leadership/management generalists and shore and sea assignments can be very different. Sometimes it was more technical; sometimes more personnel-based and generally everyone has a part to play to make it all work.

On the boats we saw that in some instances the more senior leaders needed to immediately manage an effort, especially in an emergency that required more experience although we also saw a broad pushing down of direct decision-making in preparation for contingencies and in support of individual and team development and growth. Multiple leaders commented on delegation and ensuring that the teams could operate effectively without the designated leader. Of course, this approach is also critical in an environment where accident or battle action could disrupt the management hierarchy with casualties or assignment of a senior member to lead an emergency effort.

In a previous role I was asked by a CEO, "How do you teach people to make good decisions?" My response was, "You have to let them make them and provide feedback." This is where the submarine leaders understood that you create the space to try based on the individual, give them feedback and encourage their growth at the pace they can (or need) to absorb improvement into their practice. Several leaders commented on the ability of a mentor to understand who could do what and who needed help. That ability coupled with active support results in better decision-making and judgement.

Leadership and management, influence and negotiation, effort and resistance occur at all levels within all people and are also part of the social norms, standards and individual responsibility. They are aligned to the degree that leaders clarify and express their intention through broad sharing and consistent behavior. It is the responsibility of those at the top to lead the way, and as Joe Tofalo recognized, the measurement of success is how far down (to the deck plates) it is accomplished.

Business and other organization may not be able to replicate all of these conditions and they don't need to in order to see a multiplication of value from applying some of the ideas. This is where knowledge of the context that each reader has intersects with the management paradoxes. These ten paradoxes do occur in all organizations. In most they are left to chance or are a single sided effort. The possibility through more effective leverage of both, using context sensitivity to help define the focus of the mix, can help create competitive advantage in any organization.

A Last Piece of Advice
One Way and Many Styles

When I was in PCO school we used to all get together at the end of the day and we would talk. And by the time you get to PCO school, then you think everybody does things the same way. And, of course, there are procedures as far as the operations detail. But I was surprised at the diversity of the ways that people ran ships. But again, it goes back to the personality thing. You got to do what works for you. It's that simple. I would say that's what happened to me. I learned what worked for me, and continue to do that. Mike Gray

I had an opportunity to go on a small squadron staff out of La Maddalena, Sardinia. That was an eye opener for me because they were all the attack submarines that were coming into the Mediterranean on a routine basis. I probably saw 15 or 16 different submarines and submarine COs pass through there. You realize that there is room for individual application and ways to make things work and do it much better than what you were exposed to in your previous life. Frank Stewart

*One final thought on everything we've talked about. Whatever you come up with given the culture you created and the leadership you apply, to go do whatever mission, event or task, is not a one-size fits all solution. The standards and tripwires set, the plan developed, the way you put together teams, the level of procedural detail needed, the level of supervision you use, the timeline and milestones you establish; all of that is going to be different depending on the people that are involved, with their respective strengths, weaknesses and personalities, the scenario that you're given, and the hand you've been dealt. Leadership is very dynamic, there is no one single answer.
Joe Tofalo*

In the introduction to this book I presented a framing assumption through a paradox—that you (the reader) would benefit from the wisdom of twenty-two submarine leaders and that I would not specifically know how. I suspect that there were many areas and ideas that were beneficial and inspiring. These are, of course, twenty-two unique individuals and at the same time you can feel the connection and similarity forged in their submarine service and individual commitments to effective leadership. Through their stories I believe you have had an opportunity to see more broadly into a world of high performance and dedicated leadership and be able to focus on value you can personally use on your continued leadership path.

One more paradox to consider is thinking together and thinking for yourself. There is no question that great value comes from listening and incorporating other's opinions and advice and at the same time you need to decide for yourself what to include or leave alone. This is also a paradox mastered by the submarine leaders; they understood the value and opportunities for inclusion and expansion of their perceptions and ideas, they also knew that at some point they would need to decide and to carry the weight of judgment alone. Like all of the paradoxes it isn't either/or; we do need to do both and learn which contexts fit those choices.

The purpose of this work is to describe a general direction and some of the paths toward that beacon for success. It is based on an environment that demands high performance in leadership and personal examples from those who have measured up, learned and adapted and taken a personal responsibility for individual and organizational success. As with any advice and example, take what makes sense and works for you. Be encouraged as you find and reach for your brass ring and as we would say in the Navy, best wishes for fair winds and following seas on your journey.

CPSIA information can be obtained
at www.ICGtesting.com
Printed in the USA
BVHW041303060421
604332BV00008B/50/J